English Houses
1300–1800

English Houses 1300–1800

Vernacular Architecture, Social Life

Matthew Johnson

Longman
Is an imprint of

Harlow, England • London • New York • Boston • San Francisco • Toronto
Sydney • Tokyo • Singapore • Hong Kong • Seoul • Taipei • New Delhi
Cape Town • Madrid • Mexico City • Amsterdam • Munich • Paris • Milan

PEARSON EDUCATION LIMITED

Edinburgh Gate
Harlow CM20 2JE
United Kingdom
Tel: +44 (0)1279 623623
Fax: +44 (0)1279 431059
Website: www.pearsoned.co.uk

———————————

First edition published in Great Britain in 2010

© Pearson Education Limited 2010

The right of Matthew Johnson to be identified as author
of this work has been asserted by him in accordance
with the Copyright, Designs and Patents Act 1988.

Pearson Education is not responsible for the content of third party internet sites.

ISBN: 978-0–582-77218-2

British Library Cataloguing in Publication Data
A CIP catalogue record for this book can be obtained from the British Library

Library of Congress Cataloging in Publication Data
Johnson, Matthew, 1962–
  English houses, 1300–1800 : vernacular architecture, social life / Matthew Johnson.
– 1st ed.
        p. cm.
  Includes bibliographical references.
  ISBN 978-0-582-77218-2 (pbk.)
   1. Architecture, Domestic–England.   2. Vernacular architecture–England.
3. Architecture–England–History.   4. Architecture and society–England–History.
I. Title. II. Title: Vernacular architecture, social life.
  NA7328.J53 2010
  728.0942–dc22
                                                              2010003455

10 9 8 7 6 5 4 3 2 1
14 13 12 11 10

Set by 35 in 10/13.5pt Giovanni Book
Printed and bound in Malaysia (CTP-VP)

Contents

List of Plates, Figures and Maps

Plates (*in central plate section*)

Figures

Maps

This book is for little David

Acknowledgements

The gestation of this book has been over a twenty-year period, and as such, I cannot list all the people I must give thanks to over that time. The late Alan Carter first sparked my interest in buildings. Many of the ideas discussed here can trace their origins to my PhD thesis, submitted in 1989 and later revised and published as *Housing Culture* in 1993. The thesis was supervised by Ian Hodder; I remember our discussions with tremendous gratitude and affection. Kate Pretty and Eric Mercer examined the thesis with close, critical eyes and sharp minds and tongues. Eric expressed doubts about my conclusions, but was supportive of the attempt; I learnt much from his criticisms.

Study leave to progress this book was provided by the University of Durham; the AHRB, now AHRC, funded a second term of study leave. Since my move to Southampton in 2004, my colleagues there have provided tremendous support. Collectively, I have learnt much from the Vernacular Architecture Group, particularly Sarah Pearson, Barry Harrison, and Joan Harding. I must also thank the many house owners who over the years have shown such a hospitable and welcoming nature both to me and to scholars of vernacular architecture of all stripes.

I owe a particular debt to my discussions with Adrian Green. Many of the ideas presented here arose in talks with him. John McGavin pointed out how central the idea of 'performance' was to my thinking, when I hadn't seen this myself. Penny Copeland read the whole manuscript and prepared many of the illustrations. Richard Harris kindly provided the photos of Bayleaf, and Andrea Kirkham generously provided the photo of Gracechurch Street, Debenham; both also took the time to comment and correct several points. David Hinton and my editor Mari Shullaw generously provided comments on the whole manuscript. I must also thank the Johnsons, Dana Arnold, George Bernard, Jude Jones, Jeremy Lake, Mark Leone, Gerald Pocius, Robert Blair St George, Anne and Helen Smalley, Mark Stoyle, Danae Tankard, Simon Upton, and Dell Upton. Errors and misconceptions that remain are, of course, my own responsibility.

My wife Becky, as always, was my kindest, sharpest and most perceptive critic. It takes a very special person to express enthusiasm for a weekend looking at houses in Chipping Campden.

This book is dedicated to my nephew David, who as a two-year-old was unequivocal in his evaluation of one of my previous books as 'rubbish'. I hope this book marks some improvement. It's got more pictures in it, anyway.

Publisher's acknowledgements

We are grateful to the following for permission to reproduce copyright material:

Weald and Downland Open Air Museum/Richard Harris for Plates 8 and 9; Andrea Kirkham for Plate 13.

Maney Publishing for Map 2.1, from Alcock, N. W., 'The distribution and dating of crucks and base crucks, *Vernacular Architecture*, 33, 67–70 (2002); English Heritage for Map 3.1, from Roberts, B. K. and Wrathmell, S., *Region and Place: A Study of English Rural Settlement* (2002); Jeremy Lake for Map 3.2.

Maney Publishing for Figure 2.4, based on Colman, S., 'Weepers: a small late medieval aisled hall in Cambridgeshire, *Medieval Archaeology*, 26, 158–62 (1982) (www.maney.co.uk/journals/med and www.ingentaconnect.com/content/maney/med); Bloomsbury Academic for Figure 3.3, based on Hinde, A., *England's Population: A History Since the Domesday Survey* (2003); Maney Publishing for Figure 4.2, from 'An early vernacular hammer-beam structure: Imberhorne Farm Cottages, East Grinstead, West Sussex', *Vernacular Architecture*, 36, 32–40; *Oxonesia* for Figure 4.3, from Hinton, D., 'A cruck building at Lower Radley, Berks', *Oxonesia*, 33, 13–33 (1967), reprinted by courtesy of the Editor and Committee of the Oxfordshire Architectural and Historical Society; Maney Publishing for Figure 4.4, from Alcock, N. W. and Laithwaite, M., 'Medieval houses in Devon and their modernization', *Medieval Archaeology*, 17, 100–25 (1973); Maney Publishing for Figure 4.5, from Pearson, S., 'The chronological distribution of tree-ring dates, 1980–2001: an update', *Vernacular Architecture*, 32, 68–9 (2001); Maney Publishing for Figure 4.6, from Gardiner, M., 'Vernacular buildings and the development of the later medieval domestic plan in England', *Medieval Archaeology*, XLIV, 159–80 (2000); English Heritage Photo Library for Figures 5.4 and 7.5, © Crown Copyright NMR; the Unit for Landscape Modelling for Figure 5.5, copyright reserved Cambridge University Collection of Air Photographs, Unit for Landscape Modelling; National Trust Photo Library for Figure 6.2 © NTPL/Robert Morris; the Textile Conservation Centre at the University of Southampton for Figure 7.7.

The National Trust Photo Library for permission to reproduce the author's photograph in Figure 2.1b.

In some instances we have been unable to trace the owners of copyright material, and we would appreciate any information that would enable us to do so.

1

Introduction: The Study of Vernacular Architecture

Every weekend, thousands of people, mostly from the towns and suburbs of England, engage in the most innocent of pursuits – a visit to the countryside. Picturesque villages and country landscapes within convenient driving distance of a major city are the destination of families and individuals seeking a few hours' respite from the stresses of urban living.

Visitors, driving and walking around the regions of England, see that not all English houses are the same. The houses and other buildings that make up rural landscapes vary in obvious ways in their choice of building materials, and also more subtly in their style and decoration, and their size and form. Observers soon recognise that this variation is not just a random jumble, with each house varying from the next in a merely haphazard way. Rather, there are certain patterns to be discerned in the local landscape and architecture: concentrations of different kinds of building in particular areas, use of particular roofing and walling materials, different architectural styles. These patterns must surely mean something; they must surely tell us something about the history of the household, community and region.

If our visitors look more carefully at the facades of houses as they walk past, they can begin to speculate about the stories they have to tell (Plates 1 to 4). This house has a steeply pitched roof – it may have been thatched before the thatch was replaced with ceramic tiles, the steep pitch being needed in earlier times to facilitate rainwater running off the thatch. That house has one end much higher than the other end. Could one end have been rebuilt, and if so why? This next house has a date and initials above the door. Does this date mark the initial construction of the house or does it date from a later improvement? And why is there a pair of initials, or maybe two Christian names, either side of a surname – what does this tell us about relations between the married couple? Taken together, these differences may proffer stories: the timber-framed and plastered fronts of irregular houses may give way, over time, to more strikingly regular and symmetrical Georgian brick facades.

Our visitor stands back and surveys the scene as a whole. Perhaps the houses are clustered tightly round a green, a church in their midst; perhaps they are more dispersed, isolated even. In much of England, the countryside does not conform to the stereotype of the classic 'English village' familiar from Agatha Christie novels and TV adaptations, with a church, manor and village houses in a cluster surrounded by arable fields; rather, it is a dispersed scatter of small hamlets or isolated farmsteads. And this difference in settlement form between this and that region is not random or trivial – it is linked to very deep differences between local communities, and to subtle variations in the history of human settlement, variations whose origins are often at least a thousand years old. The location of houses in the landscape, then, has as much to tell us as their form and decoration.

Clearly, our visitor rapidly recognises that the story of the houses that make up the village is not one of an unchanging rural idyll. The village, and the individual houses within it, have been transformed through the centuries. Non-local building materials could not have arrived before the transport revolution of the eighteenth century. Houses bear marks of alteration and updating in line with contemporary tastes and standards.

Different patterns can also be seen at a regional level. To travel between different regions of England is to traverse different zones of building styles, different forms of houses, set within different kinds of landscape. These differences between regions are partly conditioned by material factors – the underlying variations in geology conditioning the availability of good building stone, or proximity to woodland. Others relate to human geography – the proximity of London or a major regional centre, ease of access to major routeways. Still others, however, are the products of local choice: ordinary people, whether acting as individuals, or as part of households or communities, choosing to do things differently.

Many of these differences between houses are not immediately obvious to the casual visitor, but become apparent on close inspection. Live in a region of England for even a few months and look at local buildings closely and critically, and the visitor will quickly come to see differences between this dale and the next, this county and the next, in features that are often, at a first and superficial glance, arbitrary choices – decorative schemes, the manner of laying stone or bricks, the panel infills of timber frames.

Houses and People

This book is aimed in part at those who perhaps on casual visits to the countryside have already seen different patterns of traditional houses, and who want to know more about old houses, what these patterns might mean, what they might tell us about the history of the English landscape and the men, women and children who dwelt in that landscape.

The book has a very simple message: houses are about human beings. Architecture is a human creation, the medium and outcome of people acting on their surroundings. The form of smaller houses, then, can tell us about the lives of the ordinary people who built them and who lived in them. They are artefacts that should be understood as part of the way ordinary people lived and thought. They tell us about those lives and thoughts in often very profound and complex ways.

Many books on houses concentrate on changing architectural styles – Perpendicular, Renaissance, Palladian. This story is a fascinating one, and aspects of it will be retold in the pages that follow. However, somewhere in this cascading narrative of styles and influences the people seem to be forgotten. Such books often also concentrate on the houses of those at the very top of the social structure – the gentry and aristocracy. Where the houses of the middle classes are considered, the concentration is on the cities and towns rather than the countryside. Again, it is often forgotten that, before the Industrial Revolution, over four-fifths of the English lived in the countryside, and were not of such elevated social status.

Other books do concentrate on the ordinary houses of lesser people, but wax lyrical on changing building materials and technologies – brickwork, cruck types, scarf joints, ashlar coursing. Still others discuss economic factors behind housebuilding – changing farming practices, agricultural improvement, dairy production, the cloth and iron industries. All these themes are important, and all will be explored in the pages that follow, but in the end they are only a means to an end. *The one true end of the study of old houses is to understand something of the ways of life and systems of thought of their builders, owners and users.*

Those ways of life were very different from our own. The houses we see today appear quite familiar; the descriptive words we use often have an Anglo-Saxon plainness to them – farmhouse, stable, kitchen, barn, byre. The past, however, is a foreign country, and this apparent plainness conceals just how very different that past was. These houses were built to accommodate ways of living very different from those of the twenty-first century. These different ways of living related to very different systems of belief in terms of how a household was ordered, the different roles of women, men, children and servants, the husbandry of the fields beyond. Houses, then, relate to different cultural attitudes. The everyday movement from house to barn and byre and back again, the milking of cows and labour in the fields, the daily gathering around the table for mealtimes – all these very simple and everyday actions expressed a deep understanding of the world.

This book will ask questions about those past men, women and children who lived in houses that survive today in the English countryside. I have already shown that we can already begin to make guesses about these people by wandering around villages and landscapes with an observing eye and an enquiring mind. In the chapters that follow, I will begin to flesh out some of these guesses about what houses meant into firmer ideas. I will set these casual observations against a closer inspection of the houses themselves, against other documentary and archaeological evidence for past people, and against a wider picture of historical change at regional, national and international scales.

The Study of Vernacular Houses

The study of smaller traditional buildings is not new. Though the term 'vernacular' as applied to buildings dates to the later nineteenth century, the origins of the historical study of buildings can be sought in the perceived loss of 'tradition' itself, at the end of the eighteenth century. Many writers and intellectuals of the time, both radical and conservative, reacted with horror to the rapid changes in the world around them: the Industrial Revolution, the enclosure and privatisation of the formerly open fields, the 'dark satanic mills', and the mass migration from countryside to the growing urban centres.

This horrified reaction expressed itself in a sense of loss: that an older, pre-industrial way of life was passing away, and that the advance of industry was destroying something valuable and authentic, something that needed to be preserved. It thus led to the desire of nineteenth-century antiquarians to study what was being lost, and to the birth of the conservation movement. One of the earliest examples was the 1830s protest of the Romantic poet William Wordsworth against what he saw as the deformation of the Lake District by over-grand building, follies, and white roughcast, together with conifers and exotics: '*Singula de nobis anni praedantur euntes.* This is in the course of things; but why should the genius that directed the ancient architecture of the vales have deserted them? For the bridges, churches, mansions, cottages, and their richly fringed and flat-roofed outhouses, venerable as the grange of some old abbey, have been substituted structures, in which baldness only seems to have been studied, or plans of the most vulgar utility' (de Selincourt ed. 1906, 65). Romanticism as an intellectual and literary movement expressed a powerful sense of loss, and of opposition to modern ways of 'vulgar utility'. This opposition between aesthetics on the one hand and utility on the other went on to constitute a central formative influence on the study of vernacular architecture.

Early nineteenth-century Romanticism fed into Victorian thinking on architecture, the arts, design and material culture. Such thinking took both conservative and radical forms, and could be found equally on the political Left as on the Right. A powerful link was argued between a 'medieval' or pre-industrial way of life that involved a sense of community and closeness to Nature on the one hand and the technical and aesthetic principles of hand-made 'medieval' art and individually designed architecture on the other. Both were seen by many Victorians to relate to a sense of community and a more human, less alienated way of ordering human affairs that had been lost with industrialisation. The study of earlier forms of art and architecture, then, became for the Victorian mind a moral and political, as much as an historical, exercise. To contemplate a medieval building was not simply to look at something beautiful, it was also to contemplate a way of living, an ordering of human communities, whose passing was to be mourned. This moral imperative lay behind, for example, A.W.N. Pugin's Gothic designs (Hill 2007), John Ruskin's patient recording and explication of Gothic architecture in his great work *The Stones of Venice* (Ruskin 1884) and behind the Victorian 'restoration' of so many medieval churches, both great and small. The Oxford Movement linked veneration of the values of medieval Catholic religion, of architectural forms, and of a sense of tradition and community, in a single conservative political vision.

The classic example of such thinking and its application to architecture and material culture was the career of the socialist thinker and craftsman William Morris. Morris' understanding of socialism was expressed through his designs and his books. These celebrated the craft traditions and methods of production that, he felt, had been destroyed by capitalism and the Industrial Revolution. Morris developed a narrative of the rise and fall of the medieval craft traditions, a narrative that served as a condemnation of industrial patterns of production. He was the founder and the most prominent member of the Society for the Protection of Ancient Buildings, founded in 1877 (Miele ed. 1996, 37).

Much of this Victorian thinking concentrated on the great monuments and styles of the medieval period, most obviously the great cathedrals and churches, rather than focusing on vernacular architecture and culture as such. However, it is important to remember that nineteenth-century academic journals such as the *Archaeological Journal* and *Antiquaries Journal* grouped a wide range of objects of study under the term 'archaeology', including items of folk culture and other old artefacts (see Ebbatson 1994). In many ways, the bifurcation and academic division between different disciplines (archaeology, architectural history, folklife studies) occurred after this period; in bringing these strands back together in the modern study of vernacular architecture, scholars are going back to first principles.

Two great books, published at the turn of the nineteenth and twentieth centuries, can be seen as laying the intellectual foundations of the systematic study of vernacular houses. S.O. Addy brought an understanding of that other great Victorian theme – evolution, as expressed in the thought of Herbert Spencer and Charles Darwin – to vernacular architecture in his *Evolution of the English House* (1898). Addy argued that the form of houses had evolved in parallel with the evolution of human societies, with, he believed, earlier circular houses characteristic of matrilineal societies giving way to more modern rectangular forms indicative of male-dominated societies. In so doing he was following earlier schema of social evolution proposed by Morgan and Maine and adopted by, among others, the associate of Marx, Friedrich Engels, in his classic *Origins of the Family, Private Property and the State* (1884). Addy also related the system of the structural division of early houses into bays to the need to stall pairs of oxen, one pair to each bay, and saw the stalling of oxen in this way as fundamental to the Germanic origins of 'Anglo-Saxon' ways of living. C.F. Innocent took as his theme different building techniques in his *Development of English Building Construction* (1916). Innocent drew on his observations of cruck-framed buildings to insist on the antiquity of vernacular buildings and the evidence for pre-industrial building techniques found within them.

The early twentieth-century development of interest in vernacular buildings in England was rather different from that in other countries. In much of continental Europe and Scandinavia, peasant culture, and with it rural and vernacular tradition, was seen as something living and ongoing rather than something that had been irrevocably lost with the Industrial and Agricultural Revolutions. Rural society and culture, then, was studied as part of a living tradition, or at least as only having been eroded or threatened in the very recent past. As a result, a tradition of folklife study was often much stronger in these areas (Dorson 1972). A stronger tradition of folklife studies can also be seen in other areas of the British Isles, in Wales, Scotland and Ireland.

After the Second World War, there was a rapid expansion in England of interest in medieval and postmedieval archaeology, vernacular architecture and related themes. Much of this work must be seen in the context of postwar culture in general, in particular the Fabian reformist socialism of the postwar Labour government and an ideological commitment to the scholarly exploration of the lives of ordinary people in the past, rather than the kings, queens and princes of elite political history. Such an ideological commitment was seen most obviously at the Wharram Percy project on the Yorkshire Wolds, where from the 1950s onwards several of the peasant houses of the deserted medieval village were excavated (Johnson 2007, 104–8). The Vernacular Architecture Group was founded in 1952. This period also saw a marked expansion in extra-mural and other classes, and in amateur local history and archaeology societies. The study of vernacular buildings was perfect work for such groups. The recording and analysis of houses did not need the logistical support or have the constraints of an excavation; valuable work could be done on a Sunday afternoon, more often than not accompanied by the genial house owner's offer of a cup of tea, and, with luck, a biscuit.

Intellectual Foundations

Taken together, it could be argued that three scholars – an anthropologist, an archaeologist, and an historian – laid the foundations of the modern study of vernacular architecture. The historian W.G. Hoskins wrote a short but enormously influential article in the left-wing historical journal *Past and Present*, 'The Rebuilding of Rural England 1570–1640' (Hoskins 1953). Hoskins proposed that there had been a revolution in housing standards between these two dates, and tied this revolution in to contemporary economic and social changes. He gave potential students of vernacular architecture a narrative, a sense of how individual buildings related to a wider story about the English landscape, which he set out in lucid and passionate terms in his classic *The Making of the English Landscape* (Hoskins 1955). We shall see in Chapter 4 that Hoskins' vision is now partly out of date, but it has been enormously influential, particularly in its impact on historians' perception of the sixteenth and seventeenth centuries as being of rising affluence and assertiveness in the culture of the middling sort of people.

If Hoskins suggested a historical model, Sir Cyril Fox and Lord Raglan demonstrated the method: they showed how the study of vernacular houses could be undertaken in their three-volume study *Monmouthshire Houses* (Fox and Raglan 1951–4). Fox and Raglan looked at houses carefully within the county of Monmouthshire, utilising drawn and measured ground plans, and building a picture of vernacular architecture in a given region. (Though now part of the county of Gwent in Wales, Monmouthshire sits on the border with England and enjoys an English as well as a Welsh heritage.) *Monmouthshire Houses* was, typically for the study of vernacular buildings, an inter-disciplinary and a professional–amateur collaboration. Raglan was an unorthodox figure; he is classified in the *Oxford Dictionary of National Biography* as an anthropologist. He was interested in the anthropological study of myth and its relationship to ritual. Dismissed by many as an eccentric amateur, a more charitable view is that he prefigured anthropology's structuralist turn by twenty years. Fox was an archaeologist and curator of the National Museum of Wales. He was central to the foundation of St Fagan's open-air museum near Cardiff, one of the finest collections of reconstructed vernacular buildings in the British Isles.

The success of Hoskins, Fox and Raglan can be judged by the proliferation of studies of particular regions of England and Wales after this date. One consequence of this proliferation after the 1950s is that it is more difficult to summarise the development of vernacular architectural studies between the 1950s and the present. Such regional studies are frequently done by local and amateur groups; others have been undertaken by the Royal Commission on Historical Monuments of England (RCHME), now merged into English Heritage, and its Scottish and Welsh counter-parts Royal Commission on the Ancient and Historical Monuments of Scotland (RCAHMS) and Royal Commission on the Ancient and Historical Monuments of Wales (RCAHMW). These bodies have produced a series of detailed scholarly studies, accompanied by meticulous plans and, indeed, reconstruction drawings of great beauty (for example, Pearson 1985 on Lancashire; Smith 1992 on Hertfordshire; Giles 1992 on west Yorkshire; Suggett 2005 on Radnorshire).

A survey of scholarship in vernacular architecture today reveals a plethora of regional studies, relating local form and traditions to the economic and social history of a given region. As factual depth and detail has accumulated, however, scholars have found it more and more difficult to pull these observations together into a national synthesis. It sometimes seems as if the more we know about English houses, the more buildings surveyed, the more studies of local forms and traditions are completed, the more difficult scholars have found it to stand back and draw a picture of English vernacular houses as a whole. Anthony Quiney has even called such a task a 'will 'o'th' wisp' (Quiney 1994, 238). Proper scholarly caution, combined with the nature of the subject, where individuals tend to know one area or region as 'their patch' first and foremost, means that individuals have a natural reluctance to venture outside their own area and propose a national or wider pattern.

The apparent reluctance to tell a wider story about vernacular buildings means that we have to go back to 1961 and 1975 for two great studies at a national level. In 1961 Maurice Barley, Professor of Archaeology at Nottingham, published *The English Farmhouse and Cottage*. Barley used the evidence both of the houses themselves and of probate inventories. He made reference to improvements in material comfort and to social processes such as emulation, but he primarily saw differences in region as responses, in part, to different geographical conditions. In particular, Barley linked patterns in vernacular building to the Highland and Lowland Zones proposed by Sir Cyril Fox in *The Personality of Britain*, published and revised successively in the 1930s and discussed here in Chapter 3. Barley saw the south and east of England as more economically and socially 'progressive', owing to its physical geography and proximity to the Continent. To look at local differences, then, was to see one small element of a national pattern that was conditioned by physical geography.

In contrast, Eric Mercer's 1975 *English Vernacular Houses*, the result of his work as part of the Royal Commission, proposed that social and economic developments, rather than what he called 'geography', was the real driver of variation in vernacular architecture. Mercer suggested that all regions of England shared the same start and end points of development in house types. Regional differences in house form certainly existed, but the variation seen today between region and region was an artefact of different regions going through the same fundamental change at different paces and at different times:

> Regional peculiarities had not been wholly eliminated by the end of the eighteenth century . . . but they had become of minor importance against the background of national conformity brought about by a sequence of changes common to all parts. If the develop-ment in the South-East is regarded as the classic norm, then those in the rest of the country fall into place. The stages occurred in different regions at different times, occupied longer or shorter periods, or were even omitted altogether, but the same road was followed to the same end, and that early uniformity which began to break up in the later Middle Ages had re-established itself on a wholly different level by the early nineteenth century. . . . Looked at in this way the subject ceases to be a bundle of independent themes, connected only when one area happens to influence another, but becomes a national theme with local variations. Instead of giving a geographical account of vernacular houses in England it becomes possible to attempt a history of English vernacular houses which may perhaps be related to the history of English society (Mercer 1975, 33).

Mercer's text does not state this explicitly, but as his obituaries made clear, the underlying model was Marxist in form: Mercer saw this fundamental 'history of English society' as being one from feudalism to capitalism: from a feudal, 'medieval' social and economic structure to a modern, capitalist one.

The tension between 'geographical' and 'social' models continues in studies of vernacular architecture to this day. When scholars disagree about how to explain different patterns of vernacular building, it often comes back to whether they think they are looking at differences between the particular qualities of regions on the one hand, or change through time on the other (see, for example, recent debates on the distribution of cruck-framed buildings in different areas of England: Mercer 1996, Alcock 1997, Mercer 1998). It is a theme we will come back to several times in the course of this book.

Two developments since 1980 are of pivotal importance. First, the development of dendrochronology or tree-ring dating has given scholars an independent, scientific means of determining the age of the structural timbers in a building. Previously, scholars often had to rely on educated guesses about the date of a building, in the absence of documentary records or inscribed datestones, based on the changing form and style of decoration, framing or other elements. Such educated guesses can be subjective and unreliable, relying as they do on judgements about how fast architectural and decorative styles change and/or whether this building can be compared to that one. Other scientific techniques are generally too 'fuzzy' to be of much use; radiocarbon dating, for example, might have a 'plus' or 'minus' of at least fifty years. Tree-ring dates mean that, in principle and given the right sample, the precise date of the felling of many timbers can be determined. With caution and care, then, the construction of many buildings can be dated to within a year or two.

The second, and ongoing, development is the changing legislative and management framework surrounding old buildings (Pearson and Meeson 2001). There are currently over 350,000 buildings that are 'listed' and have statutory protection as being of 'special architectural or historical interest'. Listed buildings need statutory consent from the local authority before any alteration, either internal or external, can be made. Any building standing in reasonable condition dating before c.1700 should be listed. Though there are constant stories of damage to old buildings (the 'Nooks and Corners' section of the satirical magazine *Private Eye* always makes for interesting reading) the prevailing trend over the decades has been towards widening and deepening this protection. In the process, valuable resources for researchers have been created, most notably the house-by-house descriptions of listed buildings that are of varying but generally improving quality. Many of the leading figures in the study of vernacular architecture are employed by local authorities or by English Heritage, and their primary responsibility is in managing and caring for these buildings.

More broadly, interest in 'cultural heritage' has never been higher, and with it interest in restoring and caring for old buildings. Websites such as www.imagesofengland.org.uk, and TV programmes such as *Restoration*, reflect a very high level of public interest in historical buildings and landscapes, and moreover a level of affection for, and commitment to, their conservation.

The study of English vernacular buildings today is, then, an exceptionally vibrant and challenging field. Continuing themes and debates include the following: an interest in buildings as records of social developments, versus, or complementary to, an interest in the technical aspects of their construction; a tension between interest in regional particulars on the one hand, and the desire to tell a national story on the other; the participation of scholars from different disciplines in their study, without vernacular architecture really being central to any one discipline; the involvement of both professional and amateur; and the contested place of vernacular architecture – the thatched roof and half-timbering of the iconic 'Tudor' cottage – in a nostalgic vision of a regional and pre-industrial England, and the continuing cultural and political power of that vision, whether for better or worse.

Approaches to Vernacular Buildings

The study of vernacular buildings, then, has a very complex history, a history moreover that has always had a wider cultural and political resonance. The study of vernacular houses is consequently a field in which scholars from very different disciplines come together in what is often a sharp dialogue and debate. But this vibrancy and sharpness can also be a problem. As the Jesuits famously observed, the way a person has been educated in his or her youth moulds and conditions the way they see the world. A particular disciplinary training, as an architect, archaeologist, historian, or some other discipline, gives the scholar not just a set of spectacles but a set of blinkers as well. What the document-based historian sees as 'conclusive evidence' can be seen by the archaeologist as tentative or irrelevant, or vice versa. Scholars can end up 'talking past' each other, as their respective disciplines have very different understandings of what they are studying, how best to study it, and what criteria of evidence or proof might be. Cases where different disciplines are brought together in the study of a single traditional building are still quite rare (the study of Bowhill, a gentry house in Devon, is an exemplary study: Blaylock 2004). This difference in understanding between different disciplines is much deeper and more profound than grand, explicit visions: it extends to such apparently mundane points as how best to record a building (for example, the debate between Ferris 1989 and Ferris 1991 and others on 'objective' recording techniques), or what is architectural 'style', or how to write the history of houses (Arnold 2002 looks at a range of approaches).

Some description of disciplinary differences is therefore needed, but an exhaustive account would be tedious; many of the conceptual and theoretical issues at stake are abstruse and even dull when considered in the abstract, and are far better explored with reference to concrete examples in the chapters that follow. Here, then, for the benefit of the reader new to the study of traditional buildings, are a series of caricatures. As such, they are necessarily stereotypical, over-drawn, and over-simplified.

The *historian*, tweed-jacketed, bookish, and slightly rumpled, came to look at old buildings as part of a growing appreciation that getting immersed in the yellowing papers of the local record office was only part of the story. Looking at buildings is for such a scholar preferable to archaeological excavation, as one does not have to get one's knees or boots muddy. However, the old house is a problem as well as a source of evidence – the historian would like nothing better than to have a document giving the date of its construction and the names of those responsible, for then, and only then, it could be made to tell us something. Historians understand buildings as documents – pieces of evidence to be slotted in alongside this inventory and that survey, though they tend to trust the document rather more than the physical evidence of the building. The historian gets nervous when no corroborating documents are to be found, often equating the absence of documents to the absence of evidence.

The *architectural historian* spends most of the time on the outside rather than inside of the building, expressing deep grief over the modern Velux windows and noisy appreciation of the outside decoration. The architectural historian is never happier than when contemplating some detail of design, preferably of Classical inspiration and 'correctly' executed. He or she spends very little time in the kitchen, the adjacent farm buildings or any of the other more mundane aspects of the building. Architectural historians understand buildings as examples of types, often 'good' or 'bad' examples according to often unspoken aesthetic rules (rules that anyone of a proper, correct education 'just knows'), and use the facades of the buildings as illustrative of a wider story about the succession of types.

The *folklife enthusiast* plunges straight in to the house, revelling in the little details of the surviving latches, the witchcraft precautions, the marks of craftsmanship of the adze and saw. For such an enthusiast, the house is silent but eloquent testament to an ancient way of life, a simpler, better way than that of the present. Folklife scholars view buildings in a romantic way, as testaments to a vanished way of life that was somehow more authentic than that of modern times, and whose passing is to be mourned.

Finally, the *archaeologist*, in stripy jumper, socks and sandals. Looking around the inside of the house is all very well, but what the archaeologist would really like to do is to knock the house down, recording it brick by brick as the structure was dismantled, and then excavate the foundations; only then, when the house is reduced to nothing more than an empty hole in the ground, will the archaeologist understand every last secret of the building, and thus be really happy. Archaeologists understand buildings as a form of archaeological site, a series of accreted layers – a rebuilding of this wing, an alteration of that hall. They can be vague about dates – after all, what is twenty-five years here or there when your prehistorian colleagues study a period of several million years?

Definitions

These very different disciplinary backgrounds lead to very different views and definitions of the nature of vernacular houses, and the appropriate way to study them. Let us try to tie these different views together with some definitions.

Eric Mercer sees the term 'vernacular' when applied to houses as having 'three distinct but related meanings: first, vernacular houses are of traditional form, are built in traditional ways with traditional materials, and use traditional ornament; secondly, they are common within, and peculiar to, one or more limited parts of the country; thirdly they are small and mean in comparison with some of their neighbours'. Vernacular is thus a closely related term to 'traditional'. For Mercer, vernacular buildings are 'those which belong to a type which is common in a given area at a given time' (Mercer 1975, 1). An implicit contrast is drawn here with 'polite' architecture. 'Polite' buildings are designed by individuals with professional training, often termed 'architects' and often named. The form and ornament reflects and draws upon national and international models. Of course, the contrasted terms 'polite' and 'vernacular' here have social as well as architectural connotations. We shall see in future chapters how the term 'vernacular' raises real difficulties, but it will serve as an introduction for the time being, with the proviso that its definition will be revisited in the Conclusions.

The word 'architecture' is more familiar to the reader, but close examination shows that it has just as many difficulties. For some writers, particularly architectural historians such as the great Nikolaus Pevsner (Games ed. 2002) and Alec Clifton-Taylor (1972), and even the architectural critic and Poet Laureate John Betjeman (1970, 16), architecture is different from mere building. For a building to become architecture, it must be evident that it was designed with some sort of conscious aesthetic effect in mind. In this view, Pevsner wrote, 'a bicycle shed is a building; Lincoln Cathedral is a piece of architecture' (Pevsner 1963, 15). It is possible to extend this view to argue that farm buildings and even farmhouses, being functional buildings whose form (in this view) is governed by an utilitarian view of their everyday uses, are also not architecture.

This view has been very influential in architectural history, in part because it was inscribed into the intellectual foundations of the discipline by the great German art historians; but it is one that I oppose with great passion. A central and guiding theme in what follows in this book is that *even the smallest house, built and dwelt in by a household of the most humble status and of the most limited economic means, is a statement about the world, and a chosen way of living in it*. That way of living may be heavily constrained by external factors such as the availability of building materials, poverty or economic necessity, the demands of a higher political authority, or the wishes and desires of the landlord who built the cottage, but it is a carefully ordered and thought-through expression of a view of the world nevertheless. Moreover, that expression is thought through actively. As Upton and Vlach rightly insist (1986, xxiii), the story of houses is one of ordinary people making their own history. I therefore retain the term 'architecture' to refer to vernacular buildings such as farmhouses and barns and byres and even bicycle sheds, as I want to insist on these buildings being ordered, their design being carefully thought through by the builder and owner, and in their own way their being just as complex or profound a statement about the world as the greatest Elizabethan house or medieval cathedral.

Five Myths About Traditional Buildings

Seeing vernacular architecture in terms of people making their own history can be difficult for the modern observer, in part because, as we have seen, traditional houses carry a strong cultural and emotional baggage, a baggage placed on our backs by the Romantic tradition. Unlike prehistoric remains such as Neolithic chambered tombs or Palaeolithic handaxes, these houses occupy a very special place in the formation of contemporary views of and prejudices about the English countryside. As such, they are subject to a Romantic view that goes back to Wordsworth's and others' views of vernacular buildings as reflecting a *genius loci*: they are immediately classified as authentic, closer to the earth, more functional, timeless even, to be contrasted with a faceless, placeless modernity of 'vulgar utility' in whatever guise. Here, then, are five assertions about traditional buildings that I want to examine in the course of this book. They are myths, in the sense that they are stories that are told over and over again: this does not mean that they are necessarily right or wrong, but they can and do bear further examination.

Vernacular building was necessarily functional, as opposed to decorative. This view was expressed most eloquently by Maurice Barley, who wrote that 'Till the eighteenth century [farmhouses and cottages] remained in essence functional building [*sic*], in which purpose determined plan and form, and ornament was subordinated to them. That the builder often achieved what an architect now consciously strives for – a satisfactory relation of forms, a harmony of structure and environment, a pleasing variety of finish and ornament – was incidental to his purpose of making a machine for living in. The archaeological approach, as distinct from the aesthetic, makes it easier to relate the form of an artefact, whether it is a flint implement, a pot or a house, to the culture which evolved it and the purpose for which it was made' (Barley 1961, xix). It is closely related to the traditions of German art history and of architectural modernism that so influenced Pevsner. My response is not to deny that architecture is functional, but to question the either/or nature of this divide. 'Function or aesthetics' is a false choice. Traditional builders and owners placed decoration on their buildings, as we shall see, and it is often impossible to say where 'function' ends and the 'aesthetic' begins. Perhaps builders and owners lived their lives and built their houses in ways that made sense to them, according to a rhythm and tempo that related to a sense of tradition and memory on their part. As such, perhaps it was both deeply meaningful to them, and also a material way of making a living. Scholars should not force themselves into a position where they have to make a false choice between functional and aesthetic interpretations.

People were trying to imitate those above them on the social scale. It is often thought that changes in buildings start at the very top of the social scale, and then 'filter down' to lower levels. The underlying assumption here is that, in a deeply status-conscious society such as pre-industrial England, people habitually attempted to copy or emulate their social superiors. But the evidence for such an assumption is questionable. Very often, when historians cite 'evidence' for social emulation, they quote documents written by the elite, expounding the fear that their social inferiors are getting uppity. Such fears tell us a lot about the anxieties of the ruling classes, but are not direct, unproblematic evidence of whether the lower orders were really attempting social emulation.

Vernacular builders were inherently conservative: vernacular architecture is unchanging. One of the words associated with ordinary buildings is 'traditional', which can be taken to imply unchanging or changing very slowly. The implied comparison is with metropolitan, urban and elite buildings; by contrast, it is implied, rural dwellings were open to a narrower range of 'influences'. Behind such a notion is an image of the countryside as a rural retreat, more insular, slower to change, with a more conservative social pattern and way of life. It is certainly the case that the idea of 'traditional builders' has a very strong notion of a craft tradition, and I will look at evidence in Chapter 5 that while owners were attempting to innovate, they were often held back by builders' reluctance to part with traditional methods. But this view is not necessarily borne out by the evidence in all cases. At certain periods, as we shall see, vernacular buildings could change very quickly. Such notions of an unchanging rural retreat again go back to Romanticism and beyond to the Classical legacy of poets like Virgil, and are often ideological preconceptions of urbanites. The great cultural critic Raymond Williams showed many years ago that images of the countryside of this kind are ideological photo-negatives of life in the city (Williams 1973). Anyone who has actually lived in a rural community knows very well that, alongside deep continuities, change in such communities can be very fast and very wide-ranging.

The domestic/private was divided from the agrarian/public. It is natural for the modern reader to conceive of 'home' as a private retreat, away from the place of work, of the cares of public and professional life. But the pre-industrial farmhouse was not like this at all: rather, as Marshall Sahlins insists, households before the Industrial Revolution were 'charged with production' (Sahlins 1972, 76). Activities such as brewing, dairying, rural industry such as the spinning and weaving of cloth, took place within the structures of the home. Relations between husband and wife, then, were economic as well as domestic. And they were also political: in a patriarchal world where the husband was head of the household, and where the king was held to rule over his people just as the husband ruled over his family, the courts routinely interfered with household relations, for example, through public prosecution and punishment of women they categorised as 'scolds' or nagging wives.

If they didn't have names, they didn't have agency or culture. This is perhaps the most difficult myth to identify as such, but also the most pervasive myth of all. Very often, we do not have direct historical evidence for the names of people who built and dwelt in vernacular houses. We know that such-and-such a house was built in the later sixteenth century, and that its size and appearance suggest that it housed a yeoman or husbandman household; but the names of its occupants elude us. However, this does not mean that we do not have evidence for who they were, their view of their world, and the way they acted upon it. That evidence is there, in the form and use of the building. The addition of a wing to a building, the everyday activities of cooking, the sweeping of the floor – these were all human actions that can be seen in the archaeological record of houses, and which tell us about the human beings who dwelt there.

All these myths are not necessarily untrue. Some had particular currency at particular times and places. We will see, for example, how the eighteenth century saw a widening separation of the world of work from that of the domestic environment, and how, at specific historical periods, some people may well have presented their houses and belongings with the intention of emulating their social superiors.

However, their truth cannot be assumed for all times and for all places. If we are to look objectively at houses, and explore their full potential for telling us about people in the past, we have to start from the position that we cannot make any initial assumptions about them. Perhaps, in some periods, socially middling people did attempt to emulate those above them on the social scale; perhaps, in some periods, a division between private and public domains of the house can be demonstrated. Some of these issues will be explored in this book.

Performance, Materiality and Agency

Instead of relying on such myths, I want to introduce three ideas to help the reader understand traditional buildings: performance, materiality and agency. All three ideas have been discussed extensively and elaborately by writers on social and material life, but all three are in essence very simple.

Performance is about the way all social action, for example, the everyday actions of building and living in a house takes place in front of an audience, even if the audience numbers one, the self. (Even when humans are on their own they observe cultural conventions, for example, sweeping the floor or setting the table for a meal.) Who people are, then, is defined by the performance they put on. All actions are performance, though some actions can be more performative than others. Everyday activity is a particularly important kind of performance, as by repeating actions over and over again identities are produced and reproduced. Think of a very simple set of actions involved in and around the vernacular house: that of preparing, cooking and eating a meal. The housewife, family members and servants cooperate in bringing the food to the kitchen, out of service and farmyard areas. Preparation and cooking is a sequence of actions. At a certain time, say midday, the men return to the house from the fields, perhaps taking their turn in washing their hands before being seated in a particular order at the table, the master of the house sitting at the head of the table. Perhaps a prayer or blessing is said, either by the master or someone invited by him. Guests are defined and honoured by being offered food first. At the end of the meal, the household members rise in a particular order, and the men leave for the afternoon's work; the women then wash up and turn to other tasks.

The point here is that performance is much, much more than 'good manners'. Precisely because it is implicit and unspoken, 'what everyone knows', performance defines at a very basic level who someone is. In the example I have given, performance refers to ideas of gender, of social status, of religious belief, and of values of hospitality – that is, an understanding of what it means to be a man or a woman, master or servant, guest or host, is defined and asserted through everyday actions. Further, the rhythms of everyday action were particularly important in the pre-industrial world. Where people interacted on a face-to-face level, and where many or even more than half the inhabitants were illiterate, the importance of visual representation and performance cannot be overstressed.

Building and dwelling in a traditional house is, and was, a set of repeated performances. But it was also much more than this. The house materialised social lives. *Materiality* refers to several interconnecting ideas. The house was a physical expression of the household. People built the way they lived and dealt with each other, and they built literally as well as metaphorically. The external appearance of the house, the arrangement of rooms and spaces, its decoration – it is obvious that all these reflected ideas about social life.

Materiality is also about the way material things do not simply reflect ideas, but how they embody and even enforce ideas. People did not have abstract ideas about how to live which they then expressed in houses. Rather, the houses, perhaps built by a generation long dead and modified by each succeeding generation, influenced them. For women and men who grew up in these spaces, experiencing the textures and qualities of the house, engaging in repeated performances such as those of mealtimes, the house materialised a way of life. This meant that social ideas did not exist for people prior to the form of the house; people did not have ideas about how to live that they then 'expressed' in how the house was built and used. Rather, the house and social life acted recursively, back-and-forth on one another. At the same time, the house physically fixed and defined performance. It acted as a backdrop, a stage setting even, to the everyday rituals such as mealtime.

Materiality refers to the particular qualities of the material world, the very important way buildings and objects can fix and centre certain ideas and relationships. In our mealtime example, relations between men and women would be more effectively and lastingly renegotiated by the building of a new chimneystack for the kitchen than they would by a 'debate' on the issue of marital equality between husband and wife. More subtly, objects and fittings around the house such as treasured heirlooms, quilts, items given as gifts at life-defining events such as weddings and baptisms, served as constant memory devices and emblems. Again, the power of these objects was all the greater within a world where many could not read or write.

Agency is about the way humans used performance and materiality together in an active way. Humans did not simply passively absorb the cultural values of the day and then replay them uncritically. For example, while pre-industrial England was a patriarchal and status-conscious society, this did not mean that all members of the household, women and servants especially, always and uncritically accepted the dominant view of how they should behave. People acted in subtly different ways to renegotiate or transform the social world around them, for example, through rebuilding or modifying the houses in which they lived. Everyday clusters of actions such as mealtimes could be replayed, or subtly transformed by little actions – sitting in a different position, failing to show deference, putting the bowls down with an angry clatter, failing to offer food first to a guest, whispering or talking a little too loudly.

Agency, in this sense, might sound obvious or common sense. It has to be remembered, though, that the scholarly underpinnings of the study of vernacular architecture have often bypassed agency. Pevsner saw buildings as reflective of a zeitgeist or spirit of the age. Others see house-plans as distinctive to regions, and imply that this region gave birth to that house-plan. Others still see house forms as illustrative of wider processes of economic or social change, such as the transition from feudalism to capitalism. In all these views, in the urge to move from zeitgeist, region, economic process, or historical stage to the form of the house itself, the agency of real human beings runs the danger of being bypassed.

Structure of the Book

I will start by introducing some of the contexts of building and living in traditional houses. Chapter 2 considers how houses were built using traditional building materials and construction techniques. Chapter 3 introduces some of the wider landscape, material and social contexts for the house. Both chapters will lay out some very basic patterns in traditional houses, ranging from the influence of the underlying geology and soil type, through different aspects of the craft tradition and forms of wider regional landscape, to the social and cultural make-up of the family and household.

I will then examine how houses changed from the Middle Ages onwards. Chapter 4 discusses the late medieval house in terms of the way it expressed, encoded, enforced – in other words, materialised – an understanding of the world, in particular through the structure and meanings of its central space, the open hall. Chapter 5 looks at the loss of that open hall in the rebuilding of houses in the sixteenth and early seventeenth centuries, and asks what factors were involved in this change, including the English Reformation. Chapter 6 examines the same period in terms of the changing relationship between greater and smaller houses, the houses of the elite and of ordinary people. Chapter 7 paints a portrait of the reformed house, linking very small details of its construction and decoration, its spaces and textures, to patterns of everyday life within the household.

Chapter 8 looks at how this order in houses was dissolved and reassembled once again, through a set of changes often packaged (and perhaps oversimplified) as 'the Georgian Order'. The Georgian Order introduced a pattern in architecture and society of order, standardisation and symmetry. The process of Georgianisation has to be understood on a wider canvas than simply England alone, and the Conclusions will look at a few elements of this wider canvas, putting changes in the pattern of English vernacular architecture in the context of the Atlantic world as a whole, from the British Isles to the eastern seaboard of the New World.

Throughout, I will concentrate my discussion on rural buildings, though I will use examples from smaller towns as appropriate. Urban architecture raises a fresh set of problems, but the distinction between a small town and a large village will not always be clear to the observer, while the interdependence of countryside and provincial towns is very clear (see Giles and Dyer 2005).

1. Lancashire (cont.)
2. Westmoreland
3. Shropshire (Salop)
4. Staffordshire
5. Rutland
6. Nottinghamshire
7. Worcestershire
8. Warwickshire
9. Northamptonshire
10. Leicestershire
11. Huntingdonshire
12. Cambridgeshire
13. Bedfordshire
14. Hertfordshire
15. Buckinghamshire
16. Oxfordshire
17. Middlesex
18. Herefordshire
19. Gloucestershire

Map 1.1 Map of England, with the old (pre-1974) counties indicated.

In many senses, this book represents a revisiting of the themes I first addressed in my 1993 book *Housing Culture*, and the themes of the Suffolk-based research that were the foundations of that book. Many of the arguments presented there remain little changed. I remain convinced of the usefulness of thinking about buildings as a kind of language, in helping students to grasp the way the pre-industrial builder created houses out of raw materials; of the centrality of the century after 1540 to the understanding of change in vernacular buildings; and the importance of looking contextually at the whole landscape, including the cultural and religious landscape, in understanding that change. This book changes emphasis from my earlier thinking in several ways. First, it looks less at the formal content of religious belief – Protestantism and Puritanism – and more at the everyday performance and experience of religious change, for example, in the parish church. Second, it widens its scope – it attempts to explain houses at the level of England in its context in the Atlantic world, rather than in a particular region. Third, it takes advantage of a decade of fresh scholarship, particularly interdisciplinary work on material life and culture, and in particular feminist research on gender and women's experiences in the household.

Fourth, the style and tone of this book is different from *Housing Culture*, and I hope a little more courageous – the former book was in parts a forest of technical jargon and scholarly qualifiers; it was unduly governed by a young scholar's fear of academic disapproval. This book is addressed to a wider audience, popular as well as academic, and I hope it is a little more accessible as a consequence. Often, the plea for 'clear and simple prose' is nothing more than a complaint that the reader does not wish to be challenged by new and unfamiliar ideas and ways of thinking; I have tried in what follows to write simply, without diluting my conviction that scholarship that fails to challenge and move our thinking forward beyond easy and familiar assumptions is not worth pursuing.

My wider, governing view of vernacular buildings is updated and in some ways spelt out more clearly, but it remains unchanged in its essentials. The study of old houses is, fundamentally, about much more than the cosy material familiarity of crucks, tie-beams and thatched roofs: it is the study of the people who built them and who lived in them. It is about performance, materiality and agency – 'the study of people acting. It shows us people . . . engaged with their surroundings in a critical way, people making their own histories in the face of authorities trying to make it for them' (Upton and Vlach 1986, xxiii). If we want to understand those old houses, we have to understand something of the physical, cultural and mental landscape those people inhabited, and how that landscape changed through time and across space. Further, we must understand those people as making their own history through their houses, through the form and pattern of their construction and through the everyday actions of living in them. Such a task is desperately complex and ambitious, but anything less is to condemn the voices of the past to what E.P. Thompson (1963, 13), in his great evocation of working-class culture in the Industrial Revolution, called 'the enormous condescension of posterity'.

2
Building Traditional Houses

The building of a traditional house is, in one sense, an act of translation. The builder has an idea of what the house is intended to look like, its internal disposition and arrangement of rooms, the materials it should be built of, the technical details and decisions necessary for construction. The builder translates this idea into the physical form of the house. In this sense, the final form and appearance of the house can be seen as the embodiment of an idea, or a mental template, that exists initially only in the mind of the builder. That idea or template may never have had a material existence as a plan or elevation on paper, but it did exist nevertheless, and the final form of the house is its imperfect manifestation.

In practice, however, the thinking-through and construction of a building was always a more complex process than a simple translation by an individual craftsman from idea to physical reality. When a vernacular house was built, many different physical and cultural structures, individuals and agencies came together. Different craftsmen were involved, not simply a single designer but carpenters, bricklayers, tilers, thatchers, unskilled labourers. There was a complex relationship between the needs or desires that the client expressed and the builder's willingness or ability to build a structure that met the client's preferences. Building materials were often reused, in particular selective elements of former timber frames. And much building activity involved repairs, or additions to, or modifications, of existing structures, as much as building new houses.

The traditional builder was constrained by the materials to hand. Before the transport revolution of the middle of the eighteenth century, and to a lesser extent after this date, vernacular builders had a limited choice of locally available materials, depending on local geology and physical geography. A typical example is the late seventeenth-century house of Pasture Farm, Boarstall in Buckinghamshire, where a detailed set of documentary records survives; the timber for the house and the stone for its cellar came from less than two kilometres and fifteen kilometres away, respectively (Airs and Broad 1998, 51). In Cumbria, where admittedly good stone was generally plentiful, quarries were seldom sited more than three kilometres away from the building site; timber on the other hand had to be brought from much further afield (Tyson 1998, 65 and 76).

By contrast, 'polite' buildings could be constructed with material brought from some distance; the first Norman castles and cathedrals, for example, were in part built of stone from Caen in Normandy. Within England, stone from quarries such as those at Barnack on the Northamptonshire/Cambridgeshire border, or those at Purbeck on the Dorset coast, could be transported many hundreds of kilometres. Material which carried a particular set of meanings, for example, Roman brick, could be transported and deliberately reused in elite buildings for its social symbolism; for example, it has been convincingly demonstrated how Roman material was transported some distance for reuse in elite buildings when more economic alternatives were available (Eaton 2000).

It has been estimated that for distances of over twenty kilometres transport costs of stone, for example, would be higher than those of extracting the stone in the first place (Salzman 1952, 119). Consequently, patterns of vernacular building that can be seen today habitually reflect the pattern of local geology, geomorphology and geography: sandstone in this area, Jurassic limestone in that area, timber-framing in this third area where local stone suitable for walling was not readily available. We will discuss these geographical and geological patterns, and the way they suggest a broader pattern to buildings, in the next chapter. But this constraint of locally available materials was also enabling. Materials determined aspects of the broader pattern of English building, to use Alec Clifton-Taylor's phrase (1972), but they did not dictate them. Traditional builders used the materials to hand as a set of resources, not simply as a set of limitations. They had a close and detailed practical knowledge of the properties of materials such as different species of timber and different kinds of stone, and they used this practical knowledge in the creative manipulation of the materials at their disposal (Plate 5).

The agency of the builder – what he wanted to build – was also constrained by the relationship with the client, and the client's means, wishes and demands. With vernacular building in pre-industrial England, builder and client were characteristically part of the same social network, a network that was often close and intimate and which involved shared norms and assumptions about the way the world worked. Builder and client were often neighbours, but they were not the same person.

In prehistoric societies, building methods could be relatively unspecialised, though the techniques used could nevertheless create impressive structures. For example, the great trilithons of Stonehenge were shaped and their joints were mortice-and-tenoned in such a way as to indicate that their builders used techniques derived from the building of equally impressive, though now vanished, timber structures. In prehistoric communities, the person who built a dwelling, and the person who lived in it, were likely to be the same or at least very closely related: craft specialists in prehistoric societies were characteristically very much part of the local community. In modern societies, by contrast, there is a much wider gap between architect and client. The buildings designed by the professional architect are rarely lived in by him or her. Instead, the modern architect has a professionally defined relationship with the client, specified by the written contract and by a detailed set of architect's plans and elevations; as any student of the history of modern architecture knows, the gap between architect and client has meant the design of buildings that are not always sensitive to the client's needs. We shall see in Chapter 6 how this gap between architect and client emerged as part of the social divisions of the early modern world.

The Organisation of Traditional Building

Vernacular building in pre-industrial England falls somewhere between these two extreme situations in the relationship between builder and client. Building was to a greater or lesser extent professionalised; the profession of 'carpenter' and 'mason' was in part subject to a guild structure of apprenticeship and fellowship. There was no architect, in the modern sense of 'one who plans buildings as opposed to one who executes them, or furthermore one who plans with a view to aesthetically as well as functionally satisfactory results, as opposed to one who concerns himself only with the technical requirements of building' (Pevsner 1942, 549). Such a description might only be applied to building at an elite level after 1600, and arguably later still with traditional building.

We have a great deal of documentary information about the organisation of carpentry, brick-making, masonry, plastering and other building skills within urban and elite contexts. This information comes from a variety of sources, including building accounts, diaries, the wills and inventories of craftsmen, and essays, literary references and other didactic literature. As a result, a very detailed picture of large-scale building projects can be drawn, and an extensive literature on the planning and building of structures such as great churches, castles and country houses exists. Salzman's and Harvey's great syntheses on medieval building draw much of this material together for the Middle Ages (Salzman 1952; J. Harvey 1984); the *History of the King's Works* provides a detailed account of royal building (Colvin 1963); while Malcolm Airs' classic *The Making of the English Country House*, later revised as *The Tudor and Jacobean Country House: A Building History* (Airs 1975 and Airs 1995), does this for the sixteenth and early seventeenth centuries. Urban building is also well covered by this documentary material, relatively speaking (for example, Woodward 1995).

The pattern of building at the vernacular level and in the countryside, however, does not have the same level of documentary coverage. Both builder and client below the level of the gentry may well have been illiterate, particularly in earlier periods before the early modern rise in literacy. As a result, plans and written contracts are relatively rare at the vernacular level before the seventeenth century, though they do exist (Dymond 1998 gives five examples from fifteenth-century Bury St Edmunds). Here, for example, is a contract for a fifteenth-century house in Bedale, North Yorkshire. Harrison and Hutton comment that 'the figures do not represent the full cost of building, since timber, stone, clay and wattling materials were supplied by the lord':

Thomas Vale (1429–30)

Stipend of John Thirn for carriage of timber, by agreement		19s	0d
Stipend of Simon Wade for the carpentry of same, by agreement	5	0	0
Sawing planks and timber	1	0	0
Stipend of carter carting stones for walling, clay and sand	1	2	10
1,000 laths brought for the same		10	5
4,000 lathnails bought for the same		6	0
400 iron medilspykings (spike-nails)		1	8
200 dubelspykings		1	8
Iron bought for makying chains, crokes, hasps, and staples		3	4
Stones brought for the roofing	1	1	6
Carriage of the same		14	10
Bread and ale at the raising		2	6
	11	3	9

(Harrison and Hutton 1984, 5)

It should be noted that this house was quite expensive – Harrison and Hutton cite another example which cost less than £5.00, while costs of between £2.00 and £4.00 are often cited for medieval houses in general (Dyer 1986). Cottage housing in Cumbria cost between £7 and £20 per house in the later seventeenth century (Tyson 1993); in England as a whole, a mid-seventeenth-century timber-framed house could be between £30 and £40, though this rose to £200 by the early eighteenth century (Machin 1977b).

It is clear from the documentary evidence that builders worked on a great variety of contracts and projects of different sizes and at different social levels, both 'polite' and 'vernacular'. The fifteenth-century manorial records of Havering-atte-Bower, for example, record a request for a brickmason to come to construct a 'Dowble Chemeney of Brykke', with a suggestion that a brickmason be employed from nearby Witham, where work was going on at the much larger Faulkborne Hall (Ryan 1986, 113). More broadly, the documents show us a fascinating pattern of builders and masons being brought together by lords for major building projects. A famous example is the set of building accounts for Edward I's great castles in Wales. In these accounts, we have evidence of craftsmen coming together from the length and breadth of England to work on common projects. It has been suggested that this coming-together helps us to understand the ensuing trajectory of vernacular building in north Wales (Taylor 1974, vi; Smith 1975). Some syntheses of documentary sources have been attempted for vernacular housing in rural areas (see, for example, Airs and Broad 1998; Dyer 1986), but much remains to be done.

It is very tempting to try to extrapolate – to use this documentary material written in the main for urban and elite contexts to tell us about building at vernacular levels. This can be done, as Currie maintains at some length (2004), but only with caution. Where documents do exist for vernacular buildings, for example, building contracts at a socially middling level, they are by definition exceptional. They were drawn up by literate people, in a context where, to state the obvious, a written contract was deemed necessary, and where, very often, well over half the surrounding community was illiterate. In other words, building contracts may indeed signify a quite unusual, rather than 'normal', set of circumstances. When studying old buildings, it is tempting to have recourse to the documents as the final, deciding say in judging between arguments; equally, it is tempting to view buildings as effectively prehistoric, to view documents as hindrances rather than aids in their interpretation. Both approaches have potentials and problems.

Inventories of the houses of those involved in vernacular building suggest that, however specialised, much of such work was nevertheless part-time and seasonal; many carpenters at least in the countryside had a farm and other activities contributing to the economy of the household. Building was largely, though not exclusively, the preserve of men (there are a few references to women baking and laying bricks, for example, in the fifteenth-century brick additions to Tattershall Castle). It could involve a combination of local labourers and outside craftsmen, as at Middle Claydon in Buckinghamshire, where a total of twenty-six people were employed, including three women for preparing the straw for thatching (Airs and Broad 1998, 46).

Traditional building practices were associated with ritual practices of different kinds. When traditional buildings have been demolished or excavated by archaeologists, the discovery of foundation deposits has been common. In different contexts from a variety of dates across northern Europe, prehistoric stone axes, coins, steel, human and animal skulls and small animals were either used as foundation deposits or buried in the walls of houses to provide ritual protection (Merrifield 1987, 123–5).

Competence and the Craft Tradition

Behind the ideas and technical competence of both builder and client lay a much wider and deeper structure, what Richard Harris calls the craft tradition (Harris 1989 and Harris 1993). Like other pre-industrial craft traditions governing the design and production of artefacts such as pottery and furniture, the design of any individual vernacular building was strongly constrained, not only by the materials available but also by enduring conceptions of what was or was not an appropriate way of building, an accepted idea of what the size, form and appearance of the house should be. We will see in the context of the late medieval house just how strong and enduring these governing conceptions could be. This does not mean that vernacular building was necessarily or inherently conservative at all times and in all places; nor does it mean that a wide variety of building forms – expressing a range of ideas of what was appropriate – could not co-exist. The craft tradition could be enabling as well as constraining; in other words, as well as prescribing a range of forms for vernacular building it could also lead to the creation of new forms and enable original solutions to new problems to be found. The vernacular builder, then, was not a completely autonomous agent, with complete free will to conceive of, design and build a house just as he pleased; but neither was he a robot or a passive automaton, condemned to simply and endlessly repeat the patterns of the past in a mindless fashion.

One way of thinking about these different constraints and possibilities, and the way they came together in the mental and physical devices that the builder used, is in terms of a cultural grammar, but a grammar that governs the organisation of spaces and things rather than the organisation of language. Every speaker of language knows that it consists in part of a series of grammatical rules, which individuals follow as they speak or write. These rules are partly or wholly implicit; speakers do not consciously rehearse rules about gerunds or subjunctive clauses as they speak, even though they are implicitly using and deploying those rules. A relatively small set of simple linguistic rules, implicitly understood by both the person speaking and the person listening, can give rise to an infinite and complex set of spoken utterances. Linguistic theorists call this ability to produce sentences from rules a 'competence', and many linguists, following the work of the great Noam Chomsky, suggest that 'competence' is an innately human attribute or quality (Johnson 1993a, 33–4).

So it is with the rules of craft tradition governing vernacular building. Builders used a set of rules to generate different forms of houses, and to generate the different forms in the technical details and decoration of those houses. The rules themselves could be very simple, even if the final range of house forms produced was very wide. The rules were partly implicit. Should a builder be asked why this rather than that technique was being used, the taciturn answer would likely be the one word 'tradition', or more elliptically, 'this is the way we always do it'. Underneath such brief and partly enigmatic replies lay a deep well of practical knowledge of the structural properties of different materials, ways and means to manipulate those materials, and a dense mass of unspoken assumptions about what was or was not an appropriate or correct way of generating house forms from the materials and techniques to hand. Although many of those unspoken assumptions had their roots in a knowledge of what was or was not structurally possible or efficient, and also in an aversion to the structural risk involved in trying out new forms, equally efficient alternatives to the forms selected did exist, as we shall see, and it was the technical competence of the builder, given to him by the craft tradition, that led him to work in a certain way rather than another.

This 'competence' can be seen most clearly if we consider the set of rules that lie behind vernacular houses that are timber-framed in their construction. Timber frames also have the advantage of being some of the most complex, beautiful and appealing artefacts that were produced by the craft tradition.

Timber Framing

The simplest way to build a wooden house is to pile the logs up horizontally, one on top of another. This method can be seen in the 'log cabins' of Scandinavia, Switzerland or the 'frontier' towns of the American West, where the horizontally placed logs are trimmed, jointed and lined; it should be noted that while this method is conceptually simple, there was a great deal of complexity and craft knowledge involved in the different techniques of log construction (Kniffen and Glassie 1986; Roberts 1986). Equally, one can dig a foundation trench and build the walls out of vertical logs. However, such methods are only economic in areas of abundant woodland, where timber is cheap and easily available.

Contrary to popular conceptions, most of what became the country of England was cleared of large swathes of woodland in deep prehistory, some millennia before the arrival of the Romans. By the Middle Ages, most of the large natural forests that covered the British Isles before the arrival of humans had largely vanished; the medieval term 'forest' when found in documents often refers strictly to areas subject to forest law, rather than forest in the modern sense of the term (Rackham 1990 and 1994). Therefore, the wooden houses that characterise so much of vernacular building in lowland England are timber-framed rather than built solidly of timber – a wooden 'skeleton' bears the load, and the walls between are infilled, most commonly with lath and plaster.

The vast majority of traditional timber-framing in England is of oak. Oak can be worked with relative ease in the first few months after being felled when it is still 'green', but thereafter it hardens. Some houses are built of elm, with concentrations in particular areas such as Surrey (Copeland, personal communication); ash and aspen are also known (Rackham 1986, 86). In the seventeenth and eighteenth centuries an increasing quantity of pine as well as oak was imported from the Baltic via the Hanse trading network (Groves 2000). Oak was the preferred material in part because of its all-round strength – other species of wood have particular strengths, but oak combines tensile strength with endurance.

The sequence of actions that led to the finished vernacular house started with the growing of the tree. Carpenters cannot use any old piece of wood to construct the timber frame of a house: there is a distinction to be made here between 'timber', suitable for structural purposes, and other bits and pieces of wood. Timber of suitable dimensions or 'scantling' for use as part of a structural frame, particularly the principal or main elements of that frame, was a much rarer commodity.

Practices varied from region to region. In Rochford in Essex, a relatively modest timber-framed building took 173 trees to build, while the larger but still typical Grundle House in Hatfield Forest took 350 trees, both oak and elm (Rackham 1990, 67–8). It has been estimated that a fifty-acre wood could produce Grundle House once every six years in the sixteenth century (Rackham 1972, 6). The nature and quantity of timber needed depended in part on whether woodland or hedgerow trees were being used: on the Sussex Weald, only fifty years later, a rather smaller house was built of hedgerow trees (Kirk 2003).

Building timber took decades and longer to produce. The palaeobotanist and landscape historian Oliver Rackham has shown how the woodland that persisted into the Middle Ages was no longer 'natural' in the sense of being uncleared forest untouched by human hand. Rather, it was carefully managed in England from at least the Conquest onwards. The Domesday Book records much of this woodland as existing in the 1080s. Woodland was managed to produce 'standards' or particularly tall trees from which timber framing elements could be produced, and a smaller underwood with a variety of uses. Trees were managed in a variety of ways, for example, coppicing and pollarding where the trunk of the tree is sawn off, to produce a variety of products such as young shoots and long stems. 'Standards' or mature trees needed for the principal structural timbers of the house took fifty years or more to produce.

Much of our knowledge of this managed woodland comes from instances where it was owned by great estates such as monasteries, royalty or great households. In these instances, estate management and other accounts often survive to provide an insight into the management process. For much of vernacular timber framing, however, the timber must have come from smaller areas of woodland for which documentary sources either do not survive or never existed in the first place.

The skill and resourcefulness of the management of such woodland is readily attested by observation of the buildings themselves, both great and small. The vast roof of the Monks Dormitory, Durham, built from 1398 to 1404, is roofed with twenty-one massive timbers, each over 12.3 metres long. However, even the vast resources of Durham monastery, in a well wooded area by comparison with much of the rest of England, could not produce all the timbers required: one tie-beam is a little short and so the fork of trunk and branch has been left at one end, requiring a corresponding fork in its vertical support (Roberts 1994, 56–7; Dobson 1973).

Trees were often felled in winter, when the foliage had disappeared and the undergrowth had grown back. After rough squaring to ease its carriage, the timber was removed to the builder's yard. Once there, the tree could be reduced to structural timbers in a variety of ways, referred to by terms like slabbing, box-hearting, box-halving, and box-quartering. The traces of such techniques can often be seen on the timbers themselves, for example, 'hewing' marks and plumb and level marks (Miles and Russell 1995). For example, where a timber has been sawn, the marks of the trestle saw (where the timber is turned over half-way through the sawing process) and the pit saw (where it is sawn through in one go) leave characteristically different markings on the timbers.

These timbers would then be combined using a system of carpentered joints (Figures 2.1a and b). There is very little or no iron used in a traditional timber-framed house. Rather, the timber skeleton is held together by the intersections between different framing members being jointed, as they were in traditional furniture, and

Figures 2.1a and 2.1b A tie-beam lap-dovetail joint. Left: in diagram form. Right: an example (with arch- and wind-braces) from the gatehouse of Lower Brockhampton Manor, Herefordshire. (Photo author's own, printed by permission of the National Trust Photo Library.)

the joints being held in place by wooden pegs. The selected forms of the joints are not always the most optimal – in some periods, carpenters seem to have moved rapidly from one joint form to another, perhaps as part of a trial-and-error process. Much was made of these rapidly evolving joint forms as a possible means of dating the construction of buildings before the use of tree-ring dates (Hewett 1980).

The timber skeleton of the house was prefabricated, often at some distance from the site where it would eventually be either 'reared' or erected. The most famous instance is the late fourteenth-century hammer-beam roof of Westminster Hall, which documents tell us was prefabricated at a 'framing field' at Fareham in Hampshire and then moved piece by piece to Westminster, almost 150 kilometres away over land (Salzman 1952, 200). Evidence of this prefabrication can again often be seen on the timber frame itself, in the form of modified Roman numerals which acted as guides for the builder on which timber should go where (Figure 2.2; there are also rare examples of Arabic numerals being used: Pacey 2005). This system also meant that whole houses could be disassembled, moved and re-erected, either in the past (Moran 1989 gives examples from Shropshire) or in the present, at open-air museums (see Chapter 4).

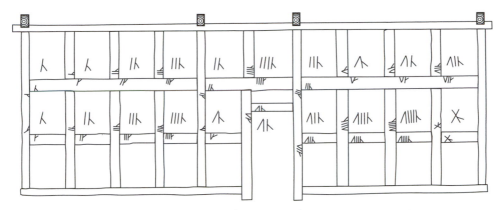

Figure 2.2 Systems of Roman numerals, from an eighteenth-century Herefordshire cottage. (Based on Harris, R., *Discovering Timber Framed Buildings*, Figure 11 (Shire Publications Ltd, 1993).)

The carpenter assembled the elements of the house together as a series of frames or panels: for a simple rectangular house with a ceiling to the ground floor, there would be two wall frames, a ceiling frame, roof frames, and a series of cross frames, including those forming the two end walls (Figure 2.3). The spaces between the cross frames are known as 'bays', and these bays often correspond to the divisions into rooms within the house. The whole structure was held together by carpentered joints. It was also given diagonal braces to hold the frame rigid, and to protect the roof against the stresses and strains of high winds. The whole was put together in such a way that, to use Richard Harris' memorable image, a giant could pick the frame up and turn it upside down without the frame or skeleton falling apart (Harris 1993, 5).

The carpenter's translation of timber from the living tree, via his yard, to the finished form of the house was a process of immense subtlety; every step was one both of constraint and choice, and every step involved some nuance of the craft tradition. In some houses, for example, where a great oak tree has been quartered, the four timbers thus produced are used as corner posts and oriented one to the other in the same relationship they had while living. No student with any understanding of timber framing could ever fall for the idea that vernacular building was somehow more crude or haphazard, or somehow less well-thought-out, than polite forms; a well-built timber frame is as structured, as formal and as sophisticated in its composition as a sonnet by Shakespeare, and it is as aesthetically satisfying to contemplate.

The techniques of traditional carpentry united knowledge and process – that is, 'one can see through them to their intention: they are obvious in their ability to achieve an accepted purpose. Timber framing, and the bracing and cutting of joints it entailed, were transparent in this way – anyone could see the effect of the brace and the joint on the stability of the frame, and although the skill of carpentry itself was restricted, what carpenters were doing was commonly understood' (Davis 2006, 15).

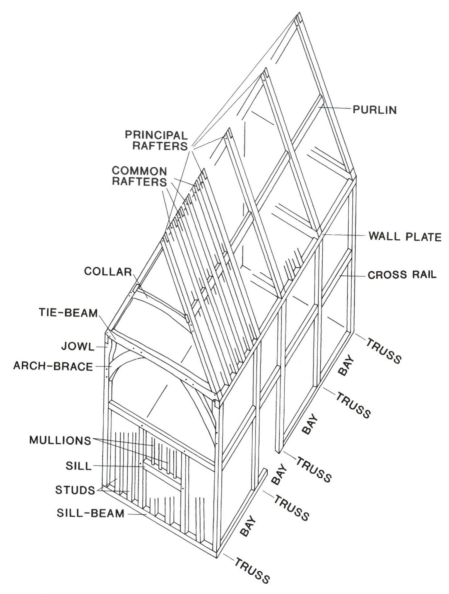

PURLIN

PRINCIPAL
RAFTERS

COMMON
RAFTERS

WALL PLATE

COLLAR

CROSS RAIL

TIE-BEAM

JOWL

ARCH-BRACE

TRUSS

BAY

TRUSS

MULLIONS

BAY

SILL

TRUSS

STUDS

BAY

TRUSS

SILL-BEAM

BAY

TRUSS

Figure 2.3 The main elements of the timber frame of a four-bay house, with bays, trusses and other features indicated.

Timber framing was also a process that combined subtlety and sophistication with economy. Countless smaller houses, particularly those surviving from later periods, use large quantities of curved or 'waney' timber. One of the particular skills of the carpenter was the intelligent and creative use of such waney framing elements. For example, a small late medieval house at Wennington, Cambridgeshire, has a large quantity of waney timber in its frame, which was built of standard trees from

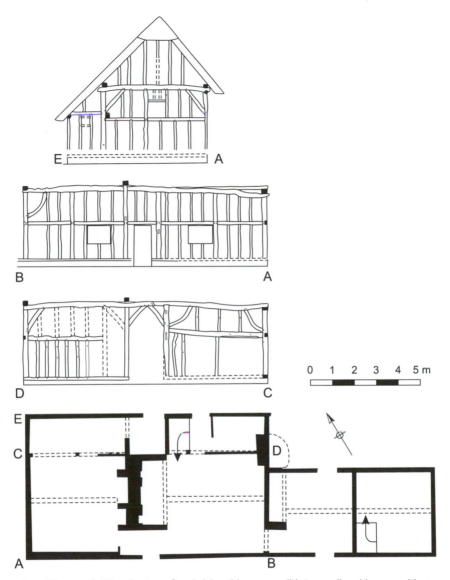

Figure 2.4 'Weepers', Wennington, Cambridgeshire: a small late medieval house with an aisle and a two-bay open hall. A chimney-stack and ceiling was inserted in the seventeenth century. The frame of the house is mostly waney timber, harvested from 'standard' trees in coppiced woodland, with great skill being evidenced by its economical use. The plan includes a later, attached byre to the east. (Based on Colman, S. 'Weepers', *Medieval Archaeology*, 26, 158–62 (Maney Publishing, 1982).)

coppice woodland. The carpenter used different forms of brace and assembly of the joints to adapt the craft tradition to this material (Colman 1982; Figure 2.4).

Large quantities of timber could also be reused from demolished houses. This can cause great confusion for novices in the understanding of timber frames, as the mortices and peg-holes in such timbers do not relate to the building in which they are now found. The popular notion that quantities of timber found in old houses are reused 'ships' timbers' is largely a myth, possibly propagated by the use of the term 'naval timber' in the nineteenth century to describe timber of a certain quality, though there is some evidence for the reuse of ships' timbers in post-medieval Norfolk (Lucas 1994).

The construction of a building was, by definition, a performative event: the process of assembling the frame combined the work of skilled individuals with the use of mass labour. The collective efforts of the whole village community, or a large part of it, would be needed for the raising of a large cruck frame. In modern reconstructions of cruck pairs, for example, at Ryedale Folk Museum and St Fagan's in Cardiff, the task required up to thirty people (Jennings 2002, 25). Physical evidence for rearing can often be found in the presence of 'hoisting grooves' on the elements of the frame (Harding 1976, 5); at Tydyn Llwydian, a cruck-framed sixteenth century house in Montgomeryshire, heel-like tapered sockets or 'scotches' which relate to the rearing of the frame demonstrated that the rearing was from upper to lower ends (Britnell and Suggett 2002, 144). Rearing the frame was also a social occasion; the Bedale building contract above on p. 23 specified 'bread and ale' to provide a meal for the group assembled for the rearing.

Cruck and Box Framing

There were two very basic grammars that governed the production of timber-framed houses in England. Both started from the most basic of problems, namely the method of support for the walls and roof. The most conceptually straightforward, described above, is to form timbers in a 'box', with vertical uprights linked at their summit by a tie-beam and with a roof structure over this. In 'box framing', as this is called, the posts of external walls of the building bear the load of the structure. As a result, the junction between post, wall plate, tie-beam and roof structure is critical: it marks the point at which three major structural timbers intersect (Figures 2.1a and b).

Richard Harris (1989) has identified four elements of a national 'grammar' of timber framing, elements that are characteristic of English framing yet are rare or not found in continental Europe. In Harris' words, these are:

1. The tiebeam lap-dovetail assembly between tiebeam and wall plate;
2. The bay system, in relation to plan and structure;
3. The rules by which the upper face of a bay-dividing frame is placed;
4. The rules by which trees are converted into frames.

However, a second tradition can be found in England, in which the load of the roof is transmitted more or less directly to the ground through the use of 'crucks'. Crucks are major structural timbers, nearly always curved, placed in pairs running across

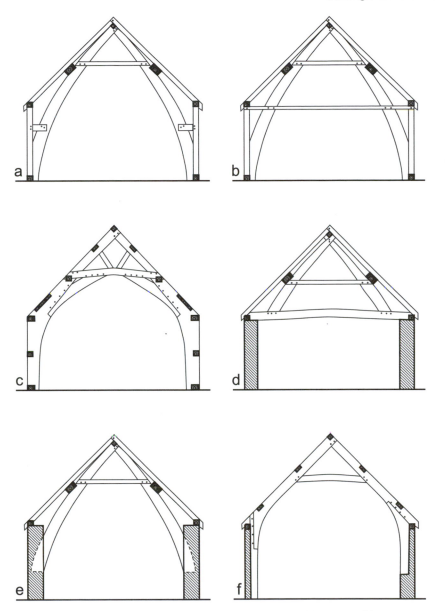

Figure 2.5 Different forms of cruck: (a) and (b) different forms of full cruck; (c) base cruck; (d) upper cruck; (e) raised cruck; (f) jointed cruck. (Based on Grenville, J., *Medieval Housing* (Leicester University Press, 1999, p. 28–9).)

the building. In cruck building, the external walls are separate from, though attached to, this load-bearing structure (Figure 2.5).

There are several different types of cruck structure. Full crucks, characteristically symmetrical and normally cut from the same piece of timber, are pairs of timber running from the foot to the full height of the building. Raised, middle and upper

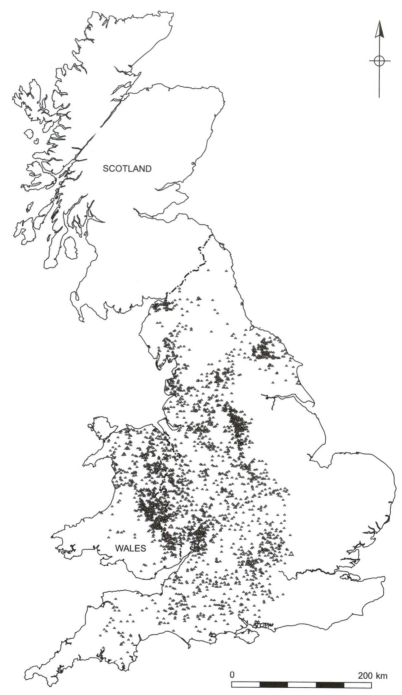

Map 2.1 Cruck and box framing: distribution map of 'true crucks'. Base crucks are omitted from this diagram: base crucks have a distribution that extends across central and southern England and the Welsh borders. (Based on Alcock, N.W., 'The distribution and dating of crucks and base crucks', *Vernacular Architecture*, 33, 67–70 (Maney Publishing, 2002).)

crucks rise to the apex of the roof, but from different points above the base of the building. Jointed crucks perform the function of a full cruck, but consist of a pair of timbers jointed and pegged in the middle. Finally, base crucks rise from the base of the building, but end at the collar of the roof rather than rising to the apex.

Cruck frames and box frames are found in different, but overlapping, areas of England (Map 2.1). It is not generally agreed what the distribution of different kinds of cruck and box framing means, despite the existence of a huge literature attempting to explain this distribution (Mercer 1996 and Mercer 1998; Alcock 1997, Alcock 2002 and Alcock 2006). There is no doubt that a distribution map of cruck framing is fascinating, and poses a very basic challenge for scholars. Box framing can be found in all regions of England where a timber framing tradition exists. Crucks, on the other hand, are confined to the north and west side of a line running across the country from Sussex on the south coast to Lincolnshire on the east coast. ('Base crucks' are found south and east of this line, but it can be argued that the base-cruck form is not derived from the larger cruck tradition, as I discuss in Chapter 4.) This line is a sharp and in most parts a precise one, but it does not conform exactly to any other border, such as county or regional boundary, geological feature, watershed, or any other sort of material culture or economic practice. It is complicated by the proximity of cruck- and box-framed structures; across much of the West Midlands and Borders, for example, in places like Weobley and Hay-on-Wye, one can see cruck- and box-framed houses sitting next to one another, while in south Yorkshire it is common to find box-framed houses sitting next to cruck-framed barns (Ryder 1979, 84). At Manor Cottage, Sutton Courtenay, cruck and box frames are found together in the same single build, dated to 1317/18 by tree-ring dating (Currie 1992). Most Midlands cruck buildings are pre-1500 in date, and the last cruck structures were built there by the end of the sixteenth century (Alcock 1981, 51); this range of dates seems to be repeated in Hampshire (Roberts 2003, 15), though they can be found from later dates in the north of England.

How we might understand the distribution seen in Map 2.1 is also complicated by the lack of survival of buildings from before c.1300: scholars are thrown back on interpretation from archaeological excavations and on documentary references, for example, references for 'furcae' or forks. Both sources of evidence can be imprecise and this imprecision has led to ongoing and often fractious debates on the origin of crucks (Hill 2005; Alcock 2006). Fortunately perhaps, the resolution of this problem lies outside the scope of this book, in that its origins must be well before c.1300.

Stone, Earth, Clay and Brick

When we stand back and look closely at a cruck- or box-framed house, then, we are examining the result of a design process, governed in part by the technical competence of the vernacular builder. What is true of timber-framed houses is also true of other building materials. It is important to note that, though less visibly and arguably in a less aesthetically striking manner, stone was used in an equally skilful manner in vernacular buildings. Both 'field stone' and stone from quarries was used in subtle combinations that were admired and commented upon by contemporary observers (Alfrey 2006).

The most common stone used for traditional building purposes was limestone, which varies in its characters and properties from place to place across England. The limestone best used for building purposes, fine-grained, relatively easy to cut and often of a beautiful light grey or honey colour, is found across England in a band from Devon, through the West Country and Cotswolds, to Northamptonshire and Lincolnshire (see Plate 5, and, for an example, Plate 6). It is this stone which gives the famous Cotswolds villages their distinctive character. Chalk has a reputation as being an inferior building material: in many houses, for example, in the Yorkshire Wolds and on the Hampshire/Sussex border, harder chalk or 'clunch' was used in conjunction with better quality stone or later brick for quoins and other details (Hayfield and Wagner 1998, 7–8). Stone of any kind needed mortar, which was a major cost factor, but again gave opportunities for complex patterns, for example, galletting (Figure 2.6).

Figure 2.6 Galletting: the use of smaller pieces of darker volcanic stone around blocks of hard white chalk, from a house in Selborne, near the Hampshire/Sussex border. (Photo author's own).

In some areas of England, walls were made of earth, but without a timber frame to support them (Hurd and Gourley 2000). Earth walls were common in the later Middle Ages, and could be used for a range of buildings (Dyer 2008). The Devon word for mud walling is 'cob' (Beacham 1990). Devon's mud wall tradition lasted later than most, possibly due to the structural properties of the local mud (Devon mud has a low level of volumetric instability and good local aggregate in the form of fragments of slate called 'shillet': Harrison 1984). Cob was often mixed by cattle treading; it was then raised with a pitchfork, tamped down, pared off, and left to set. The cob walls of houses, particularly vulnerable to damp and rain, were then protected with lime plaster render. The colour of the local earth lent itself to the structure – thus the red Devon sandstones lent a distinctive red colour to many walls, often now covered with white limewash. Devon cob was used in houses of quite high social status; Sir Walter Raleigh's E-plan house, Hayes Barton, was built in part of cob.

Clay lump was used in parts of East Anglia. It is possible that clay-walled houses were built in medieval Norfolk (Longcroft 2006), though others believe that clay lump did not enjoy widespread use as a building material until the nineteenth century (McCann 1997 and McCann 2007). The 'mud-and-stud' houses of Lincolnshire have walls made of mud and straw, supported on a carpentered frame supporting rails and laths (Cousins 2000). The 'clay dabbins' of the Solway plain, north of the Cumbrian hills, have crucks with walls '0.6 metres thick, constructed of pebbles and sand in a clay binder'; many of these walls have survived over five centuries, from the end of the fifteenth century to the present (Jennings 2002, 20).

Brick buildings were first constructed in Britain by the Romans; many great medieval monuments reused large numbers of Roman bricks, most notably the great abbey church at St Albans, now a cathedral, dedicated to a Roman martyr and partly built of reused bricks from Verulamium a few kilometres away. Bricks were not produced on a large scale until the later Middle Ages, and their use was then largely confined to large buildings, for example, the great fifteenth-century castles of Tattershall and Caister. At the vernacular level, the use of brick walling on a large scale was much later, in part due to cost. In Norfolk, for example, known for its lack of suitable building stone and therefore likely to take up brick building relatively early, large numbers of vernacular brick houses were not built till the eighteenth century (Lucas 1997). Vernacular builders did use brick for features such as chimney-stacks and gable ends from the late fifteenth century onwards, as we shall see in Chapter 4; and when they did, very frequently their use was related to 'polite' building projects proceeding a few kilometres away (Campbell and Saint 2002). 'Brick nogging', or the use of bricks rather than lath and plaster for infilling timber frames, was present from the sixteenth century or even earlier (McCann 1987). Fired earth or terracotta could also be used for door and window frames and other details (Anderson 2003).

Ceramic tiles were mostly used for roofing, but were often also found cladding the walls of timber-framed buildings in the south-east. Tiles were used earliest and most frequently in towns, where fire was a major concern (though fire risk should also not be forgotten in rural areas: Currie 1989, for example, shows its effect on the Cambridgeshire village of Swavesey). Wooden tiles could also be used, either on the roof or as cladding for framed walls. Tiled roofs became more common in the seventeenth century; the most common roofing material in many areas before this date was thatch. Thatch could be made of cereal straw, water reed, or less common materials such as heather and wood chippings (Moir and Letts 1999). These different materials gave thatched roofs a strong regional character, and the way thatched roofs were finished was, and continues to be, a strong statement of local tradition. For example, 'combed straw' is found in Devon; 'curched' or 'long straw' in other areas, and water reed thatching is found in Norfolk (Cox and Thorp 2001). In the Solway Plain, wheat stapple thatch and occasionally turf was used (Jennings 2002, 23–4).

In many areas, stone slates were used for roofing. In the nineteenth century, Welsh slate came to dominate the market and was transported by rail across the whole country and beyond. In the centuries before this, however, more locally produced slates of other fissile material such as Yorkshire limestone were often used. These choices of roofing material in turn had an influence on carpentry traditions. Thatch needs a relatively steep pitch to be effective. Conversely, the great carpentered king-post roofs of the North are often of quite flat pitch, their massive dimensions in part due to the weight of the great stone slates.

The combinations of materials and style gave each region of England a distinctive texture and feel, what is often referred to as 'character'. It also had implications for the organisation of labour in the local community. The owner of a thatched roof needs to make sure that it is regularly repaired every few years; when such a roof was replaced with tiles, such regular repair, and the constant interaction and dialogue with local craftspeople that went with it, was lost.

Conclusion: Local Dialects

I have given a rather dry recitation of different building materials and methods. The reader can easily forget that behind each individual house is not just a series of techniques, but a series of builders and owners, each using the materials to hand in a creative way to make a particular statement. Each house presents its own material narrative of building, rebuilding and dwelling, and it is important to remember that each is slightly different from the next. Each house presents a human narrative of creative interplay between different geographical and temporal scales. Building follows a national pattern, but the particular shade and texture of different materials is conditioned both by the availability of different local stones and clays, and the admixture of different materials – straw, sand, and so on.

Within the national 'language' Harris suggested for timber framing, there were different local 'dialects', in other words, different mannerisms or stylistic differences.

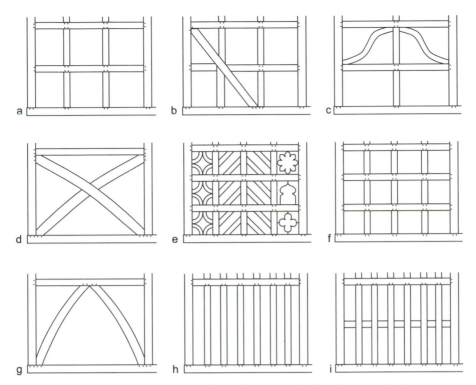

Figure 2.7 A selection of some of the different framing styles found across England.
(a) large square panels; (b) large square panels with descending brace; (c) ogee bracing;
(d) cross or saltire bracing; (e) decorative panelling; (f) small square panels; (g) storey high
bracing; (h) close studding; (i) close studding with middle rail.

A classic example is different systems of infilling the panels between the major
structural elements of the timber frame (Figure 2.7). In much of East Anglia, the
panels have vertically set timbers or 'studs'; in much of the Midlands, a middle rail
is used and the area divided up into squares in what is known as 'square framing'.
There is no obvious or immediately apparent reason why the two areas should have
such different manners of framing. More generally, framing in the West Country
is of heavier dimensions or scantling, and tends to use curved timbers more, for
example, in elaborately curved braces in the roofs of open halls.

Many of these differences might be on account of local environmental circumstances; for example, it is possible that the greater use of heavy and curved timber
relates to the greater availability of timber in the west of the country as opposed to
East Anglia. However, such constraints can be debated back and forth, and it is
difficult to avoid the conclusion that these are distinctive regional styles that are
not solely determined by the availability of materials. Why are so many roofs in
Hampshire half-hipped, and why are the panel infills of brick nogging rather than
plaster? Why were house-owners in Somerset so fond of moulded plaster friezes and
ceilings? Why do different areas of Essex have concentrations of subtly different

patterns of arch- and tension-braces (Stenning 1997)? The patterning of these different zones, and the boundaries between them, can be compared to the complex patterning of local dialects within the English language. Like dialect, it does not often follow obvious lines such as county boundaries or geological zones, as previously discussed with the cruck/box-frame boundary.

The use of flint in vernacular building is a good example. Flint nodules are very far from being an ideal building material. In particular, it is difficult to use them to frame windows and doors, or to construct quoining at the corners of buildings. Nevertheless, in the absence of other building materials, flints are used. The knapping of flints was a large-scale industry; skilled flint knappers could produce squared flints of different sizes, or at least give the flint nodules a flat face. Where flints were not squared, the intervening gaps between the flints were filled with mortar and then studded with small chips of galletting, a technique also found with other stone (see Figure 2.7 on p. 36). As a result of these variations in local technique, a flint building in Hampshire and a flint building in East Anglia look superficially very similar, but vary in very subtle ways in their architectural details.

In many cases, particular features and styles are often so distinctive, and the boundaries between different styles so sharp, that a student of vernacular architecture can look at a photograph of a building and locate it to within a fifty- or even twenty-five-kilometre radius. One of the themes I shall take up later in this book is the particular regional quality and texture of ordinary buildings. The peculiar shade and finish of local brick or stone, the colour and texture of roofing slates, the relative popularity of pargetting or moulded plaster patterning in a given area, elements as basic as the choice of traditional colours – all these factors give traditional buildings a particularly local quality and strong regional pattern. This character is so distinctive and powerful that it is often seen as rooted in the soil, rather than being the product of human actions. These fine-drawn variations can be picked up by the keen student of vernacular architecture, and would certainly have been observed by the craftsmen who built them. How far a medieval or seventeenth-century observer would have appreciated these differences, and what meanings he or she would have attributed to them, is a subtle but important question that we shall return to.

The landscape historian W.G. Hoskins stated that vernacular buildings are 'adapted to their particular environment. . . . Buildings speak to an historian as a musical score speaks to a musician. They speak objectively and do not lie' (1966, 19). Alec Clifton-Taylor took this statement further and commented that regional identity gave vernacular buildings 'a closeness to the soil on which they stand, a down-to-earth honesty and lack of pretension, and often a true countryman's strength', and that this gave such buildings the quality of 'sheer lovability' (Clifton-Taylor 1972, 24 and 326). The student of vernacular architecture may shy away from such emotive language, and feel that identity comes from the lived experience and agency of human beings, not from regions in themselves. However, he or she cannot avoid the conclusion that the complex patterning to be found in different regions must surely be telling us something interesting about the nature of traditional building, the choices made and constraints faced by local builders, and the relationship between building traditions, local communities and national traditions.

Buildings make complex statements about relationships between materials, structure, and technique that are also material statements about the people and communities who created and used them. As such, buildings were and are perhaps not always as objective as Hoskins imagined, or as directly sprung from the soil as Clifton-Taylor surmised. Houses are statements not just about building technique and the soil, but also about material, social and cultural landscapes. I shall try to unravel some of these complex strands in the course of the next chapter.

3
Houses in the Landscape

Houses, particularly traditional houses, do not exist in splendid isolation. While a very few have been physically dismantled, moved around and reassembled, most sit in a specific location in a particular landscape. Houses form part of the wider landscape, most obviously in their use of local building materials, but also more subtly in their choice of site, their orientation to the winds and to the surrounding community, and their relationship to other landscape features such as field boundaries and neighbouring houses.

The wider landscape setting of houses is superficially an obvious and physical one: this house stands in the middle of a village, that house on the shoulders of a hill or dale. A traditional rural house was more often than not at the centre of a working farm. Those heads of households engaged in rural trades, such as carpenters, nevertheless frequently worked at their trade alongside their other occupation as a farmer. The house, then, must be understood in terms of its role at the centre of that farm, the ancillary buildings and fields around it.

However, the landscapes that surround and give context to houses are more complex and layered than the simple dimension of physical location. Houses sit within a local landscape, but they also need to be understood within a regional, national and international context. The working farm produced wheat, cheese, meat and other products not only for the consumption of its inhabitants but also for the local market. In later centuries an increasing proportion of its produce was destined for major provincial centres, for London and even for export; the household produced and consumed goods (ceramics, furniture, tobacco) that travelled back and forth between England, continental Europe and the Atlantic world.

Economic connections across the landscape become visible in the house itself. A house of a particular form and appearance might be unusual in Wensleydale, but common across North Yorkshire. A seventeenth-century house might be of a local form and pattern, but constructed of a building material such as pine imported from the Baltic. A prominent window on the first floor of the house, providing a well-lit room for weaving, might relate to the production of cloth for trade, cloth that was exported to continental Europe via warehouses in coastal towns.

Houses also sit within human as well as material landscapes. The working farm was not just a centre of economic production. Its master and mistress, and its household, occupied a particular social position within the local and regional community. Again, therefore, the house materialised these human relationships: the date and initials over the door, the form and ostentation of the furnishings, down to the smallest detail – whether the kitchen door was open or closed to visitors, precautions against the external threat of witchcraft round the hearth, the placing and position of the benches, stools and chairs around the table where the household ate together.

In its own way, a traditional house is itself a small-scale piece of landscape. The landscape outside the house, through its pattern of villages, churches, woodlands, fields, roads and trackways, structured the encounters and experiences that made up the daily lives of people living in rural communities. Through the structuring of everyday experience and the framing of backdrops to face-to-face encounters, the landscape materialised the experience of community itself, and of people's individual and collective identities – in other words, what it meant to be an inhabitant of this household, this village, this county, this nation, of Christendom, of the world. The walls and partitions of the house in their turn structured encounters and experiences at the family and household level, as well as between host and guest. House and landscape, then, were tied together in the everyday ordering of experience.

It is a truism that these different kinds and scales of landscape changed through the centuries. As we have seen, the English are fond of referring to the immemorial continuity of the countryside, just as they were in the past, but the truth is very different. What was built as the dwelling of a socially middling yeoman in the sixteenth century may have been divided into labourers' cottages in the eighteenth century, before being brought together again as a Londoner's second home in the country in the twentieth, leaving unexplained partitions and features in the wake of such a sequence to puzzle and frustrate the twenty-first-century observer. The rapid changes to be seen in the countryside today are not a novel phenomenon: as we shall see, much of the landscape of the English countryside has been utterly transformed from that of the Middle Ages. It is this transformation that has left in its wake both traces in the physical landscape, and a literature of both conservative and radical protest of rural enclosure and dispossession from the sixteenth to the nineteenth centuries, from Thomas More's *Utopia* to Oliver Goldsmith's *The Deserted Village* and the poetry of George Crabbe.

What is true of material landscapes is also true of cultural landscapes. There were patterns of living and ways of thinking that were as foundational to people's lives as the roofs over their head and the boundaries of the fields in which they worked. Indeed, the boundary between the two was not always clear: when communities wished to protest against enclosure, for example, they did so through the physical pulling-down and levelling of hedges and ditches. Social commentators drawn from the literate upper classes repeatedly used metaphors deriving from the material landscape to express social and political points. When they wrote about ideas like the 'commonwealth' and the 'kingdom' they used both material and cultural references, for example, likening the nation to a house and household (Wrightson 2003, 64 – 8).

It is also true that pre-existing landscapes structure and precondition the patterns of human life that go on within them. To put it another way, as Karl Marx remarked, humans make their own history, but they do not do so exactly as they please. This chapter will look at different kinds of landscape context in turn: geology, geography, and the economic, social and cultural surroundings of the traditional house and household.

Geology: Patterns of English Building

As Alec Clifton-Taylor observed (1972), the way a house was built, and the materials of which it was built, were determined in part by what lay deep under its foundations: the underlying geology. Geological formations are superficially quite complex, but have at their heart a very basic pattern. The geology of the British Isles, put very simply, is tilted from south-east to north-west, so that the uppermost and youngest rocks in the sequence can be found in the south and east and the older rocks in the north and west (Plate 6). Taken as a whole, the younger rocks are also the softer and more easily eroded. This is a vastly over-simplified explanation of why the southern and eastern regions of England tend to be undulating lowlands, with postglacial clay and gravel deposits on top of younger rocks such as chalk, whereas the north and west, and Scotland and Wales beyond, is characterised by craggier and more precipitous hills and mountains composed of older and harder rocks.

This geological pattern was first described in detail by the engineer William 'Strata' Smith, who, in his travels from project to project during the Industrial Revolution, noticed the same basic relative sequence of layers of rocks at different absolute depths in different locations across the country (Winchester 2001). Since the pattern determines what building materials are close to the surface of the land and therefore whether they are or are not locally available to the vernacular builder, it accounts for some striking similarities between different parts of the country, for example, along the band of chalk and flint stretching from Hampshire to Norfolk, or the Jurassic limestone extended from Devon to Northamptonshire and beyond.

The great Sir Cyril Fox, who we encountered as the co-author of *Monmouthshire Houses* in Chapter 1, characterised the division between north-west and south-east as the 'Highland Zone' and 'Lowland Zone' of the British Isles, respectively. He saw this division, along a line drawn roughly between Exeter in the south-west to Hull in the north-east, as a basic feature of the 'personality of Britain' that stretched back from recent history to the early prehistory of Britain (Fox 1938). Over sixty years on, Fox's original words are well worth reading, for while he had a keen sense of the importance of this division, he was careful to avoid a vulgar geological determinism in his writing. For Fox, the character of the two zones was also determined by human geography, the south and east being proximal to continental Europe and hence to influences and invasions from that direction, the north and west open to a range of contacts with the Irish and Atlantic worlds.

The distinction made by Fox has been enormously influential in the way we think about patterns of vernacular architecture, but in the process the careful distinction he made has sometimes become over-extended and vulgarised. In the first place, it is easy to slip into the assumption that the south and east are somehow, by their very nature, inherently more 'progressive' than the north and west, and the north and west somehow more inherently 'conservative' or even 'backward'. Such notions are all too frequently found in the writings of scholars based in or around London. In some areas of cultural practice, for example, dialects, traits can move from north to south.

It is easier still to slip still further from such notions of the primacy of the south and east into an assertion that geology and soil type have determined the regional character of communities and even individual humans. Alec Clifton-Taylor wrote that 'there are a good many English people, especially in the North, to whom charm, and indeed all smoothness, is slightly suspect, and some of these will be found to prefer the Carboniferous Limestones . . .' (Clifton-Taylor 1972, 97). This attribution of human character to geology and soil type is not new: three hundred years earlier the seventeenth-century scholar John Aubrey wrote of people on the chalk soils versus the claylands that:

> In North Wiltshire, and like the vale of Gloucestershire (a dirty clayey country) the Indigenae, or Aborigines, speake drawling; they are phlegmatique, skins pale and livid, slow and dull, heavy of spirit; hereabout is but little tillage or hard labour, they only milke the cowes and make cheese; they feed chiefly on milke meates, which cools their brains too much, and hurts their inventions. These circumstances make them melancholy, contemplative, and malicious; by consequence whereof come more law suites out of North Wilts, at least double to the Southern parts. And by the same reason they are generally more apt to be fanatiques: their persons are generally plump and feggy: gallipot eies, and some black: but they are generally handsome enough. . . . On the downes, sc. the south part where 'tis all upon tillage, and where the shepherds labour hard, their flesh is hard, their bodies strong: being weary after hard labour, they have not leisure to read and contemplate of religion, but goe to bed to their rest, to rise betime the next morning to their labour.
>
> (Britton ed. 1847, 11)

Aubrey was writing about Wiltshire and Gloucestershire, and believed that there really was a direct link between the composition of the soil and the make-up of the character of the individual. As we shall see in the next section, for historians such as David Underdown, who is interested in patterns of regional culture and society, and for those interested in how such patterns affect traditional houses, Aubrey was on to something (Underdown 1985b).

Geography: Patterns of English Landscape

The human settlement that overlay this base of geology was already many thousands of years old by the time the earliest surviving traditional houses were built. The accretion of traces of human settlement, layer by layer through the millennia, had already divided and structured the landscape in very deep and profound ways before the Middle Ages. It had been over four thousand years since the first Neolithic farmers cultivated the land. Prehistoric people cleared much of the formerly forested landscape, created great monuments such as Stonehenge and Avebury, built dykes and banks that marked boundaries between territories, created trackways and drove-ways, and laid out and managed extensive field systems, some of which endure in part to this day. The Romans added to this pattern a system of urban centres and metalled linking roads. Though urban life in Britain failed after the end of the Roman Empire, most of the town sites continued to be places of importance, and were often re-founded in later centuries. Roman sites, then, went on to become major provincial or metropolitan centres such as York, Colchester, Winchester, Exeter and many others, most notably London.

The nature and degree of Roman influence on the later structure of the countryside is much debated; it is agreed, however, that much of the basic fabric of the English rural landscape that we see today was created in the centuries before c.1200. In the centuries after re-conversion to Christianity in the seventh century AD, the basic structure of English minsters and parishes, each parish a territorial unit with its parish church, was created. The parish structure went alongside that of the secular and civil community, the township and manor. Before the eighth century, human settlement had shifted from place to place on a regular basis, as it had done for millennia. In the centuries after this date, much of the classic landscape of the English village, a nucleated settlement with church, manor house and peasant houses, surrounded by large-scale open fields and often termed 'champion' landscape, so named after the French term 'champagne', was created (Jones and Page 2006).

Champion landscapes only existed across part of the country: a broad belt stretching from the South, through the Midlands, into Lincolnshire, Yorkshire and up into lowland county Durham, termed the 'Central Province' by Roberts and Wrathmell (2002). On either side of this belt, but outside the highlands and hills, lay areas of 'woodland' landscape. In these areas, large nucleated villages were rare, and the open field systems characteristic of champion landscapes absent. In much of this latter area, patterns of landscape and human settlement seem to be much older than that of champion areas, representing a degree of continuity with earlier, even prehistoric, patterns of settlement, and hence these areas either side of the champion area are often termed 'ancient landscapes'.

The pattern thus drawn is vastly over-simplified: in much of Norfolk, for example, there were nucleated villages and open fields, but organised large-scale field systems on the Midlands model were largely absent. However, the pattern can still be seen today in maps and aerial views of the English landscape (Map 3.1; compare with Plate 6). The open field systems that survived were replaced in the eighteenth and nineteenth centuries by enclosed fields, with straight, regular lines, contrasting with the dispersed settlement, more irregular fields, greens, and patches of woodland that give their name to 'woodland' areas.

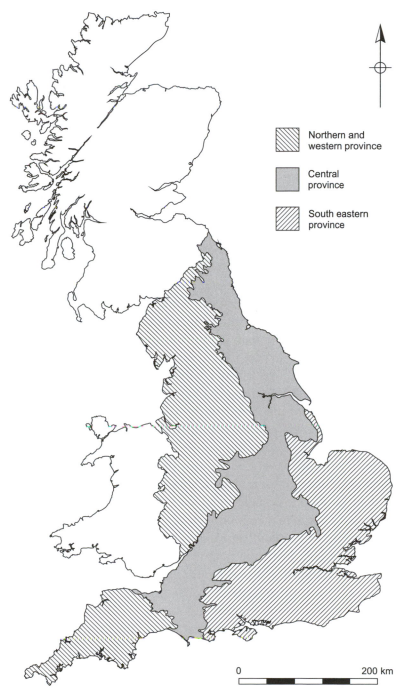

Map 3.1 Map of England, showing the different 'settlement provinces' outlined by Roberts and Wrathmell. The central province is broadly that of nucleated villages and open fields, with ancient or dispersed landscapes found in the northern and western provinces and the south-eastern province. The render should compare this pattern with Figure 3.5 and Plate 6. (Based on Roberts, B.K. and Wrathmell, S., *Region and Place: A Study of English Rural Settlement* (English Heritage, 2002).)

Again, I stress that the pattern I have just drawn is over-simplified: the complexities have been extensively delineated and debated in a vast literature (for example, Jones and Page 2006; Roberts 2008; Williamson 2002). It is nevertheless helpful because it composed much of the basic structure of the English landscape, a material structure to the countryside within which most traditional houses are placed. A traditional house built after 1300 was rarely placed on 'virgin ground', whatever that might be taken to mean. More often than not, the traditional house we see today occupies a much older site of human habitation in the landscape. Many houses in Suffolk and Essex, for example, are partly or wholly surrounded by a moat, or sit adjacent to a moat. Such moated sites have been shown by fieldwork and excavation to be thirteenth century or older in date; they are, then, a visible marker that the site of the house is often several centuries older than the surviving fabric of the house itself (Aberg 1978).

Such a pattern can also be seen in the basic structure of the English village. Villages, particularly in the north of England, often have regular layouts that may well have been the outcome of deliberate planning, often best seen through Ordnance Survey maps or from aerial photographs. The layout, with church, manor house, and narrow plots of land facing on to a main street or rectangular village green, is clearly medieval in origin, though the surviving houses that sit on these plots are almost always much later in date. The underlying medieval structuring of space has persisted, then, even in the face of change; where the old medieval plots have been bought, sold, or otherwise changed hands, the property lines have persisted, and continue to structure the layout of the village to this day. In particular, the pattern of tofts, tenements and other property boundaries persists (Dyer 2006a; Roberts 2008).

Traditional houses, then, very often sat within a landscape the wider structure of which was centuries or even millennia old before their construction, and which structured their location, orientation and surrounding boundaries in a very direct way. The fabric of a house may only be a few centuries old, but it needs to be understood within an immediate landscape that is hundreds or even thousands of years older. Scholars are only just beginning to come to terms with the subtlety and complexity of the relationship between vernacular houses and the wider landscape. The Historic Landscape Characterisation scheme of English Heritage has shown just how complex this can be; for example, Lake and Edwards have explored the relationship between farmsteads of different forms and sizes and the surrounding landscape types (Lake and Edwards 2006).

Farming Landscapes and Regions

These landscape differences also had economic implications. Most obviously, the north and west of the country were poorer than the south and east. Taken as a whole, the soil was less fertile and the climate less kind; as a result, human settlement was sparser. One index of affluence was the eating of bread made entirely or largely from wheat grain. Before the eighteenth century, the consumption of bread made wholly of wheat was socially and geographically restricted: though most social classes could afford it in the south, wheat bread was only eaten by more affluent families in the north. Barley was more frequently used to make malt for ale or beer than for bread, while oats were used as fodder; they were also eaten by humans in the north of England (as Dr Johnson's famous definition of oats as 'a grain, which in England is generally given to horses, but in Scotland appears to support the people', failed to acknowledge: Overton 1996, 14).

Before the transport and Industrial Revolutions, transport costs affected the production of food, just as they did the distribution of building materials outlined in the previous chapter. It was rarely cost-effective to transport large quantities of grain and other staple foodstuffs from one region of England to another. As a result, all regions of England to some extent had a mixed economy, growing arable crops such as wheat and barley alongside the raising of sheep and cattle. This is part of the reason why, in upland regions of England, one often sees 'lynchets' and other signs of arable cultivation in areas that would not now be seriously considered as land suitable for arable crops. Agriculture in both champion and woodland areas was always a balance between arable and pasture – the cultivation of grain versus the raising of sheep and cattle. In the open-field village, and in the absence of modern chemical fertilisers, the balance between the two was critical, since the animals provided the manure that was one of the few ways to keep the arable fields fertile.

Farming in 1500 involved the cultivation of a much narrower range of crops that those known today: wheat, rye, barley, oats, peas, vetch, beans, together with the raising of cattle, sheep, pigs, and poultry. It was mostly done by human and animal power, though windmills and watermills were an essential part of the agricultural round (Overton 1996, 10; Thirsk 1957). As such, farming was also a fundamentally insecure activity: no matter how prosperous, farming practice sat on the edge of constant peril. Though outright famine was very rare, a run of bad harvests or disease among the livestock could spell disaster for the household and the utter ruin of all its members (Clarkson 1975).

Life in pre-industrial households in the countryside was structured around the activities of the farming year, which imposed a definite rhythm and pattern on rural life. After harvesting the corn in August and September, the land had to be ploughed. The mouldboard of the heavy plough, pulled by teams of oxen or horses, turned the stubble and weeds into the soil. The soil was then harrowed, or left till the spring for spring crops. Wheat and rye were sown in September and October, and oats, peas and beans in late February to April: the seed was scattered by hand, then the ground was harrowed again, and weeded if the labour was available. Farmers timed the servicing of cattle and sheep for September and October so that most animals were born in the spring: the mothers could then produce milk from the new spring grass, before the calves and lambs were weaned and most of the males castrated. They were also careful to 'fold' or pen in sheep at night-times on arable land, so that the manure was concentrated on these areas (Williamson 2002, 55).

Harvesting started in June and July with the hay harvest: the hay was mown with a scythe, left to dry, then stacked or taken to the barn to feed livestock in winter. In August and September, the corn was harvested. Wheat and rye were reaped with a sickle by women and men, barley and oats mown with a scythe by men. The corn was then bound into sheaves and stacked into 'stooks' to dry, before being carted and stored in a barn. The fields were then gleaned by women and children, who were allowed to keep the gleanings; this custom, mentioned in Flora Thompson's *Lark Rise to Candleford*, was abolished in the nineteenth century (Bushaway 1982, 25–6). Grain was threshed when it was needed, by being beaten on the barn floor with a flail. It was then winnowed by being shaken in a wicker basket, and weed seeds were sieved out. Grain was then put in sacks to be ground, either on the farm or by the local miller, or to be sold. Sacks of grain are found over and over again in inventories, stored on the upper floors of houses; in later centuries grain was also stored in staddle barns, set on raised stones to stop rats, mice and other vermin getting in (Figure 3.1).

Figure 3.1 A weather-boarded granary, near Exton, Hampshire. The staddle stones are modern. The half-hipped roof is characteristic for the region. (Photo author's own).

Most farming households consumed much of what they produced; in many respects, the household was a self-sufficient unit in terms of what it ate. Before the eighteenth century, production for the market was important, but only certain specialist crops (hemp for ropes, flax for linen, hops to flavour beer, woad and saffron for dyes) were made exclusively for the market. The obvious exception was wool and woollen cloth, which was England's principal export after grain until the Industrial Revolution and of the first importance to the national economy (hence the Speaker of the House of Lords has been seated on the Woolsack, a symbol of national wealth, from the fourteenth century to the present day: Britnell 2004, 413–19).

The farming activities of women and men were very different. At critical points of the year, most notably harvest time, women and men worked together in the fields, but at other times tasks and daily rounds were strongly prescribed by gender. Broadly, men worked in the fields and with the livestock, and were responsible for the maintenance and care of hedges, ditches and buildings. Women were responsible for household activities, such as brewing, the making of cheese and butter, gardens, the preparation of food, and childcare (Mendelson and Crawford 1998). As a result, the daily experiences and everyday social worlds of women and men were very different, though they came together at key points in the day, most notably around the table at the midday meal and at bedtime.

In all areas of England there was a degree of agricultural specialisation, and this became more marked between the fourteenth and the eighteenth centuries. The medieval farmer consumed much of the food that he grew, but the growth of urban centres and transport networks meant that, over the course of the period covered by this book, it became more and more possible to buy and sell food at market. This meant that the farmer could specialise, and also meant that the household became less and less of a self-sufficient unit and more and more tied in to, and dependent on, regional, national and international economic networks (Wrightson 2000; Overton 1996).

Religious Landscapes

Closely tied in with the basic reality of people's lives in the pre-industrial countryside was the Church. The sound of the bells ringing from the tower and the dim and mysterious spaces of the parish church structured people's lives very directly, and at every stage, in a way that can hardly be imagined today. For earlier ages, religion was important. It was not just an ideology or a false consciousness, and it was certainly not a 'private' or purely personal affair. For an age before Darwin and modern secular society, religion was not simply something one did on Sundays; the material and symbolic vocabulary of the Church formed the most basic understanding of the world for people of all social classes, even if their attitude towards the Church varied. And it did so in the most material way; the parish church was (and characteristically remains) the largest, most prominent, and most enduring building in the parish, physically standing over all the traditional houses in the community and outlasting most of them (Duffy 1992 and Duffy 2001; Marks 2004).

Every member of the rural community started their social life in the church: they did not have a name or social identity until they were baptised. And every member ended their life there, through funeral in the church and burial in the churchyard. Between this universal beginning and ending, the church mapped out the temporal and cultural landscape of virtually every aspect of people's lives, from baptism, to marriage, the safeguarding of women during childbirth and their subsequent 'churching', to death and burial in the churchyard.

The regular tolling of the church bell could be heard across the whole parish, and defined the working day in the fields. In many areas, such as East Anglia, the church tower could be seen from most parts of the parish. The whole community was enjoined by clerics to come together once a week on Sundays; in addition to the religious service, royal proclamations and news of political events were read from the pulpit. The farming year was defined and structured through religious observation: the lean time of Lent, Harvest thanksgiving, Christmas celebrations, servants' hiring fairs on saints' days. Religious celebrations and saints' days meant that up to a third of the working days of the year were taken off prior to the Reformation, when many of the minor saints' days were removed (Hill 1966).

The church structured and defined social differences. Seating became common in churches in the fifteenth century. The seating plan was carefully laid out according to social rank; in some churches, people were generally seated by status from front to back, while women and men sat on opposite sides (Marsh 2005). Even in death the location of burial was determined by social position, those of higher status being buried inside the church or along the main path to the south door; their memorials, and the memorials of the ancestors of the leading families of the parish, gazed down upon the congregation from the walls of the church. Suicides and others deemed to be outside the social matrix were ordered to be buried on the north side of the church. Women and men, often illiterate, learnt the differences in work roles between the genders from paintings on the church walls and in the window glass in the church of Adam labouring with a spade, and Eve spinning and caring for children (Duffy 1992).

The fabric of the parish church today bears the marks of this central role in rural society. On first appearance, to the untutored eye, one parish church can be very much like the next. They differ in matters of architectural detail, and these differences appear to be chance variations; this church has a Perpendicular tower, that a spire, this other one no tower at all. But if these differences are read not simply as narratives of architectural style but as markers of the social life of the communities they served, these differences become important and fascinating (Roffey 2001). Even where a church was largely rebuilt by a single donor or small group, today it bears the marks of successive generations of the community, through its tombs, monuments, internal organisation, and notices, even its graffiti. To walk around a parish church and observe its many details is to excavate the changing identity of the community that created it and of which it is an expression (Plate 7).

Domestic Landscapes

If religion was not a private affair, neither was the domestic world. Pre-industrial communities held strong ideas about the nature and composition of the household, and how it should be ordered. These ideas were reflected to a greater or lesser extent in the everyday life of the household, and thus in the structure and use of the traditional house.

The word 'house' itself could apply to any dwelling, animal or human; seventeenth-century uses of the term found in inventories included pig houses, cow houses, hay houses and barn houses (Machin 1978, 7). A house for humans was a dwelling house, or 'hall house': in a sense, the use of the term 'hall' in this context shows how central the idea of the hall was to human life, and its distinction from the natural world.

The origins and etymology of the word 'house' show the strength and endurance of this structure of ideas. The *Oxford English Dictionary* records the origin of the word 'house' as being Old English. In other words, the idea of the house as expressed in the English language dates back to the early Middle Ages. It was at this early date also that the word was used both as a collective term applying to the members of the house, both in the sense of the immediate nuclear family living inside the physical house, and also as the wider lineage or collection of descendants forming a political or social group. The term was further used to apply to the dwellings of farm animals, themselves part of the traditional community (Thomas 1983) and which were sheltered under the same roof as humans in longhouses; and also to a religious community of monks or nuns in a 'religious house' such as a priory or nunnery (Gilchrist 1994). The application of the values of the house to the 'household', designating not simply family members but also servants and other followers as part of the house, is a little later, in Middle English or the fourteenth century, when, for example, it applied to the great households of the later Middle Ages (Heal 1990). The idea of the house, then, as a structure with social and cultural resonance, was a very old and enduring concept by the early modern period; and it was an idea whose power can be observed in many societies (as seen in the variety of studies from around the world gathered together in Beck 2007). We have seen how houses are set within the matrix of what was often a much older landscape: that older landscape was cultural as well as physical. The structure of Old English linguistic terminology for the house, community and landscape goes hand-in-hand with the physical ordering of the landscape from the elements of the house up to the parish and county community (Hines 2004).

The basic social unit that dwelt in the house was the nuclear family, that is, husband, wife, and children, and their servants. The prevalence of the nuclear family was in contrast to some other areas of early modern Europe, where extended kin such as pairs or groups of brothers and their wives might live under the same roof. J.T. Smith has argued for many years that pairs of conjoined houses may well be artefacts of a 'unit system' in which brothers or two households related by kin lived together (Smith 2002). The problem with this argument that there is very little documentary evidence for such an arrangement in England, in an age when written documentation of family and household relationships, at middling as well as upper social levels, is relatively copious. There are well-documented examples of pairs of houses adjoining on common properties (for example, at Yetminster: Machin 1978, 17–24) but this is not the same thing as a single kin-related unit; in other instances, the arrangement may well have been temporary, not lasting for more than a single generation. There is also more convincing evidence for a 'unit system' from Wales, where the importance of kin ties outside the nuclear family may have been greater (Suggett 2005).

The idea of the house in early modern England was very different from the twenty-first-century notion of a private, domestic retreat, away from the cares of the workplace and public affairs. In the first place, the house was 'charged with production' (Sahlins 1972, 76). In other words, the rural house was not set apart from the world of work, but was typically the centre of a working farm. Its kitchen, butteries and brewhouses were centres of production; the wheat and rye grown in the fields and stored in granary and attics, were, in part, consumed by the household itself, as well as taken to market. As a result, relations between husband and wife were not simply or solely domestic or emotional in nature: marriage and domestic relations between husband, wife and children were also economic transactions.

The cultural metaphor of the 'family' and its reciprocal rights and duties was extended to cover servants; servants were given food, a bed and clothing, as well as a cash wage. Adolescent boys and girls were hired into service and spent a number of years serving another household, often using this time to save their earnings and in time set up households and perhaps employ servants of their own. Hiring fairs for servants punctuated the economic and cultural cycle: they were at definite points of the year, for example Martinmas (11 November), Michaelmas (29 September), and Pentecost (fifty days after Easter Sunday). Hiring fairs were critical points in the life of a servant, and rare moments of a degree of power, when they had some choice to move to a different employer and work and live under a different roof (Kussmaul 1981).

The formal structure of the household was one of patriarchy. After all, who could be ignorant that Eve was created for Adam, and not the other way round? The head of household was master of the house, and in the legal and moral jargon of contemporary commentators held dominion over his wife, his family, and his servants; men 'of good credit' occupied most of the parish offices. In tax records, it is often the male head of household's name alone that is recorded, leaving the modern scholar with the problem of guessing how many individuals there were within the households they headed. The very language of social status reflected this primacy – 'yeoman', 'husbandman' – inscribing the patriarchal order into the most basic language of social identity (Johnson 2007, 101–4).

In practice, there was a great deal of variation around this norm. In the last few decades, feminist historians have given us a much more varied, complex and more realistic picture of how the families and households occupying traditional houses actually lived. Men controlled land, but many women retained rights, for example, over household goods and personal possessions. Men were responsible for the farm and for most trades, but women ran the household. In many areas, responsibility for activities such as dairying gave wives a great degree of economic control, particularly in wood-pasture areas where the dairy economy was of greater relative importance (Underdown 1985a; Mendelson and Crawford 1998, 100–1).

This complex division of duties and powers within the house meant that the house and household were politically charged. The house was 'a little commonwealth'. The relationships between different family members might be loving and companionable, but ultimately they were also seen by many contemporaries as a version writ small of the reciprocal rights and duties that lay between a monarch and his subjects. Disorder within the household was held to threaten the order of the community and the commonwealth. Court cases were routinely brought against women classified as 'scolds', in other words considered by their male judges to be unduly assertive, and husbands who failed in their God-given duty to discipline their wives were often subject to public ritual humiliation by the community, as Chapter 6 will show with the Montacute frieze (Underdown 1985a and Underdown 1996, 14–15).

Finally, it is also difficult for a modern audience to grasp that the house and household relations were also charged in religious, spiritual and even magical terms. The presence and number of books found in inventories increases through the sixteenth and seventeenth centuries with the steady rise in literacy and the availability of the printed word, but the first book to be found recorded in probate inventories is invariably a Bible. It was second nature to perceive the wind howling round the rafters not merely as an irritant, but as providential (Underdown 1993). Threats to the house came from the witch, a figure whose existence was not discredited until the end of the seventeenth century, who often embodied many of the fears and anxieties of the early modern world.

Further, the house was regarded as a body, just as the political and spiritual commonwealth was a body, with the monarch at its head and the different elements of society being likened to commentators to the different organs. The idea of house-as-body is very deeply ingrained in the structural language used to describe it – we have already encountered hips, shoulders, head ('loft'), and other terms. Robert Blair St George has argued that the English house was conceived of as a body, with the frame forming the skeleton, the front door the mouth, the hearth corresponding to the soul, and so on. He cites the poem by Robert Underwood, published in 1605, entitled *A New Anatomie: Where the Bodie of a Man is Very Fit and Aptly (two wayes)*

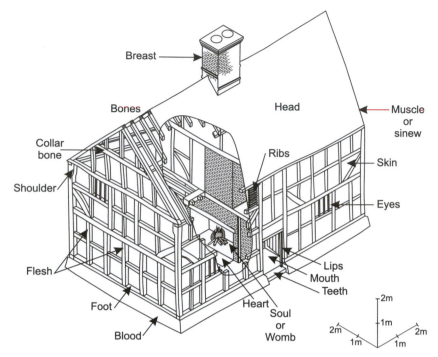

Figure 3.2 The human house and its parts: adapted from St George's illustration of seventeenth-century New England houses. St George discusses how Robert Underwood, George Herbert, John Donne and other English writers saw the house as a body in quite specific ways, expressing a view of contemporary cultural and political thought which linked up the bodies of the person, the household and the commonwealth.

Compared 1. To a household 2. To a citie. Underwood's scheme was a particularly complex elaboration of correspondences that were contrived for poetic effect, but his poem would not have been understood by contemporaries if the scheme it represented was not present in the thought of the time (St George 1998; Figure 3.2).

Population

Traditional houses were built to shelter people from the elements, and the number of people they had to shelter changed through the centuries. Historians have debated absolute figures and short-term fluctuations, and have produced subtle studies of mortality rates, life expectancy and fertility, but the larger picture for pre-industrial England is very clear (Figure 3.3). After a steady rise in the number of people in England up until the end of the thirteenth century, the population fell sharply in the fourteenth. It remained low for the rest of the later Middle Ages, only recovering in the middle of the sixteenth century. This rise then levelled out in the later seventeenth century, only to pick up again in the second half of the eighteenth century, with the Agricultural and Industrial Revolutions (Wrigley and Schofield 1981).

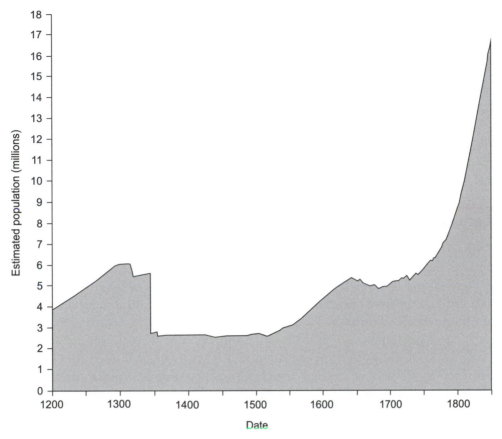

Figure 3.3 A simplified population curve for England, AD 1300–1800. (Based on Hinde, A., *England's Population: A History Since the Domesday Survey* (Bloomsbury Academic, 2003, pp. 2, 25, 181).)

Behind this overall population curve lie long-term processes and trends that the student of vernacular architecture must understand to make sense of the patterns of building in pre-industrial England. The sudden decline in population of the fourteenth century was the result of a lethal combination of agricultural crisis, malnutrition, and climatic change, and these factors themselves tied up in turn with a deeper failure of the medieval social and economic system. In this sense, the famous outbreak of plague, the Black Death of 1348–9, has been perceived by population historians to be a symptom rather than a cause, and should be seen as the most calamitous of a series of plagues, famines and other crises that marked the fourteenth century. For the population that survived these crises, life became much easier. After the fourteenth century, times might be hard, but the English population as a whole never experienced the extremes of famine again. The conditions of scarce labour and low grain prices of the later Middle Ages shifted the balance of power between landlord and tenant. The population remained at low levels until the early sixteenth century; these changes formed the context for the building of many of the houses of late medieval origin discussed in the following chapter. A century later, that pattern was reversed. The rise in population after 1550 led to a rise in demand for bread and for land, and thus a rise in rents and in the price of grain (Wrightson 2000); in Chapter 5, we shall see how many prosperous yeomen took advantage of these conditions to rebuild their houses, and in the process better accommodate their large families.

It is important to remember, however, that behind these very broad trends lay literally millions of human life stories, of individuals and families. Historians have emphasised how these very broad patterns of population rise and fall need to be heavily qualified with respect to region, social class, and above all individual experience (Wrigley and Schofield 1981).

Landscapes in the Atlantic World

One of the key broader processes that determined the pattern of vernacular building was the increasing size and range of the social and economic networks in which it was set, and within which it was understood. The house of a socially middling head of an English farming household in 1400 was built of local materials. Within the house, the food consumed was largely from the farmer's own gardens and fields; other foodstuffs, and much of the material culture, came from the local market.

By 1800, if not earlier, this situation had been totally transformed. First, the farm was much more specialised. The growing penetration of regional and national markets into local economies meant that farmers could concentrate on particular crops and activities, most broadly arable farming in some areas and pastoral in others. More production, then, was oriented for the market and less for the consumption of the household. At the same time, with the steady advance in levels of literacy, most if not all of the household could now read and write (Cressy 1980). This ability tied people into new social networks; where the farmer formerly relied on scraps of gossip picked up in the church or alehouse, he could now read the local news in the newspaper. Visits to provincial towns were much more regular, and many people of all social classes had visited London at some point in their lives. Some of the male heads of household could even vote, depending on the local conditions of the franchise, and many took an active interest in national politics.

One of the cardinal errors that has been made in the past by writers on the English landscape, including myself, is that the story of houses has been told in exclusively local terms, of this or that region. Where a more general picture has been sketched, it is at the national level – 'the English landscape', 'English vernacular houses'. This error is closely tied to an affection for the particular, regional quality of English landscape that sees its scale of operation as small-scale and comfortable, and it is also related to a laudable insistence that the everyday actions of ordinary human beings, people engaging in local and material lives, are just as important and worthy of study as the great deeds of kings and princes on the national and international stage.

In fact, many of the very simple, everyday actions of humans in and around houses tied them in to much wider processes and to networks of production, consumption and trade that stretched around the world. Smoking Virginian tobacco in a clay pipe, drinking tea, consuming potatoes, wearing Indian cotton – all these very simple actions tied the inhabitants of traditional houses into a much wider network or chain of connections with foreign lands and other peoples. These actions also made for mobility across the landscape of travellers, 'masterless men' and vagrants (Beier 1985). And consciousness of these connections, as they grew in scale and complexity between the fourteenth and the eighteenth centuries, made them much more aware of their own identity as English or British, as opposed to villagers of Nether Wallop or of the county of Lancashire.

The landscapes that surround traditional houses, then, are not only complex and multi-layered. Their material and human structure changed radically through the centuries. It is now time to look at the houses themselves, and ask some very basic questions about how these changes were reflected in their numbers and antiquity.

Houses in the Landscape: Numbers and Distribution

Thousands of traditional houses can be seen as 'living archaeology'; that is, they still stand today and are still occupied. However, different numbers of surviving houses are found in different parts of the country. We have a clear idea of exactly how many surviving houses there are, because one of the statutory duties of local authorities is to list and describe all houses and other buildings still standing in a reasonable state that date from before 1700. Of houses built after this date, those of 'architectural merit' are also listed (Pearson and Meeson 2001).

In extremely basic terms, there are many such houses in the South-East of England, quite a few in the Midlands, and ever fewer the further north one goes in the country. A visitor to a Kentish or Essex village may well observe scores of houses dating to the fifteenth, sixteenth and seventeenth centuries; a Cumbrian village, on the other hand, is unlikely to have more than three or four at most. The pattern continues into Wales, where older houses are likely to be concentrated along the area known as the 'marches' along the English border and the easily accessible river valleys (Smith 1975).

It is easier to describe this pattern than to say what it means. The obvious explanation is that of wealth. The south and east of the country were, generally speaking, richer for most of the later Middle Ages and pre-industrial period than those of the north and west. In these lowland areas, agricultural land was richer and more productive, and the metropolis of London provided a growing market for any agricultural surplus. In such communities, then, there were more people who could afford to build a house that was built to last, that did last until the present – and who thought that such an investment was worthwhile.

However, one might propose a reverse explanation. Much of the north and west was affected quite profoundly by the Industrial Revolution. In these areas, late eighteenth- and nineteenth-century populations possessed money, and they spent much of it on new houses. As a result, landscapes in these areas were dramatically transformed during this period. Old houses in these areas are more likely to have been destroyed. A Lancashire valley might have had its old houses swept away by the landscape of textile mills and industrial production; conversely, a forgotten, still predominantly rural corner of the Sussex countryside might retain its old houses precisely because of its relative lack of dramatic landscape change at this period.

In any case, when we examine it closely, the pattern is not so simple as a south-east/north-west divide. Within particular areas, the numbers of old houses may vary strikingly. In the southern Pennines, areas of Devon, in Herefordshire and Shropshire, large numbers of medieval houses have been found; by contrast, the Breckland in East Anglia, an area of poor glacial soil transformed by the intro- duction of sugar beet in the nineteenth century, has very few houses before c.1750 (Johnson 1993a, 25). The Solway Plain, in the far north of England beyond the Cumbrian hills, contains some numbers of houses dating to the sixteenth century and earlier (Jennings 2002). Numbers of old houses can vary strikingly between village and village, even within the same kind of landscape.

Much of this variation may be to do with the chance outbreak of fire – in pre- industrial England, fire was a constant hazard, and might sweep quickly through a densely nucleated village as it did through many towns. Chris Currie studied historical records for the Cambridgeshire village of Swavesey and found that the risk of fire was a critical element in survival rates (Currie 1988). In some cases, variation might be due to the difficulties of later generations in converting different kinds of houses to up-to-date requirements. Sarah Pearson has argued, for example, that later owners found aisled and low-walled houses in Kent difficult to modify in later centuries, and so such structures were later demolished and are now under- represented in the present (Pearson 1994, 60–4). In still other areas, differences in the numbers of houses point to social and legal differences, for example, between different kinds of manorial structure, as Chatwin found in two parishes in the Sussex Weald (2003).

Different kinds of manorial structure conditions involved different systems of tenure. Security of tenure often played a key role in the decision to build or rebuild, and the form of the house that was chosen. The legal conditions under which land was held – freehold, copyhold, and many variations thereof – gave different degrees of security to tenant farmers. The level of rents was a matter of national concern in the later sixteenth century, with the grasping landlord being routinely condemned in popular pamphlets, though the reality was more complex (Wrightson 2000). A farmer who felt secure on his land would feel much more incentive to rebuild than his neighbour who lived under the threat of arbitrary rent rises and summary eviction. At Sawbridge in Warwickshire, Alcock and Woodfield contrasted the 'complex carpentry and elegant mouldings' of Hall House and the 'solid but plain' Old House, 'a difference in mental attitude between a freeholder with pride in his own house, standing on his own land, and a tenant at will whose home and fields might arbitrarily pass to another family at his death' (Alcock and Woodfield 1996, 68–9).

The Middling Sort of People

If the houses that survive today are only a small fraction of those that stood in the past, then a further question arises. Perhaps surviving houses do not reflect the full range of kinds of house, from the largest to the smallest, from the most substantial to the most flimsy? Perhaps instead the houses that do survive, and that we now think of as 'typical', are a biased sample – are they built by the more prosperous and higher-ranking members of rural communities, while the houses of the labouring poor have entirely disappeared?

The study of vernacular architecture has been popularly termed 'the study of the middle classes by the middle classes', and the argument of this book will be that there is some truth in this observation, though it is an oversimplification. Traditional houses, by definition, are not those of the elite (though this statement raises a series of further questions about who were the elite, and whether and why different groups of people chose to build in different ways, questions I will discuss in later chapters). Equally, it is difficult to look at many of the solid and substantial houses in many of the illustrations in this book and conclude that they were typical dwellings of the landless, labouring poor.

A famous edict of Elizabeth I referred to 'the erecting and building of great numbers of cottages, which are daily more and more increased in many parts of this land' (Hamilton 1878, 27). Less than a century later, the Hearth Tax of the 1670s recorded large numbers of one-hearth houses, whose occupants were often exempted from the tax owing to poverty. The vast majority of these houses have vanished. Occasional examples of very small cottages surviving from a very early date have been found. Only 3 per cent of the houses listed in the Hearth Tax Returns survive in the northern county of Durham, as opposed to 28 and 30 per cent for Suffolk and Kent, respectively (Spufford et al. 2006; Barnwell and Airs 2006).

However, the issue is a little more complex than this. In the first place, the inhabitants of many traditional houses included servants. Service for many was an age grade rather than simply a social class – in other words, through the cycle of their lives, many people would move from being children and then servants in adolescence and young adulthood to marrying and being heads of households and employing servants of their own (Kussmaul 1981). As a result of this pattern, many of the lower social orders lived under the same roof as their masters.

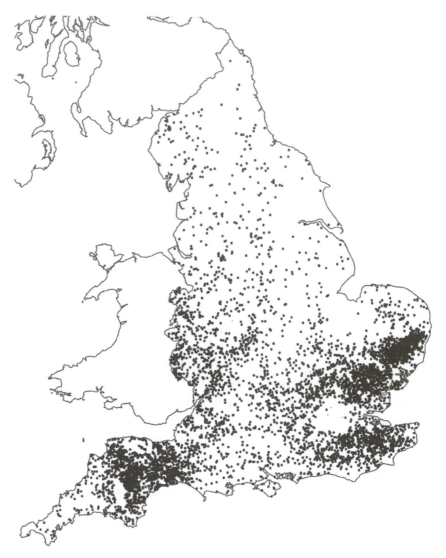

Map 3.2 Distribution of surviving farmhouses in England. Left: surviving houses built before c.1550. Right: surviving houses built 1500–1750. (By permission of Jeremy Lake).

Secondly, it is likely that particular types and classes of building have survived more or less well and thus 'distort' our picture in other ways. For example, many medieval cruck buildings, however well-built they were, may well have failed to survive because of the difficulty of converting them. Smaller cruck-frames were often built for a ground-floor pattern of living, with limited roof space. When changing living patterns dictated the insertion of floors and greater use of upper storeys, they could only be adapted with difficulty. Many were probably demolished entirely in later centuries where other buildings (for example, those with box-frames) were

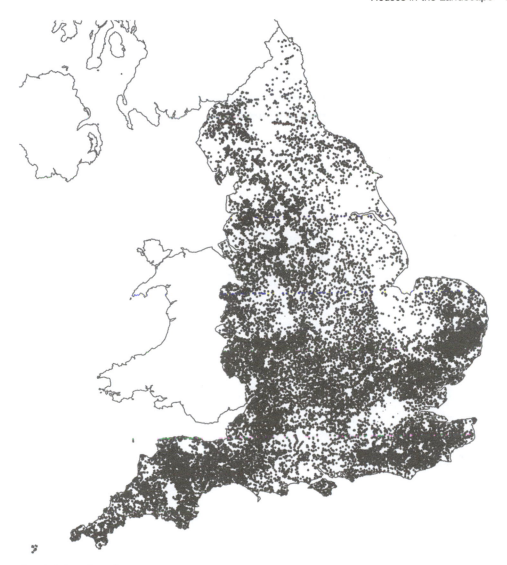

Map 3.2 (continued)

preserved through conversion. Similarly, Adam Longcroft has argued that medieval clay-walled houses largely disappeared from Norfolk because of their single-storey construction (Longcroft 2006).

It is difficult to avoid setting aside the many necessary details and qualifications offered by Currie and others and see the big picture captured by Map 3.2. Stated very broadly, the steady rise in the numbers of traditional buildings, and the presence of larger numbers of earlier buildings in the south and east of England relative to the north and west, is related in however complex a fashion to the rise in numbers, affluence and political and cultural presence of the middling sort of people. Every century from the fourteenth through to the nineteenth has been identified by historians as being that of the rise of the middle classes. Such a characterisation tells us more than simply how historians often concentrate on too narrow a time-span: it draws attention to a very long-term process that unfolded over a number of centuries.

The rest of this book will examine and discuss some of these issues in more detail, starting with the houses of the later Middle Ages.

4

Houses in the Later Middle Ages

One of the most fascinating and appealing aspects of traditional buildings is that they have been used and reused by successive generations, and in most cases are still occupied today. A house that stands today, first built in the 1400s, is also, by definition, a sixteenth-century house, a seventeenth-century house, and so on. The changing needs and desires of successive occupants have meant that each generation has, literally, left its mark on most old houses – the addition of a wing here, a new roof there, and more ephemeral traces such as wear on a floor or plaster on a ceiling. Even careful restoration to a building's 'original state' by the current owners is a new mark of sorts – a changing preference for authenticity and antiquity so characteristic of the modern age. Old houses, then, have layer upon layer of accretions. In this respect, they are much like the historic landscape as a whole.

The changing and accreted form of houses, however, is also frustrating. One very rarely sees a medieval house in its 'original state', however that might be defined. Walking around an old house and observing this extension and that addition, one can mentally peel away the later accretions and reconstruct its earlier form in one's mind; one can even prepare reconstruction drawings, that is, how the building 'might have looked'. But in the vast majority of cases, where the house is still in use today, such a reconstruction can never be more than in the mind. Most modern house owners and their families are happy enough with, even encouraging, students of vernacular architecture to clamber up and down their roof spaces and prepare plans and drawings, but understandably they draw the line when it comes to the physical removal of ceilings, chimneys and other later additions.

To see a later medieval house in its original form, then, one must visit reconstructions in open-air museums; and I want to start this chapter by considering one of the best, Bayleaf, a house of medieval origin reconstructed at the Weald and Downland Museum at Singleton in west Sussex. Bayleaf has become iconic, its form reproduced on postcards and tea towels (Plate 8), but its form is typical of hundreds of medieval houses both surviving and vanished, and the central elements of its plan are, as we shall see, characteristic of many of the features of late medieval vernacular houses as a whole.

Bayleaf

Bayleaf is a timber-framed house; its roof is now tiled, but was formerly of thatch. It is of more than one phase, as the solar end was rebuilt in the early sixteenth century. Its front elevation is as it would have been seen in c.1530, and as seen now is a subtle combination of symmetry and asymmetry, a composition which reveals the arrangement of space inside, and the structure and organisation of the household it was built to house. Further, this material ordering is a physical expression, a materialisation of the social and cultural ordering of the human relations that made up the late medieval household.

The front elevation of Bayleaf is marked by two upper floor projections, supported by jetties or overhangs; the main structural timbers are exposed, forming a distinctive pattern, with a regular rhythm of curved braces at both ground- and first-floor level. Bayleaf is clearly laid out with symmetry in mind, with jettied upper floors with windows to left and right, but it is nevertheless not quite symmetrical. The two projections balance, yet the right-hand one is slightly longer than the other and the jetty at this right-hand end is carried around both the front and the side of the building. At its corner the jetty is carried on a diagonal 'dragon-post'.

The centre of the house is recessed between and behind the two jettied first-floor ends; it has a huge window offset to one side, lighting one end of the hall within. The window, like the other windows at Bayleaf, is not glazed; instead, like most windows in medieval vernacular houses, it has wooden mullions and is backed by wooden shutters. The roofline above the hall window is not recessed; the wallplate runs straight across from jetty to jetty, forming an overhang in front of the front wall of the hall, and supported by two of the distinctive arched braces. This overhang between the two jettied stories and the continuous roof it enables is the diagnostic feature of a particular type of medieval house, the 'Wealden', named for its popularity as a house form in the Weald of Kent and Sussex (though it is found elsewhere, as far afield as Stratford-on-Avon, Oxford and Suffolk: Rigold 1963, Munby 1974 and Johnson 1993a, 46). The front door is placed at the other end from the window, tucked under the right-hand jettied projection.

One of the keys to understanding medieval houses is that the distinction between exterior and interior is not marked in the way that it is in a modern house. Rather, the external appearance and disposition of features, doors and windows, act as a clear signal for the outside observer of the layout and appearance of its internal spaces (Figure 4.1). A medieval visitor to Bayleaf might understand and interpret, from the pattern described above, the internal layout of the house, before he or she even went inside the building. This is in part because the internal layout would be familiar, unspoken and indeed second nature to him or her from countless other houses of different sizes but of the same pattern.

For the modern visitor, however, to walk through the front door of Bayleaf is to engage with one of the most visually arresting and even moving sights of the Middle

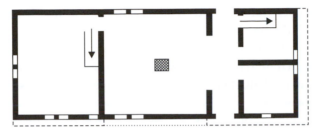

Figure 4.1 Bayleaf: plan. The arrows indicate stairs. (Based on Harris, R., *Discovering Timber Framed Buildings* (Shire Publications, 1993, p. 66).)

Ages, in its own way as profound and as carefully composed as any of the interiors of the great medieval castles and cathedrals (Plate 9). Once through the door, one's eyes take a few seconds to get used to the dimness of the interior. One then turns to the left, past the spere truss and also perhaps a moveable screen in the space now left by the truss, to stand on the edge of a great hall, open to the roof. In the centre of the hall an open fire crackles and burns; one's eyes are led upwards, where the grey wisps of smoke disperse amidst the rafters. The visual 'pull' upwards is accentuated by the great arch-braced tie-beam across the centre of the hall. This beam is 'cambered' or curved upwards, has a carefully moulded soffit or underside, and is surmounted by an ornamented crown-post at the centre of the roof.

Looking back down, one's gaze is drawn to the great windows already observed from the outside, and the way they cast light downwards on to the far end of the hall. Peering dimly through the smoke, one can see that the far end of the hall has a fixed bench with overmantel; behind it, a door leads off to 'private' rooms at this end of the house. Back to the visitor's right, a symmetrically placed pair of doors lead to a pair of 'service' rooms, where food and drink would have been stored. At either end of the house, stairs give access to the upper storeys, now furnished with reconstructed beds and other furniture.

There are two abiding impressions which remain with the visitor to Bayleaf. The first is how subtly crafted the architecture is. For example, the hall is of two bays, and that housing the fixed bench is clearly the superior or 'upper' bay. It is lighter, being lit by the pair of windows front and back. In fact, the whole house has been oriented by the carpenter towards this upper bay of the hall, in ways that a casual visitor might not notice. For example, the carpenter used wooden pegs to secure the joints in the timber frame. These were hammered in with the hammered, flat end, or 'fair face', flush with the timber, with the pointed end projecting from the other side. Now the 'fair face' at Bayleaf, and in hundreds of other medieval houses, always points towards the upper bay of the hall. In some houses, even the main posts are so arranged that the heartwood of the timbers always faces towards the centre of the upper end. Again, one can compare the tie-beams in the two upper rooms. That at the lower end of the house is placed as normal, from front to back;

but that at the upper end is turned by ninety degrees, so that it runs along rather than across the building. The upper end is thus elevated, conceptually, from a simple room into a 'wing' running at right-angles to the hall. Now this architectural subtlety is clearly tied in to cultural ideas of the household and social order: 'upper' and 'lower' ends to the hall, then, are designations that merge physical, architectural and social connotations.

The second abiding impression is how spartan and, to our eyes, physically uncomfortable the interior of Bayleaf is. There is very little furniture; its interiors would satisfy the most dogmatic modern minimalist. The houses of higher social orders might have had wall-paintings, painted cloths or tapestries (Davies 2008, 32–4), and interiors may well have been brightly coloured, but there are few fixtures and fittings, few movable items. The open and lofty hall is visually arresting but draughty and cold; the smoke gets everywhere, and after a while forms a layer of grime on every surface, whether on the walls, the furniture, including that of clothing, or on the human body. Analysis of human skeletons from medieval cemeteries has in several cases revealed the characteristic traces of sinus infection, caused by everyday living in smoky environments (Lewis 2002).

The Medieval House

In many respects, though not in all, Bayleaf is a particularly impressive example of the many hundreds, and even thousands, of late medieval houses standing in the English countryside today. The defining characteristic of almost all of these houses when they were first built was a central hall, open to the roof. Many were much smaller than Bayleaf, and many had open halls that were smaller and in particular much lower than Bayleaf's lofty rafters. However, all but a very few had this central feature, to the extent that they were referred to in terms that stressed their strong relationship ('dwelling-hall', 'fyrehous', 'hallehous': Poos 1991, 76).

There was a reason for the centrality, and ubiquity, of the hall. The hall, in its physical layout and in what it meant to medieval people of all social ranks, was a basic building-block of late medieval society. Its basic form, with opposed doors and sometimes a screens passage at its lower end, and a combination of elements marking the upper end such as a fixed bench, a raised dais, a canopy, and provision for lighting, can be found in halls both large and small, ranging from the very top of the social scale to far down the social scale, from the greatest of noble or royal households to modest peasant dwellings. A medieval peasant could have walked in to the very largest of them all, the great Westminster Hall at the centre of the premier royal palace in the country (Figure 4.2), and understood the space he was in. The scale would have been stunning, and there might not have been a raised dais or canopy in his own hall, but the doors at the lower end, the dais or bench at the upper, the social ordering implied by this spatial ordering, and the cues for correct behaviour implied by this ordering, were all there.

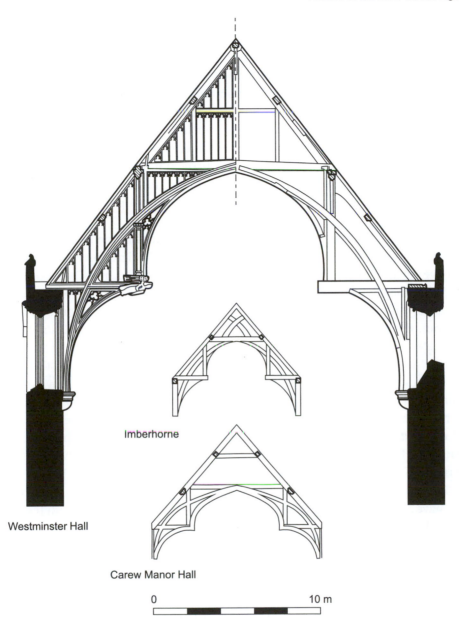

Figure 4.2 Hammer-beam roofs: Westminster Hall and comparatives, very different in size but similar in construction and appearance. (Based on Clarke, J., 'An early vernacular hammer-beam structure: Imberhorne Farm, *Vernacular Architecture*, 36, 32–40 (Maney Publishing, 2005).)

The specific form of the great hall was also distinctive to England, although halls are found across medieval Europe, to the extent that they have been considered the characteristic and defining feature of the architecture of medieval Christendom: 'the most characteristic building of the Middle Ages was not the cathedral, or even the castle, but the hall' (Coldstream 2002, 23). At the elite level, French houses had the 'grande salle', but its layout was subtly different from the English later medieval hall (Girouard 2000, 79; see also Virágos 2006 for Hungarian elite dwellings). In areas of the Welsh borders of cruck construction, halls were often dominated by a great cruck-framed open truss with its cusps, which may well have had references to 'the international Gothic architectural vocabulary' (Suggett 2005, 22).

In smaller houses, the hall was less impressive, being smaller in terms of both floor space and height, and simpler in its roof structure and decoration, but just as meaningful in its layout and decoration. Smaller halls could be only one bay, but there the cross-passage or opposed doors were often housed in a second bay. Where the open hall was of two bays, as J.T. Smith found, for example, in Hertfordshire, the upper bay is often slightly wider than the lower, emphasising its superiority in the off-centre placing of the open truss (Smith 1992, 39–40). Ornamentation was mostly seen in the timbers, but could also be found in the layer of thatch laid directly on to the timbers. In Devon, patterns of straw or decorative wattlework still survive, again drawing the eye of the observer upwards (Cox and Thorp 2001).

The authority of the open hall sprang in part from the perception by contemporaries of the antiquity of the hall, its identification with tradition and ancient custom. One of the most common ideological buttresses in pre-industrial society was reference to the past, to 'custom since time out of mind'. Nobles referred to lineage and ancestry, and used a visual language of heraldry to express this lineage and ancestry. Peasants referred to custom and tradition, accepted ways of doing things and rights sanctioned and honoured by generations of practice. The hall was part of a visual language that made reference to this ideology. There are examples of open halls that deliberately retained older forms to retain a sense of cultural authority: for example, Fyfield Hall in Essex, which 'retained the old twelfth-century form, as if to preserve an air of ancient authority' (Walker 1999, 125).

The hall was certainly a cultural preference on the part of housebuilders and owners. We have already noted its physical discomforts, and the sparks rising with the smoke from the open hearth posed a constant fire risk to the thatch and timbers of the roof. Chimneys had been commonly used at elite levels since the twelfth century, and could often be found within larger halls, particularly where the hall space was at first-floor level above a cellar or basement; it was not therefore a necessity to have the hall open to the roof to disperse the smoke. Elaborate louvers and hooded open summits of gables could be used (Gee 1987; Adams 2005). It was also inconvenient to have the hall divide the upper levels of the two ends of the house: there is at least one example, at Wickham in Hampshire, of a gallery being built across the hall to communicate between the upper floors of the two ends. This complex arrangement shows that builders would go to great lengths to allow communication between first floor levels without losing the open hall itself (Roberts 2003, Figure 4.14).

One of the reasons the open hall carried such a heavy load of cultural meanings was because of related symbolism and imagery in late medieval religious belief. We have seen how central the Church was to people's experience of the world (Marks

2004). The Catholic religion was a fundamental and structuring part of everyday life in the later Middle Ages; the Church was central to the most mundane of activities in a way that is difficult for the modern mind to understand. The rituals of the Church utilised a series of symbols that had very complex theological meanings but which also had resonance in everyday life: blood, wine, oil, water, saliva. Holy Communion could be conceived of as a meal; the altar as tablecloth. So, as Pam Graves has argued, the local church derived its cultural authority and power from the way it articulated the Mass in terms of everyday, domestic activities. As a deliberate result, ordinary people might not be expected (or encouraged) to be versed in the finer points of theological arguments, but might nevertheless share in the mystery and in the power of the ritual (Graves 2000). And, equally, the mystery and power worked in the other direction: the repeated patterns of everyday life, such as the mealtimes hosted in the hall, had a spiritual and symbolic significance that went far beyond the mere action of eating.

It is difficult not to see a close link between the experience of domestic space and experience of religious space, and common principles structuring both. Where the hall was divided into upper and lower ends, the church was divided into nave and chancel. The altar was in the position of the bench and table in the hall, and stood on a raised platform, just as the dais end was in larger halls. The visitor to both church and house entered at the lower end, and in entering through either the south porch or through the cross-passage, turned their body towards either the altar or the high table. And the liturgy of the Mass, whatever the endless doctrinal debates among the literate clergy over its precise meaning, was experienced by the congregation in a way that brought to mind the ritual of eating within the hall. Both church and house framed a complex structuring of public and private space, the church with its chantry chapels (Roffey 2001). In elite, ideological depictions of the house and the family there were often Eucharistic references: for example, the famous fourteenth-century Luttrell Psalter depicts Sir Geoffrey Luttrell sitting at the centre of his table, in a dominating position over family and guests, with the words of Psalm 115 above him: 'I call upon the name of the Lord' (Camille 1998, 105; see also Gardiner 2008, 60–1). In great houses, when the meat was carved at the lord's table for a grand meal, the 'towel, second napkin and girdle [of the carver] were worn in exactly the same way as a priest wears a stole, maniple and girdle for mass' (Girouard 1978, 47). The great house employed an array of distinctive sights, sounds and smells to express the cultural values of the household (Woolgar 2006, 248–66).

Such discussion may seem speculative to some readers. It is certainly difficult to point to this or that written document stating how the form of the open hall was specifically understood by people, and there are relatively few documentary references to what activities specifically went on in the open halls of peasant houses. But it is not difficult to point to texts that assume the importance of the hall at upper social levels, and that engage in moral condemnation for those not using it. The most famous example is Langland's *Piers Plowman*, which complains of the lord who forsook the dais but rather sat 'by him-selve . . . in a privye-parlour. . . . Or in a chambre with a chymnye [having left] the chief halle' (cited in Lloyd 1931, 48). But this lack of written documents discussing the meanings of the hall should not be taken at face value. We have established that the hall was ubiquitous, part of the accepted structure of society. In this sense, it was part of an accepted world of custom, and custom, by definition, is something that rarely needs overt articulation. The hall materialised social relations so effectively that those relations were taken for granted.

Families, households and communities get on together, create their own social world, through what anthropologists have called 'habitus'. Habitus is the dense layer of accepted, everyday meanings and actions that define who we are, though we rarely articulate them (Bourdieu 1990). Habitus is a shared understanding of how to get on, how to behave; it is reinforced by everyday actions whose meanings are so 'obvious' that they do not require explanation. For example, actions like knocking before we enter a room define ideas of privacy and the individual; the arrangement of space in a house embodies ideas of masculine and feminine, parent and child, master and servant. These ideas are obvious and common sense to us – however, any serious historical study of changes in everyday life shows that such ideas and practices were very different in the past.

The structure of the hall, then, acted to materialise or to fix in place certain ideas that were central to the late medieval habitus. Its fixed bench, its orientation in terms of upper and lower ends, its lighting of the upper bay, its placement of doors at the lower end, acted to peg social expectations and relations in place, as securely as its wooden pegs held its timber-framed joints in place. One of the characteristics of habitus is its implicit and unspoken nature. It reflected a shared understanding, and shared understandings do not need to be articulated or written down. It was important, and it governed and directed patterns of behaviour securely, precisely because it was 'obvious', taken-for-granted and therefore never put down on paper.

Indeed, one of the reasons why spatial structures such as the hall were so important in communicating social rules was because the great mass of medieval society was illiterate. Outside the clergy and aristocracy, very few of the late medieval population could read or write. The lived experience of a preliterate world is very different from our own (Goody 1987): it is a world in which cultural values are expressed orally, through gestures, bodily movement or through material things, in a much more important way. It is a world where communication through material symbols was central. It is difficult to stress too strongly how far the later Middle Ages was an age of cultural expression in terms of bodily gesture, dress, colour, form, and the richness of different meanings that attached to the senses of sound, taste, smell, vision and touch (Woolgar 2006). As a result, the visual language of architecture and material culture was much more important, and of a very different quality, than it is today.

The hall was central to the life of a community with a strong sense of status and hierarchy. It laid out, in material form, a strong grid of expectations of authority and responsibility. This authority was expressed and reinforced through the daily performance of people's face-to-face actions: the lord rising to greet his guests; the deference shown by those of lower social status at the lower end of the hall. The hall structured that interaction very closely; its layout made it very difficult for the visitor not to be overawed, or to fail to show deference. It controlled the movement of people from one end of the house to the other, and displayed different ranks of people much as a stage displays the bodies of the actors. The head of household, sitting in the middle of the bench at the upper end, was the first to sit down; in this way, the arrangement of the hall structured even the temporal rhythm of movement. Households at relatively humble social levels shared in this everyday rhythm: the smallest hearth was placed in a hall which, however humble, was still open to the roof, still had upper and lower ends, and around which different family members sat in a hierarchical pattern.

One of the distinctive features of late medieval communities was the way different people could move around, but the formal social grid remained intact. In many households, particularly at upper social levels, the male head of household might be away for much of the year, serving king or lord, but his wife would still be there, moreover occupying the same fixed bench at mealtimes (Archer 1997). So at the same moment as a man might sit down at the lower end of the hall of a great household, showing deference to and receiving hospitality from a great noble, his wife might be sitting at the upper end of a much smaller but nevertheless similar hall, receiving as his wife, and in her own right as the mistress of the household, the performance of deference from a smaller group of family members, servants and farm hands. The labourers themselves might be moving around between communities more and more, as a result of social and economic dislocation (Goldberg 2004; McRae 1996), but they occupied the same social place within each of the households they moved between. The physical structure of the house, then, served to fix and define relations between people. At lower social levels, even when the peasant farmer was out tilling the fields, the bench remained as a visual reminder of his authority.

The structure of the hall varied but carried the same system of visual referents. Earlier houses are often aisled in form: that is, the weight of the roof was carried in part by a pair of aisle-posts. Earlier halls are often fully aisled in form. Aisles can be found in later medieval houses in the south-east and in southern East Anglia, though examples can be found elsewhere, for example, the early sixteenth-century dwellings in the southern Pennines (Sandall 1986, 23; Giles 1992, 26–36). However, so important was it to 'free up' the interior of the hall, that a variety of solutions were adopted to eliminate the aisle-posts from this central space. The most elaborate means of so doing was the hammerbeam roof found in great halls and churches, most notably Westminster Hall, in which the aisle-posts rest on a plate, itself supported by braces rather than running down to the ground; a manorial, arguably vernacular, example has recently been discovered at East Grinstead in Sussex, where it was tree-ring dated to 1428 (Clarke 2005; Figure 4.2, see p. 69).

More prosaically, but more commonly, the aisle-posts might be replaced by a pair of curved timbers, or what are termed 'base-crucks'. The term is possibly misleading, as in the view of some scholars they are not necessarily anything to do with the cruck tradition. Rather, it is possible that they were invented independently by carpenters who previously worked in the box-framing tradition – though this contention is much debated. If they were, then their origins lie in a desire to clear the floor space of the hall of the internal posts, creating an open space (for example, in Essex: Stenning 2003); though their origins may also lie in the need within barns to clear the internal space of posts that would hinder carts.

Around the hall, there was more variation in the structure and layout of late medieval houses. Not all halls had a room at their upper end, though most had a room or rooms at the service or lower end. Also, not all houses had jettied ends or wings. Almost all houses had upper and lower ends that were unheated. (There is a very rare example of an upper end heated by a smoke bay served by a louvre at Cuttle Pool Farm at Knole in Warwickshire, and a smoke bay at the service end of a Wealden-type house at Rougham in Suffolk: Alcock 1998, 82–3, and Johnson 1993, 46.)

The majority of larger vernacular houses probably had detached kitchens, although most have been destroyed. In recent years, a number of examples in Sussex, East Anglia and the west Midlands have been found of buildings most plausibly interpreted as detached kitchens (Martin and Martin 1997; Meeson 2000; Walker 2000). According to map evidence, nearly two-thirds of late medieval farmhouses in one manor of rural Essex had an outside kitchen, of which one-third were thatched and the rest tiled (Ryan 2000, 15). Some houses had a kitchen open to the roof on the other side of the service rooms from the hall (for example, The Old Rectory House, Northfleet, Kent: Barnwell and Adams 1994, 22).

In the north and west of the country, many later medieval houses had a byre for cattle at the lower end of the house, below the cross-passage. This type of house is called a 'longhouse', and has attracted a great deal of scholarly attention. Many medieval and later examples have been excavated, being identified most characteristically by the byre at the lower end with a drain for the manure to flow away (Plate 10; Hurst 1971). Surviving longhouses from the later middle ages, however, are often difficult to identify with certainty, as the lower or byre end has frequently been rebuilt, and it is impossible to be sure what type of structure (if any) predated the rebuilding.

Bayleaf is not exceptionally large, but it is one of the larger and more impressive examples of surviving late medieval houses. Smaller houses are well known, but are often very difficult to identify from external survey alone (for example, Figure 4.3). Later builders, as we shall see, became very skilled at converting these earlier houses by inserting a ceiling and brick chimney stack into the formerly open hall. As a result of these and other alterations, many open-hall houses are indistinguishable on a

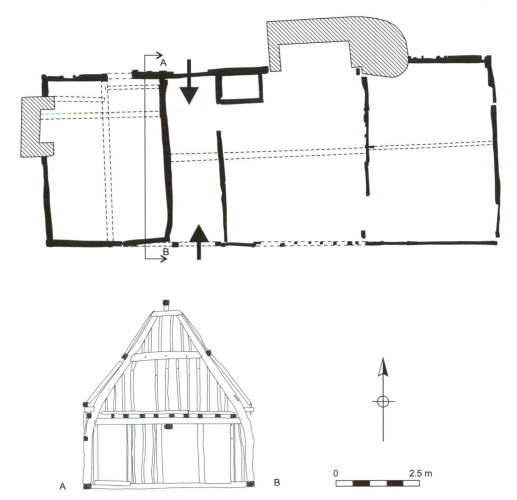

Figure 4.3 A four-bay medieval farmhouse at Lower Radley, Berkshire. Externally this small houses had an unremarkable appearance; its medieval origins were revealed by careful archaeological examination during demolition. (Based on Hinton, D., 'A cruck building at Lower Radley, Berks' *Oxonesia*, 33, 13–33, 1967 (by courtesy of the Editor and Committee of the Oxfordshire Architectural and Historical Society).)

superficial examination from later houses. It is often only when one clambers into the roof space to discover rafters, and occasionally thatch, caked with soot from the open hearth, that one can establish the true antiquity of the house (Letts 2000).

In many cases, these smaller houses only had one storeyed end, or in some cases had no storeyed ends at all. A group of houses in Devon studied by Nat Alcock and Michael Laithwaite (1973), for example, started life as only one storey high throughout. These dwellings were divided into rooms by wooden partitions that were over head height but did not reach the roof. They subsequently had ceilings for a first floor inserted into them that were jettied-in over the partitions, thus preserving them for modern study (Figure 4.4). Elsewhere, houses of greater height

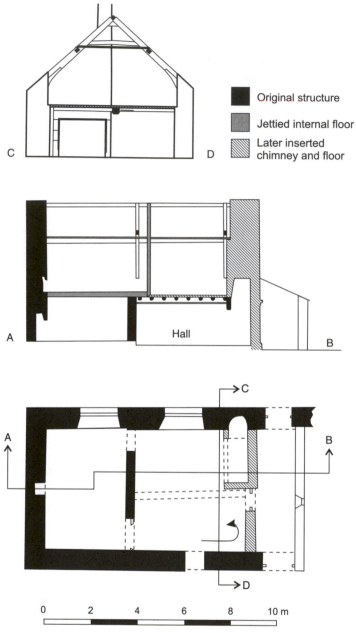

Figure 4.4 Pumpy Cottage, South Tawton, Devon: in the earliest phase of this medieval cruck house, there was probably a low partition between single-bay hall and inner room, which were both open to the roof. The inner room was then provided with a ceiling and a partition rising to the roof while the hall remained open. Chimney-stack (indicated in dashed lines) and hall floor (indicated with dotted lines) were added subsequently, and any former partition between hall and inner room replaced in stone. (Based on Alcock, N.W. and Laithwaite, M., 'Medieval houses in Devon and their modernization', *Medieval Archaeology*, 17, 100–25 (Maney Publishing, 1973).)

nevertheless had partitions that did not reach to the roof, evidenced by smoke-blackening all the way along it (Smith 1992, 44). The symmetrical appearance of Bayleaf itself was only arrived at piecemeal: the open hall and service end has been tree-ring dated to 1405–1430, while the present upper end was rebuilt in the earlier sixteenth century.

As we have seen, there are large numbers of traditional houses that survive from before the Middle Ages, but their distribution is highly concentrated. We saw in the previous chapter that, broadly, more vernacular houses survive from earlier dates in the South and East than do in the North and West. Specifically, very large numbers of medieval houses can be found in Suffolk, Essex, Kent, Sussex and the Home Counties. There are also groups of houses that survive in Devon and the West Country. Areas of the Midlands and South outside these areas have rather fewer, and surviving medieval houses from the North below manorial level are, with exceptions in certain areas, quite rare. An important exception is the southern Pennines, where a group of houses survive from the first part of the sixteenth century (Giles 1992).

Historical Origins

Overall, later medieval houses survive in their thousands. Their numbers have been underestimated in the past, as we have seen, owing to the difficulty of ascertaining the date of the house from external observation alone, and also to a general belief that medieval houses of relatively humble social origins must necessarily have not survived. In Suffolk alone, my research suggested a rough estimate of between one and two thousand open-hall houses surviving (Johnson 1993a, 21).

How old are these houses? The vast majority of surviving houses have been dated, either by tree-ring dating or other evidence, from the late Middle Ages, that is, after 1350. Programmes of tree-ring dating have found ever larger numbers of earlier houses that survive from the earlier fourteenth and thirteenth centuries, and even a few examples of twelfth-century houses, but these very early examples have usually been discovered as part of a wider programme of identifying medieval houses in general. In Kent, most surviving open-hall houses were built after 1460 (Pearson 1994, 68). Construction of houses in smaller towns also seems to have accelerated in the fifteenth century: the period 1430–90 'stands out as a period of house construction' (Dyer 2003, 112). Twenty years of tree-ring dating has confirmed that most surviving open-hall houses were constructed in the period from the mid-fifteenth century onwards (Pearson 2001; Figure 4.5).

Archaeologists and historians have disagreed about what this pattern of dates of surviving houses means in terms of past processes. In particular, it is very difficult to evaluate how the houses that have survived above ground today might be compared with the much larger number that have not survived. The majority of later medieval houses have either disappeared altogether or left only below-ground traces recoverable through archaeological excavation.

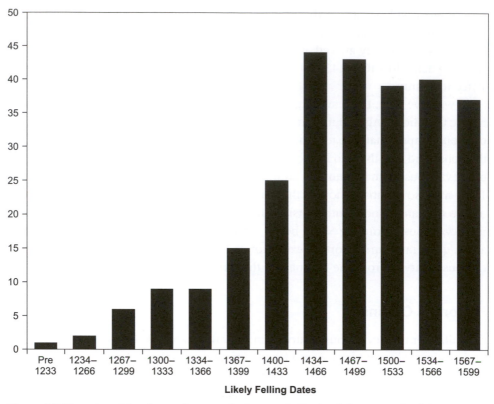

Figure 4.5 Tree-ring dates for rural vernacular houses in England, from samples taken between 1980 and 2001. (Based on Pearson, S., 'The chronological distribution of tree-ring dates, 1980–2001: an update', *Vernacular Architecture*, 32, 68–9 (Maney Publishing, 2001).)

Archaeologists have excavated a large number of medieval peasant houses from deserted or shrunken medieval villages (Gardiner 2000), and over the last few decades these excavations have changed scholarly views of such structures. It used to be thought that the arrival of numbers of late medieval houses marked a decisive and quite sudden change: that prior to this change, medieval peasants had lived in flimsy, insubstantial hovels that had to be rebuilt every generation. The arrival of large numbers of surviving houses, then, dating from the later Middle Ages, was interpreted as the result of a major change in peasant building, from 'impermanent' to 'permanent' ways of building.

However, the archaeological and historical evidence has been reassessed (Wrathmell 1989). At the famous site of Wharram Percy, for example, phases of rebuilding found by excavators have been reinterpreted not as wholesale reconstruction, but rather as repairs. At the same time, historians have found plenty of evidence to show that medieval houses after the twelfth century were well-built and lasted for much longer than a generation. Christopher Dyer, in a review of documentary information for the building of peasant houses, has shown that they were well built of large timbers by specialist craftsmen, and cost between £2 and £4 – a considerable sum for the time (Dyer 1986).

It does seem that the growing numbers of houses that survive from the later Middle Ages testify to a general rise in standards of building and levels of investment in building. In other words, over the centuries, rural households built houses that were more substantial and that were meant to last longer. This process of improvement, however, was much more gradual than earlier scholars have supposed. It happened over several centuries, rather than being a sudden change towards the end of the Middle Ages, and its pattern seems to have varied strongly according to region (Wrathmell 1984). What did this pattern mean?

It was argued by an earlier generation of scholars that the hall represents a very deep cultural tradition, over a thousand years old by the end of the Middle Ages. It used to be thought that the plan of the hall dated back to the early halls of north Germany and was brought in to England with the Anglo-Saxon settlers in the centuries after the fall of the Roman Empire (as argued by the great S.O. Addy 1898 and Thompson 1995). However, in recent decades scholars have moved away from seeing an uninterrupted continuity between early and late halls. A thousand years is a long time, and there were at least two major breaks in building tradition in the early medieval period, identified through careful archaeological excavation and inter-pretation of village and high status sites (James et al. 1984). These early buildings were generally lacking in internal divisions until the ninth century, and although they had opposing doors, the later divisions associated with the cross-passage were absent (Gardiner 2000, 168–9). Many of the functions that would be integrated into the later medieval plan were instead dispersed between the detached hall and other buildings.

The distinctive arrangement of the service end in high-status buildings, with symmetrical buttery and pantry separated by a passage connecting the hall with the kitchen beyond, persisted throughout the later Middle Ages, in part because it allowed the ostentatious display of hospitality through the presentation of large quantities of food and other goods, through the ceremonial movement of food from the lower end up into the hall and past the other tables to the upper or dais end (Gardiner 2008). However, this specific arrangement in one building, with service end separated from hall and upper end by a cross-passage as at Bayleaf, did not come together until the early thirteenth century (Figure 4.6).

It also used to be thought that the open-hall plan was a form of building with its origins in the countryside, and that surviving open halls found in towns were secondary adaptations of this plan (Pantin 1962–3). Again, recent scholarship has shown that matters are more complex. Sarah Pearson (2005) has suggested that influences moved from the town to the country at least as often as from the other direction, from the country to the town. It may well be, for example, that the earliest examples of elements of the Wealden form of house are to be found in urban rather than rural contexts. Jane Grenville (2008), in response to Pearson,

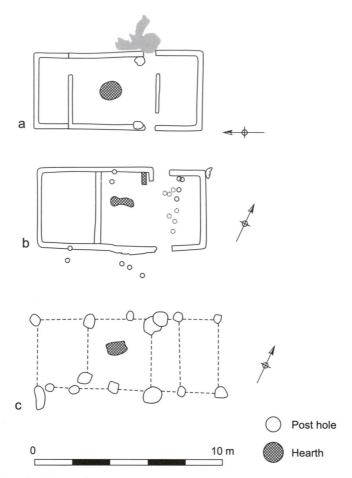

Post hole

0   10 m   Hearth

Figure 4.6 Simplified plans of excavated houses from the thirteenth century, antecedents of the late medieval plan. Above: Wintringham, Huntingdonshire. Middle; Hangleton, Sussex. Below: Tattenhoe, Buckinghamshire. (Based on Gardiner, M., 'Vernacular buildings and the development of the later medieval domestic plan in England', *Medieval Archaeology*, XLIV, 159–80 (Maney Publishing, 2000).)

has pointed out the strong parallels between peasant and urban building in smaller houses, for example, between the excavated houses at Wharram Percy and those at York, and has suggested that urban halls do indeed repeat a spatial pattern first seen in the countryside. Both Pearson and Grenville have identified important points, and in a sense both are right. Both rural and urban open halls were freighted with a common set of values, values which were exceptionally powerful. In a sense, the direction in which 'influence' flowed, whether from country to town or from town to country, is not the central point: the common pattern that both scholars discern is testament to the cultural authority of the open hall.

Later Medieval Society and Culture

We have seen that surviving medieval houses are strongly concentrated in certain areas. They are also strongly concentrated in particular kinds of landscape. Bayleaf itself, and the many open-hall houses in the Weald of Kent and Sussex, belong to a very particular landscape. The Weald was a heavily wooded area relative to other areas of England. Its farming economy was heavily pastoral in emphasis, and there was a strong concentration of rural industry – in particular, the Weald was famous for its manufacture of iron, though the glass, tanning and cloth industries were also important (Zell 1994; Pearson 1994, 13). The founding of iron required the proximity of woodland for the fuel needed for the smelting process. Large nucleated villages are rare in the Weald; instead, houses often occur in small groups, or occupy isolated locations on the edge of woodland. Instead of the large open-field systems characteristic of the Midlands, farming in this area was already taking place in small enclosed fields at the end of the Middle Ages.

In many respects, the Weald was unusual, but the pattern of settlement and economy was typical for areas of England where large numbers of surviving medieval houses are still to be found. These characteristically share a pastoral emphasis in farming. They also tend to concentrate in areas of rural industry. The chief such industry was cloth production, though other industries, for example, iron production and salt panning, were also important. Much of England pro- duced large quantities of wool; until the fifteenth century, most raw wool was exported to the Low Countries to be spun and woven into cloth. A critical change in the later Middle Ages was the growth of native manufacturing. The English now moved away from the export of raw materials to the Continent towards that of manufactured goods – in other words, from raw wool to finished cloth. This shift has been hailed by sociologists and historians as a move away from a traditional peasant economy, and towards a capitalist system of production (Britnell 2004, 351–5).

Late medieval houses also tend to concentrate in regions that fall outside the champion and upland areas of the country. It is not a common experience to walk down the street of a nucleated English village in the 'champion' landscapes of the Midlands and see a succession of medieval houses, though there are excep- tions to this. Nat Alcock, for example, records over nine medieval houses in the Warwickshire village of Stoneleigh, on the boundary between the open-field Felden and the more heavily wooded Arden (Alcock 1993, 40). The areas that possess large numbers of pre-1550 houses tend to belong to areas outside the Midlands, often classified as wood-pasture landscapes. Medieval houses below the manorial level are found more often in small hamlets or isolated locations. Bayleaf, for example, before its move to the open-air museum, sat in an isolated location in an area of dispersed settlement (Tankard 2009).

The causes of this distribution are often difficult if not impossible to disentangle in specific cases, but the general pattern is much clearer (Dyer 2003; Britnell 2004). In the first place, it was the farming economies of wood-pasture areas that were gaining in wealth in the later Middle Ages. The last chapter discussed how all regions of England had farming economies that mixed arable and pastoral, but that there was a relative emphasis on corn in champion areas, and cattle and sheep in wood-pasture areas. The fourteenth-century population decline meant that the price of corn fell steeply. At the same time, the rising prosperity of the surviving population meant that many could afford more meat and dairy products in their diet, rather than subsisting on bread alone. The cattle and sheep raised in wood-pasture areas thus brought in more wealth than before, while the reverse happened with the corn produced in champion areas. It was also the wood-pasture area where the pattern of agriculture allowed more time to engage in rural industry (arable cultivation can be more labour-intensive than pastoral farming). As a result, different areas of England became more specialised in terms of agricultural production, and the balance between the two areas as shifted dramatically in terms of relative patterns of wealth between the early fourteenth and early sixteenth centuries, in other words the very moment at which the majority of surviving medieval houses were being constructed.

There were social and cultural factors involved also. Particular circumstances varied from community to community, but in champion areas such as much of the Midland claylands, manorial structures were often strong, with relatively tight feudal ties. The balance of power between the lord of the manor and his tenants was, in these areas, often heavily in favour of the former, with peasant farmers lacking security of tenure. At the same time, the communal decision-making of the village community left individual farmers quite restrained in terms of their ability to work independently – to accumulate land and wealth, and introduce new agricultural techniques on their holdings. By contrast, feudal ties in wood-pasture areas were often weaker and the rights of tenants correspondingly stronger. Tenant farmers may well have thought of themselves as being more secure from the threat of eviction; in Kent, for example, the tenurial practice of 'gavelkind' meant that 'men were personally free and could dispose of their land at will' and normally only owed light obligations to the lord (Pearson 1994, 15). The absence of large-scale field systems in wood-pasture areas also meant that individuals could innovate more freely in terms of introducing new crops and new farming practices, and could more easily build up larger units of land. In Devon, for example, those rebuilding 'barton' farms were also enclosing fields around those farms in a regular pattern, into compact, independent blocks (Turner 2007, 66–7). It is also these latter communities, particularly in East Anglia and the West Country, which saw an early growth of the cloth industry, supplementing the incomes of farming households.

If the social setting of the household was complex, so was its internal composition and structure – the number of people in the family, their relative ages, and their relations to each other. Medieval demographers have hotly debated the size of the household and the nature of the kin relationships within it; the evidence for these relationships is very difficult to interpret (summarised, for example, by Goldberg 2004, 15–16; see also Poos 1991, 141–58). What is clear is that many of the tensions within later medieval society were contained within the house itself: between the roles of women and of men; between the head of the household and the servants; and between different family members. The house acted as a frame, around which these tensions were played out in terms of everyday performances.

One very broad pattern seems to be that families and households were getting smaller. The smaller nuclear family of the sort familiar to Western societies today – mother, father and children – is not the only family form in the world, and it was not the only form in the Middle Ages. In some areas of the Midlands, earlier forms of 'stem' family were common. The structure and appearance of the late medieval house, then, is tied up in part with the rise of the nuclear-family-plus-servants form of household.

The larger pattern remains clear. Wealthier tenant farming families and households had greater opportunities to build up land and other forms of wealth in wood-pasture communities. These areas also had a different social and cultural make-up, one that was more conducive to individualism and less binding in terms of community ties. Taken as a whole, it is these wood-pasture communities which, when examined today by students of vernacular architecture, have greater numbers of surviving medieval houses.

Medieval Contradictions

We find the open halls of medieval houses, then, not amidst the densely occupied, nucleated villages of midland England, but at the end of crooked lanes, in isolated hamlets, and on the edges and margins of parishes, outside these more heavily and classically feudal areas – on the claylands of Suffolk and Essex, the Weald of Kent and Sussex, and amidst the rolling hills of Devon. Medieval halls were strikingly similar in their layout and visual references, and the social imagination that they materialised was traditional and conservative. However, this traditional and conservative social imagination is contradicted by the location of these newly built, permanent hall houses, and it is also contradicted by the relatively affluent and assertive social position of their owners. Their appearance and layout was an overt expression of feudal values; the very presence of houses of this size and scale, however, pulled at the frayed edges of those values and hinted at underlying tensions. The old system of authority expressed in the dominance of Church and castle was changing and was beginning to accommodate new social elements, elements that would come to be called in succeeding centuries 'the middling sort of people'.

Many open-hall houses were built by prosperous farmers who were much more affluent and of a higher social status than labourers, but who were below, or formed the bottom level of, the ranks of the gentry. Their concentration is often most dense, paradoxically, in regions where there are fewer gentry, as seen, for example, when comparing one parish to another in the Sussex Weald (Chatwin 2003). Many historians would term those dwelling in such houses 'peasants', the term peasant being defined in the anthropological sense that they consumed a large part of the agricultural produce, the crops and livestock, that they produced (for example, Schofield 2003; Thirsk 1957). The contemporary terms used were more likely to be 'yeomen' and 'husbandmen'; though these terms were to subtly change their meaning and become tighter and more schematic in definition, in succeeding centuries.

Peasant farmers could be quite wealthy, just as the 'kulaks' or prosperous farmers in pre-Soviet Russia were (indeed, a generation of Marxist historical scholars drew parallels between prosperous late medieval farmers and this 'bourgeois' class: Hilton 1979). Wealthy and successful peasants, often perceived by their contemporaries as aspiring to gentility, might be referred to as 'franklins', the most famous example of such being Chaucer's Franklin:

'It snewed in his house of mete and drynke . . .
His table dormant in his halle always
Stood ready covered al the longe day'.
(Chaucer, *Canterbury Tales*, Riverside edition, general prologue, lines 345, 353–4)

The open-hall house, therefore, is perhaps surprising in that it appears to be a 'conservative' expression of social values, but it is often the chosen architectural form of a new social class. This conservatism is seen both in the form of the hall, and also in its architectural details. One of the striking things about late medieval houses is how stylistically uniform they are. The styles of timber framing would vary regionally, between cruck- and box-frames and between the different regional styles within these two larger groups. However, in terms of the chronology of details and technique, there was very little change between the 1380s and the 1520s: it is very difficult for the modern scholar to date between later fourteenth century and the earlier sixteenth century on the basis of structural form, style and decoration alone, without tree-ring or documentary dates. In Suffolk, I found that late medieval builders used very similar forms of chamfer-stops, door-heads, joint form, and other architectural details for more than a century. This period of very little change was followed by a period of very swift stylistic change in the mid-sixteenth century, and arguably was preceded by a sharp change from earlier framing styles in the late fourteenth century (Johnson 1993a).

This lack of change has usually been seen as a scholarly 'problem'. Before the advent of tree-ring dating, it was very difficult to date late medieval houses between these dating brackets, particularly if the house was of a simpler form and never had ornate elements such as a crown-post roof. But this lack of change should be telling us something. It is an expression of visual stylistic stability and conservatism.

It was a stylistic conservatism that existed in the face of a crisis of authority that was profound, but also implicit. The Peasants Revolt of 1381, with its famous demand for the abolition of serfdom, was proof that not everyone in medieval England thought about social status and obligation in the same way. But while there were peasant revolts all the way through the fifteenth and early sixteenth centuries, running from small-scale disturbances to much wider revolts on a regional and national scale, these occurred to a specific, prescribed pattern (uprising, march on London, a standard check-list of demands) and did not involve a basic challenge to the existing social order. The great Marxist historian Rodney Hilton noted this lack of ideological challenge (Hilton 1975, 17).

At the same time, there were tensions within households, between master, mistress and the servants who were part of quite modest households. The bargaining position of labourers was strong after the Black Death (Goldberg 2004, 96). For example, Hettinger (1994) has discussed tensions between masters and servants: she concludes that 'our knowledge of what transpired in the [household] is limited to the reports we have of instances when those disputes spilled out into the community and into the courts' (207). My point is that our knowledge is not limited to documents – the form of the hall is a material expression of the tensions that lurked below the surface of the documentary evidence.

At the same time as they were rebuilding houses, using what was perceived as an ancient and customary form, these affluent peasants were also playing an active role in rebuilding churches, placing their mark on what in such a view was the most traditional of institutions. A Marxist would argue that it was these very groups that should have been seeking to throw off feudal shackles, not perpetuating their material expression. The form of both houses and churches, then, used a vocabulary of elements that was part of what was perceived to be an ancient structure of authority, though they were being built by new social groups.

However, many of these households in the later medieval countryside were also drawn from social elements that would very quickly go on to build very different forms of houses in the next two or three generations. In other words, it is these areas that also show the most rapid change in house forms during the sixteenth century. The direct descendants of the builders of these medieval houses, houses that assert certain kinds of social relations most insistently and with such repetition, were the first to abandon them in succeeding decades and centuries. It would be easy – too easy – to conclude that broader patterns of change simply did not happen, and that history has no shape. Rather, I prefer to suggest that these contradictions are telling us something profound about the nature of historical change, and its relationship to the experiences of households.

Nikolaus Pevsner, in his great book *The Englishness of English Art* (1955), approaches this problem from a different perspective. Pevsner discussed the later medieval architectural style of English 'Perpendicular', of which he saw timber-framed buildings to be a part. Pevsner noted the severe, rectilinear style of Perpendicular and its contrast with the flowing, 'flamboyant' late Gothic style of Continental Europe. Being committed to a view of architecture that reflected the zeitgeist or spirit of the age, Pevsner argued that the Perpendicular style was reflecting a particular kind of English middle-class rationality (Games ed. 2002, 207 and 209). Fifty years later, one can say that at best Pevsner's argument was over-simplified, but equally it is still very possible to suspect that Pevsner was on to something, with the severe rectilinear patterns of close studding on East Anglian houses resonating with the rectilinear flushwork, panels and mullions of Perpendicular churches.

Conclusion

Much of the authority of late medieval traditional building came from the way it materialised much wider ideas about social and cultural order. People understood houses, large and small, stone and timber-framed, lordly and peasant, because they shared a common pattern in the organisation of space that in turn referred to a common social and cultural pattern, a late medieval conception of cultural authority centred on the open hall. Their everyday performances – walking to and from the fields, sitting at mealtimes, working in and around the hall – reinforced and affirmed this conception.

The next two chapters will show how this common system and structuring of authority was transformed in the sixteenth and seventeenth centuries. In Chapter 5 I will discuss how traditional buildings abandoned the open hall, and arguably began a long-term shift away from the system of values that went with it. In Chapter 6 I will look at how the strong architectural cross-referencing between houses and households of different social scales was eroded. So the story of the sixteenth and seventeenth centuries is not just about the loss of the open hall and the values that went with it, but also about the creation of a distinctive idea and pattern of regional tradition, set within a matrix of an English nation that was increasingly self-conscious, and about the emergent divide between the cultural domains of the 'polite' and the 'rustic'.

5
Rebuilding and Reformation

The century after 1530 was a time of profound transformation in virtually every sphere of material, social and cultural life in England. Three generations of Englishmen and women saw the world utterly transformed. Changes included the rebuilding of houses, the changing form of those houses, and in particular the loss of the open hall, the 'rise of privacy', and new levels of material comfort in the home, the transformation of the rural economy, the generation of new forms of bureaucratic documents as part of what historians have termed 'state formation', the rise of literacy, religious reformation and its impact on the local community, population rise, encounter and trade with the New World, a new consciousness of community and region, and with it a new consciousness of the English nation.

All these, and many other, changes are sometimes grouped under the term 'the rise of capitalism' or 'the origins of the modern world'. A very small scene, then, has a very wide context, and a single book cannot hope to trace all the connections between these different processes, each one of which has generated a vast specialist literature. However, in this chapter and the rest of this book I shall trace a few of them, with the aim of showing how the changes seen in the building of, and dwelling in, ordinary houses engage with a few of these wider processes.

In the rest of this chapter, I shall first describe some of the changes which took place in the building of ordinary houses during the sixteenth and early seventeenth centuries. I will then look at the factors listed above, and suggest that far from being random or contingent, they were all closely related one to another.

The 'Great Rebuilding'

Many thousands of ordinary houses in the countryside were newly built or rebuilt in the later sixteenth and earlier seventeenth centuries. The great landscape and economic historian W.G. Hoskins, writing in the 1950s, was the first to suggest that this period was particularly active in terms of change in vernacular architecture. Hoskins characterised the period 1560–1640 as that of the 'rebuilding of rural England' (Hoskins 1953). He suggested that three major changes could be seen through this period: the building of new houses, the conversion and improvement of existing houses, and new furnishings and levels of material comfort within the house.

Hoskins' idea has proved extraordinarily influential: it is routinely cited by historians (for example, in the title of Margaret Spufford's book, *The Great Reclothing of Rural England*, 1984). Nevertheless, fifty years on, it is in need of substantial revision. In particular, it is no longer believed that the processes of rebuilding and improvement of houses were concentrated into a mere eighty years. The previous chapter has already implied one revision to Hoskins' thesis: in many parts of the country, large numbers of substantial houses were built in the two centuries before 1560. Hoskins himself made this point on a visit to a medieval cruck-built house being surveyed by David Hinton in the 1960s, in a conversation subsequently recollected by Hinton (Figure 4.3, see p. 75; Hinton 1967 and personal communication). It should be noted, however, that the majority of these open-hall houses were almost all rebuilt in the sense of being converted and 'improved', with the insertion of chimney-stack and ceiling in the hall before 1640, a process that I will explore below.

It is also true that the process of rebuilding went on for centuries after 1640. Robert Machin showed how Hoskins' idea of a 'Great Rebuilding' needed to be pushed later, as well as earlier. He compiled the evidence for dated houses across the whole of England into a single graph, which showed a steady rate of rebuilding through the sixteenth and seventeenth centuries. Indeed, Machin's figures suggested a peak of dated houses in the later seventeenth century rather than earlier, though this peak may reflect the growing fashion for date-stones, rather than the rate of rebuilding as a whole. Machin himself rightly argued that we should talk of a much longer-term process than a specific rebuilding (1977a).

Rebuilding in the later sixteenth and earlier seventeenth centuries was also geographically restricted: not all areas of the country saw dramatic improvement in houses in this period. Hoskins himself excluded the areas of England to the north of Yorkshire and Lancashire from his thesis. Other writers, for example, Eric Mercer, have implied that rebuilding was a steady process that unfolded at different rates from north to south of the British Isles as a whole, with the 'black houses' of the Hebrides off the north-west coast of Scotland being the last surviving remnants of a form of living that the 'Great Rebuilding' replaced some centuries earlier in the southern areas of the British Isles (Mercer 1975, 8).

It is, however, the case that the century after 1530 is the period when we first see large numbers of vernacular houses across much of midland England. Before this date, as we saw in the last chapter, large numbers of surviving vernacular houses can be found in perhaps less than half of all English counties. Many more counties, however, have large numbers of houses surviving from the period between 1530 and 1640. It has been suggested that Hoskins' conclusion of a general rebuilding sprang from a narrow 'corridor' across the country – what he saw out of the window from the train journey he made every week, from his place of work in Leicester to his home in Devon. It cut through a swathe of the English countryside that included the east Midlands, the Cotswolds, and areas of the West Country, and it therefore included a concentration of communities and regions where great numbers of late sixteenth- and early seventeenth-century houses can be found.

It is certainly true that many of the regions where we find such large numbers of medieval houses have relatively fewer houses from the later sixteenth and seventeenth centuries. Much of Suffolk and Essex, for example, have large numbers of open-hall houses and also large numbers of houses with ceilings and chimney-stacks built before the end of the sixteenth century. Thereafter, we see in these wood-pasture regions of East Anglia at best continuity and at worst a slow decline in the overall number of surviving houses that were built and rebuilt at this time.

One explanation for this regional shift in the pattern of building is economic. After the middle of the sixteenth century, the woollen cloth industry went into crisis. While some areas responded with the development of the 'New Draperies', much of southern East Anglia never completely recovered. It is worth observing, following Chris Currie's insights discussed in Chapter 2 (Currie 1988), that this subsequent decline was as responsible for the survival of these houses as the former prosperity – that is, houses in 'high Suffolk' and Essex survived not just because they were well built in a period of economic prosperity, but because the subsequent long centuries of relative continuity meant that there was little incentive to rebuild. Conversely, the presence of a growing textile industry in the Lancashire Pennines contributed indirectly to the building of substantial stone-built yeoman houses in the sixteenth century (Pearson 1985, 146).

The pattern of evidence on the ground, then, is much more complex than the idea of a single eighty-year-long rebuilding might imply. What is striking about Hoskins' idea of a rebuilding of rural England is what a compelling and influential story it has been, and how many archaeologists and historians still refer to it and have extended the idea to other contexts such as towns and to material culture as a whole, for example, clothing (Spufford 1984). It suggests that while we query the dates, the idea of a rebuilding refers to a deeper underlying pattern of thought; it captures some key insights about the period. The underlying truth may be that the period of the later sixteenth and early seventeenth centuries was a crucial moment of transformation, not just in patterns of vernacular houses, but in English landscape and architecture as a whole, as Maurice Howard has argued (2007); and beyond that, that this was a moment of social and cultural, as well as architectural, transformation.

In the rest of this chapter, I will look at the evidence for the rebuilding of rural houses in the mid-sixteenth to early seventeenth centuries. I will then turn to the economic, social and cultural context in which that rebuilding should be understood.

The Closure of the Open Hall

The last chapter looked at the cultural authority of the open hall, and the way the house was a material expression of the grid of rights and responsibilities that made up the household. However, by the first decades of the seventeenth century, the open hall had all but disappeared at vernacular levels. New houses were built with a ceiling throughout, while older open-hall houses, virtually without exception, had ceilings inserted into them. Both new builds and conversions had a brick or stone chimney-stack to replace the open hearth or timber firehood.

This change unfolded over the period from around 1500 to the early seventeenth century, according to the different evidence provided by documentary sources, tree-ring dates, and stylistic and archaeological dating. Mercer notes that 'in 1500 at Cranbrook in Kent a builder was contracting to erect a house which was to be wholly lofted over and to have a chimney with two fires in it' (Mercer 1975, 28). Even a decade or two earlier than 1500, some houses in the small provincial town of New Buckenham in Norfolk were being built with ceilings and chimneys (Longcroft 2005); the same is probably true of the Suffolk cloth-producing town of Lavenham. A building contract for a house in the nearby town of Bury St Edmunds hints at a possible conversion of this kind, while a second specifies a new, fully ceiled house; both are as early as the 1460s (Dymond 1998, 274 and 277). This also seems to be true of Hampshire, where chimney-stacks are found in the halls of both gentlemen and yeomen leasing manor or priory farms, for example, a stack dated to 1505 at the Court House, Overton, or Great Funtley Farm, Titchfield (Roberts 2003, 61).

Most medieval houses were converted, with the addition of ceiling and chimney-stack, a little later than this. The majority of conversions are dated to the decades after 1540, according to both documentary and archaeological evidence. The yeoman Robert Furse took the rare step of recording in his Household Book the changes he made to his Devonshire house: between 1572 and 1593, he records that he constructed a new porch and entry, inserted a ceiling into the hall, and glazed the windows (Hoskins 1955, 46). Eric Mercer lists a 1571 conversion at Hookswood Manor, Charlwood, in Surrey, and a 1581 replacement of the hall by a two-storey block at Trout's Farm, Ockley, also in Surrey (Mercer 1975, 5). In Kent, conversions might be as late as the early seventeenth century (Pearson 1994, 115). Just across the border into Wales, many Monmouthshire houses seem to have fully ceiled halls from the mid-sixteenth century onwards (Fox and Raglan 1951–4, 98). In western Suffolk, I found houses of the new form from 1500 onwards, with no new open halls built after this date (Johnson 1993a, 87). Finally, every house recorded in Yetminster from 1568 onwards had a fully ceiled hall (Machin 1978, 12). The presence or absence of chimney-stacks in houses, and windows to upper storeys indicating the presence of ceilings, can often be seen on early maps. Two maps of the manor of Ingatestone in Essex, one in 1556 and one in 1601, provide revealing information in this respect. In 1556, of fifteen single-storeyed houses depicted, nine houses had been rebuilt or modified to a fully two-storeyed form. Two generations later, by 1601, most of these houses had brick chimneys (Ryan 2000, 18). A late example may well be the closure of the open hall as part of a wholesale renovation and rebuilding in stone of a house at Walderton, west Sussex, probably some time after the death of its owner in 1634 (Tankard and Harris 2008, 11).

In some cases, the conversion of the open hall was not a single action but a piecemeal, step-by-step process. In some late medieval houses, particularly in urban contexts, 'smoke bays' had been constructed. A smoke bay was a single, often narrow, bay of the hall that was open to the roof. The open hearth was placed under the smoke bay, and the smoke drifting upwards often left traces in the form of blackening on a distinctively narrow area of the roof. Thus, the hall could be given a ceiling across half or more of its area. Smoke bays were either constructed as part of the first phase of a building or they were inserted into earlier open halls, and smoke bays were often replaced as quickly as a generation later by brick chimney-stacks (Figure 5.1). Because the brick stack was placed in the position of the smoke bay, it destroyed much of the evidence for the former arrangement in the process, so it is probable that many more of these features existed in the past than is sometimes suspected. In Sussex, for example, a number of houses were converted in two phases. First a chimney and ceiling were inserted, and then a generation or so later replaced

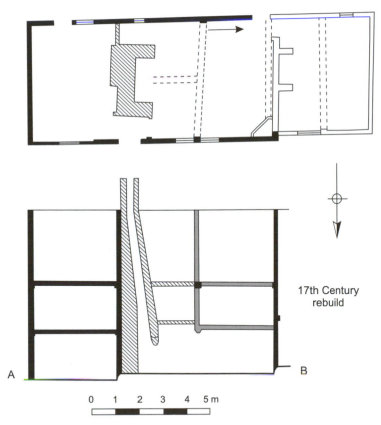

Figure 5.1 Tudor Cottage, Brent Eleigh, Suffolk: far from being a 'Tudor cottage', this is in its origins a late medieval open-hall house. The plan above, and section through the building below, indicates the late medieval house in black. It has a smoke-bay inserted into the open hall indicated in solid grey, and subsequently a ceiling and timber chimney-stack inserted into the smoke-bay. This was then replaced by a brick chimney-stack, though part of the frame of the timber stack remains.

with a larger brick chimney-stack with fireplaces and flues serving both the ground floor and upper floor rooms (Martin 2000). There are probably many more houses across the country that followed this step-by-step pattern in their development, but the later insertion of the brick stack has completely erased or concealed all traces of these earlier developments.

In other contexts, timber and wattle smoke bays or firehoods were constructed over the open hearth, which was placed at one end of the hall, with the firehood built against the partition wall. This is the original form of a group of houses found in the southern Pennines and thought to date from the earlier sixteenth century. The open halls of these Pennine houses are aisled in form. Subsequently, the timber framing of these Pennine aisled halls was usually given an outer skin of stone. This had the consequence of concealing their older origins from the outside world. Again, these Pennine houses seem to be found in areas where wealth from the cloth industry was concentrated (Giles 1992).

A large number of sixteenth-century houses, then, had chimney stacks constructed of timber with wattle-and-daub infill rather than brick stacks. Occasionally, structural evidence of a timber stack remains in the form of mortices or other fragments, though to my knowledge none survive in functioning condition except those recreated at open-air museums (a complete example survives at Dormer Cottage, Petham, Kent: Barnwell and Adams 1994, 134). In many cases, they must have been replaced quite quickly in view of the fire risk, though such risk was lessened by the plastering-over of the timbers. Although such evidence is now rare, timber stacks were common practice in the first generation of houses built by English settlers in Virginia and New England. This practice suggests that knowledge of, and familiarity with, their construction was common among the English at least in the first half of the seventeenth century, when these areas were settled (Cummings 1979). Smoke bays and firehoods have also been found in the context of kitchens, sometimes against the gable wall, as at Mannings, Stocklinch, Somerset (Penoyre 2005, 76), or at the rear of a service wing, as at Layers Breck, Rougham, Suffolk (Johnson 1993a, 46).

The most common replacement for the medieval open hall, however, involved the insertion of a brick chimney-stack into the building, and a ceiling into the old hall. This could be done in a variety of ways, depending on the location of the chimney-stack. The stack could be placed in line with the upper/lower axis of the hall, or, in other words, along the front or back wall. This pattern is common in areas of Devon and Cornwall (Figure 5.2) though it is also found elsewhere, particularly in larger houses (Pearson 1994, 108).

However, a more common method was to place the stack at right-angles to the orientation of the house, within the hall, so that the fireplace threw its heat on to either the upper or lower end of the old hall. This solution meant that much of the heat was retained within the building rather than being lost through the externally placed back wall of the stack. Contemporary advice on gardening specifically advised the planting of certain plants against this back wall to take advantage of

Figure 5.2 Elley, Colebrook, Devon: a cob-walled farmhouse of later medieval origins. The lateral chimney-stack, with bread-oven on its right, has been added. (Photo author's own).

this heat. However, where the house was timber-framed, placing the stack axially rather than against the side wall also meant that the new stack had to be carefully constructed so as to fit through and around the older frame. Stacks of this kind could be inserted into the old cross-passage, or into the old space between the opposed doors. Alternatively, they could be inserted into the upper bay of the hall, or even occasionally into the chamber beyond. At ground floor level, they could house a single fireplace serving the hall, or two fireplaces placed 'back-to-back', the second fireplace serving either the kitchen or the chamber at the upper end of the house (Figure 5.3). In some cases, the house was 'reversed', with the chamber/parlour end becoming the service end, and vice versa, which, as David and Barbara Martin have shown, was a common pattern in Sussex (Martin 2000).

Open-hall houses that have been converted in this way are often very difficult to detect from the outside. The arrangement of visible doors and windows is identical to that of a post-1550 house. It is often the case that external observation suggests that a house dates to the sixteenth or seventeenth century; it is only when one enters the hall and detects signs of an inserted ceiling that there is any clue that the building has been converted and is actually a century or two older. As noted in the previous chapter, the most revealing sign is a roof space caked with soot.

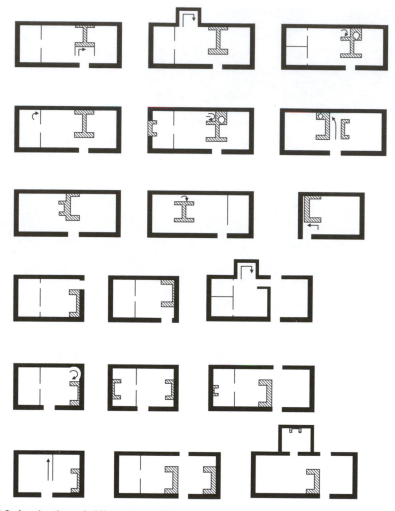

Figure 5.3 A selection of different possible post-medieval plan forms. These forms could be produced either by 'new build', or by insertion of chimney-stack and ceiling into an open-hall house, often with similar end results. The different plan forms illustrated have different and complex regional distributions, though it is important to stress that exceptions can always be found. (Based on Brunskill, R.W., *Illustrated Handbook of Vernacular Architecture* (Faber & Faber, 2000, pp. 107–9).)

An important but neglected aspect of this conversion is the impact it must have made on working patterns in the landscape. My research in western Suffolk showed very striking similarities in the methods, structural techniques and decorative details used in converting the open hall from house to house. In other words, conversion was carried out either by teams or by individual builders quite quickly in some areas, with one house following suit very rapidly after its neighbour (Johnson 1993a, 87–8).

New Houses

It is often difficult to tell the difference between a converted medieval house and a newly built house, and for good reason. The range of forms of newly built houses closely matched the different solutions to conversion of older ones adopted by vernacular builders. In other words, the form of a house in c.1600 might have been arrived at through a conversion, or through a completely new build: the final form in terms of the pattern and arrangement of space, and of the use of rooms, was in many cases practically identical.

By the middle of the seventeenth century, a traveller in England would have seen a series of different types of houses, with different forms of houses concentrated in different regions of the country according to a clear pattern. However, before the mid-seventeenth century, earlier generations of houses were much more diverse in many areas, as a variety of arrangements and solutions were adopted to the arrangement of space after the end of the open hall.

Some of these houses bear intriguing signs of this often very rapid change. In the first generation of houses that had ceilings throughout, from c.1500 onwards, there are a series of houses where analysis of the timber frame suggests that the carpenter and the builder of the chimney did not collaborate, and/or that the wishes of the client were not fully understood or carried out by the builder. In many of these very early examples, there often seems to be confusion between builder and client about what the final form of the house should look like. This confusion can be traced by close observation and analysis of the timber frame of the building. Adam Longcroft found many houses of this type in the small Norfolk town of New Buckenham (Longcroft 2005), and Edward Roberts (2003, 155) has found examples in Hampshire, for example, 73–7 Winchester Street, Overton, where 'the decision to insert a floor necessitated a special trimmer to support the floor joists around a large window that had been intended for an open hall'. A house I surveyed in Glemsford in Suffolk, dating from around 1500, appeared to be a fully ceiled three-bay, two-cell house, into which the stack had apparently been inserted on the evidence of the Roman numerals and form of the hall ceiling; the carpenter apparently framed and numbered the hall to have a ceiling, and then 'cut back' the ceiling to receive the stack (Johnson 1993a, 82–3). Jenkyns Farmhouse in neighbouring Essex, a fully ceiled house of three bays, was framed-up in such a way as to suggest to Cecil Hewitt that 'the builder, the customer, or both, had no fixed ideas about the ultimate form the house should possess' (Hewitt 1973, 64); this may well be another example of a client specifying a house of the new form, but the carpenter framing-up the building in the old manner. It is probable that both are examples of houses specified by the customer to be fully ceiled with stacks, but prefabricated in the old manner by the carpenter, who modified his ideas on site.

In a sense, one of the things the introduction of new forms and elements to house plans in the sixteenth century did was to disrupt the mental template of the builder. As we have seen, medieval houses were built to a relatively narrow range of forms, which were generated by a simple and tight competence. In other words, medieval builders had a strong sense of what the building should look like and the way to produce that form and appearance, very often down to the last detail of door and window positioning and the form of the joints and other structural details. The strength of this tradition was such that builders deviated little from accepted models. This competence was disrupted in the sixteenth century, for reasons I will explore later in this chapter. Disruption of the craft tradition left builders with a much greater freedom of choice between different models, and a greater ability to innovate. It is a testament to the creativity and originality of the traditional builder that this opportunity was taken up vigorously in many areas. By the early seventeenth century, in many regions of England, a simple and tight competence could once again be found, reflected in a particular range of house forms.

Whatever the final form or solution arrived at, the layout and appearance of the house were changed quite drastically. Most obviously, the insertion of a ceiling into the hall meant that circulation within the house at the level of the upper floors was now possible; in other words, one had the possibility of arranging doorways to allow passage from upper to lower ends of the house at first-floor levels without impediment. Inventory evidence suggests that sixteenth- and early seventeenth-century houses still used the ground floor for sleeping, and indeed for most household activities, and the upper floor largely for storage. It is also the case that many of these 'transitional' houses maintained the old pattern of separate access to first-floor rooms at upper and lower ends, as David Martin found in a study of sixteenth-century houses in eastern Sussex (2003). However, over the decades and centuries that followed, this ground-floor pattern of living began to gradually unwind and unravel as succeeding generations dwelt in the house differently.

The more immediately dramatic change in terms of layout depended on the changed location of the front door to the house, and the choice of site for the staircase to the first floor (Figure 5.3, see p. 94). In some converted houses, the pair of opposed doors or the screens-passage was retained, but in others it was lost. The front door often now gave on to the side of the chimney stack. A visitor might enter and instead of turning to be faced with the sight of the hall, would face a blank brick wall with doors to either side, or possibly a staircase. One door would give access to the hall, the other to either the service/kitchen end or the parlour. So the old hall, then, lost its old role as the central point in the circulation pattern of the house. These arrangements would vary according to the placing of the doors and the size of the entrance lobby; with some smaller lobbies, such as those in north Suffolk described by John Walker (2003), the front door is often positioned in such a way as to block the parlour entrance when it opens, forcing the visitor to step aside into the hall before closing the front door and gaining access to the parlour. At a particularly early example of a three-cell lobby entry, the brick-built Old Hall Farm at Kneesall in Nottinghamshire, built as a hunting-lodge for Sir John Hussey in about 1536, the stair is placed to the rear of the stack (Reed 1986, Plate 20).

But perhaps as important as the change in the pattern of circulation around the house, the old hall lost much of its former appearance. Where the chimney had been inserted into the hall, the ground surface of the hall was much smaller. Instead of a central hearth dominating the room and reducing visibility from one side to another, the fire was now off to one side, contained by the fireplace of the chimney-stack. And instead of the eye being drawn upwards to the mystery of the smoke dispersing in the rafters, a functional (though often ornate) ceiling of closely set joists now blocked off that view.

At the same time, the organisation of the hall was disrupted and the texture of the room transformed. The fixed bench at the upper end of the hall was no longer there in many houses where the chimney-stack now occupied this position. (In other cases, however, it was retained: mortises for a fixed bench can be observed in Ashley Cottage, Ashley in Hampshire, tree-ring dated to 1567/8.) The window at its upper end was no longer of the same size and scale; the quality of lighting was different, the room less dim, less smoke-filled and mysterious. Objects kept in the hall could be kept cleaner; they were no longer covered with a layer of sooty grime. Where houses were less than two full storeys high, the new pattern of circulation at upper floor level could be impeded by the presence of tie-beams running across the building. A series of solutions could be adopted to solve this problem, including the use of 'anchor-beams' to provide structural support at the level of the ground floor ceiling, or an interruption to the tie-beam in the attic space, for example, in Hampshire, where in one case an old pair of crucks was also used to fulfil this function (Roberts 2003, 33).

One reason that has sometimes been cited for the closure of the open hall was the onset of cold weather. England in 1600 was a cooler place than it had been in 1300. Climatic historians have interpreted this period as that of the Little Ice Age, in which the climate was much colder and wetter than that of the twelfth and thirteenth centuries (Fagan 2000; Lamb 1982). From the fourteenth century onwards, this colder and wetter weather had a profound effect on the countryside. Many of the later medieval changes, such as the shift from arable to pastoral agriculture on the claylands, were directly or indirectly related to this shift; as the weather declined, it became more difficult to plough the intractable clay, and more tempting to turn the area over to the pasture of sheep and cows. Houses that were more snug and warm may have been another indirect response to these changes. However, it is difficult for climatic theorists to explain how and why the majority of households persisted with open halls for a century-and-a-half after the onset of cold weather before making the change. The climatic theory would also suggest that open halls would be abandoned first in the colder and wetter north and west of the country; in fact the reverse is the case.

It is easy to over-draw the distinction between open-hall houses and their successors. In many areas of England, particularly in the north and west, cross-passages of different kinds were kept (Plate 11). This meant that the old medieval arrangement, with a screens passage having external doors front and back, and giving access to service end and to hall, was retained as a cross-passage; in longhouses, this separated the 'house-part' from the byre or cattle end of the house. At the same time, many early examples of halls with chimney-stacks and ceilings, particularly at upper social levels, still retain much of the grandeur and centrality of their medieval counterparts. In particular, the ceiling in such structures is often particularly ornate, with the principal and common joists being elaborately chamfered or carved. The fireplaces in sixteenth-century houses are often large and important visually, with a great wooden lintel and often space within the stack for an inglenook where one or two people could sit in a cosy and confined space, adjacent to the warmth of the fire (Figure 5.4). In areas of the north, this inglenook could even have an external window. The later sixteenth- and seventeenth-century hall, then, remained an important space, retaining many of the meanings and much of the importance of the earlier open hall. The central chimney-stack also meant in some instances that an outside kitchen was not needed, though in many cases external kitchens may have been retained. In some houses, it was not so much that the hall was less

Figure 5.4 Spout House, Bilsdale, North Yorkshire: a traditional arrangement common in the north, with flagged floor, heck-post, and seating around a fireplace and oven. (English Heritage Photo Library. © Crown Copyright NMR).

important, as that the adjoining parlour became less subordinate to it and more a focus of household activity in its own right. More parlours were heated, either with their own chimney-stack, or with a fireplace on the other side of the hall stack. Larger houses often had two or more parlours (Barley 1961, 51).

New houses from this period were often built of stone, particularly in the villages that lie on or close to the Jurassic Limestone belt stretching from Dorset through the Cotswolds up into Northamptonshire and Lincolnshire (Plate 6). At the excavated village of West Whelpington, houses were built of stone walls by the end of the sixteenth century, where they had previously been timber-framed (Evans and Jarrett 1987). If the late medieval preference was for timber-framed building over stone, after c.1540 this preference began to be reversed, with long-term implications for the appearance and texture of buildings. In north Yorkshire, this change happened quite suddenly in the mid-seventeenth century (Harrison and Hutton 1984). According to Machin (1977b), early sixteenth-century stone houses cost three times as much as timber-framed houses; by the later seventeenth century, they cost only one-and-a-half times as much, and only half as much by the middle of the eighteenth century.

Techniques of timber-framing also saw changes: 'whereas in the early years of the sixteenth century in East Anglia a house was being built with a large number of woodland oaks by a carpenter who still maintained the medieval conventions of his craft, in the Weald of Sussex, possibly only half a century later, timber from hedgerow trees was used to construct a frame in a manner which combined essentials from both medieval and early-modern practices . . . it is evident that by the late sixteenth century the quality of both saws and sawing was improving rapidly' (Kirk 2003, 19).

If there was tremendous variation in the plans and layout of houses of this period, the same was also true of structural forms and decorative details. Later medieval houses changed very slowly in these respects, and later, in the seventeenth century, structural and decorative change was again slow in many regions. However, in this intervening period, after the break-up of a spatial and technical competence framed around the open hall, things moved fast. In Suffolk, Robert Reyce commented in 1618 that 'the careless wast of this age of our wonted plenty of timber, and other building stuffe, hath enforced the witt of this latter age to devise a new kind of compacting, uniting, coupling, framing, and building, with almost half the timber that was wont to be used, and far stronger as the workmen stick nott to affirme, butt the truth thereof is nott yet found out soe' (Hervey ed. 1902, 51).

New Goods

The rebuilding of houses was just one part of a much wider change affecting people's domestic lives. Houses were not just being built in new ways and to new forms; the things that people kept and used within those houses were also changing. Specifically, there was an increase in the number and quality of movable goods to be found within the house. The relatively bare interiors of the late medieval houses became rare. Material things, ranging from functional implements to utensils for food preparation to objects that were cherished and became heirlooms to pieces of furniture – there were more of all of these, and sixteenth- and seventeenth-century households spent more money on acquiring and maintaining them.

Evidence for a rise in the level of material culture in the home comes from a variety of sources. First, there are commentaries and other written accounts. The contemporary observer William Harrison, for example, has frequently been quoted by historians in his testimony on the recollections of the old people of his Essex parish. Harrison wrote that the 'old men yet dwelling in the village where I remain' cite 'three things to be marvellously altered in England within their sound remembrance': the replacement of the open hearth with fireplaces and chimney-stacks, the 'great amendment of lodging' including the replacement of straw mattresses with featherbeds, the use of a bolster or pillow instead of a 'good round log', and changes in furniture. Harrison's elderly informants also cited a general rise in the number and standards of movable goods, for example, the exchange of wooden tableware for that of metal – 'for so common were all sorts of treen [wooden] stuff in old time, that a man should hardly find four pieces of pewter . . . in a good farmer's house' (Edelen ed. 1968, 200–1).

Many of Harrison's comments are echoed in the descriptions of household goods contained in probate inventories. As inventories are rare before c.1550, it is difficult to compare houses before and after this date. His words are, however, also confirmed by the millions of fragments of pottery and other artefacts that have been excavated by archaeologists. Excavation of archaeological sites from this period has taken place disproportionately on urban sites rather than rural dwellings, but it is clear that many of these goods were also finding their way into rural contexts. Archaeological excavation of sixteenth- and seventeenth-century dwellings has produced a range and variety of goods, including brightly coloured slipwares, stoneware mugs for drinking beer (the addition of hops to ale to produce beer was a fifteenth-century innovation), and a variety of glazed red earthenwares, including chamber-pots.

Glazed windows replaced wooden shutters; in 1577 Harrison commented that window glass 'had become so plentiful and within a very little good so cheap'. Even so, before 1600, window glass was classed as a movable good and therefore listed in inventories; after this date, glass was more plentiful and windows were classed as fixed. Window glass was often specifically bequeathed in wills before 1600 (Campbell 1942, 232). For example, in the 1590s Thomas Sturgeon's will specified that 'all the glass windows were to remayne in my house' in Ingatestone in Essex (cited in Ryan 2000, 18); in 1590 Robert Birks of Doncaster bequeathed 'all doors, glass windows etc. of his house' to his son but leaving the house itself to his wife (Innocent 1916, 258). The first mention of glass at Yetminster in Somerset comes from 1624; in this year George Payne was fined for removing the glass from the parlour of an empty house belonging to Henry Oldis (Machin 1977a, 2).

Population and Privacy

Why, then, were these changes taking place? Rebuilding of houses was, I suggest, one small part of the rebuilding and reformation of the social lives of households. Changes in houses materialise changes in patterns and ways of life as a whole; when people rebuilt their houses, they also rebuilt their lives.

There were more people around, and they were living longer. The population of England started to rise again in the sixteenth century, after the dramatic fall in the fourteenth century and stagnation of the fifteenth. In itself, a population rise had clear implications for houses: there had to be more of them, and more provision within existing houses for larger families. The mortality rates of children, always perilously high in pre-industrial societies, may well have been lessened by the smaller and snugger rooms of the new houses.

Population rise was also as much about people living longer as it was about more children being born and surviving. Heads of household, on average, had more years in which to accumulate savings to the point where they could afford to pay for a new house. Elderly widows often required part of a house for their own; seventeenth-century wills are full of careful specifications for dividing existing houses between space for the widow and space for the succeeding son and his family.

There may also have been a more subtle mental shift arising from the expectation of living longer. In the medieval world where life was uncertain and death might lurk around every corner, the incentive to invest money in long-term projects such as the building and rebuilding of houses rather than in immediate consumption was very limited. The longer one's life expectancy, and the more secure and less risky one's future was in material terms, the more incentive there was to accumulate savings and put them into long-term projects such as rebuilding.

The population rise also meant that the English nation had more mouths to feed, and this meant bigger profits for farmers. The laws of supply and demand meant that the price of bread rose in the later sixteenth century, and with it the price of wheat, barley and oats. In many areas, then, tenant farmers benefited disproportionately from this change. Depending on the particular conditions and security of tenure in their community, they paid rents to their landlords that were fixed, but the price of their agricultural produce was rising. At the same time, the growing population meant a ready supply of labour: as a result, the wages they paid to day-labourers and servants in husbandry remained relatively low. Hoskins wrote: 'The sequence in England seems to be: Savings – rebuilding and enlargement – decreased mortality and perhaps higher fertility – rise of population – new building and development of congestion – rise in mortality rates' (Hoskins 1953, 57). In Lincolnshire, for example, yeoman households could afford double the value of household goods in 1600 that they could in 1530 (Thirsk 1957, 54–7). In other places, such as Stoneleigh in Warwickshire, there may have been no objective rise in wealth, but rather a perception of prosperity among the middling sort nevertheless (Alcock

1993, 54). As Hoskins himself pointed out, however, the motives for rebuilding ran deeper than this. Rising levels of wealth and the increase in population identified some of the reasons why people could afford new houses, but they do not explain why people wished to live in different manners and styles from those of previous generations. A house like Bayleaf could equally well have accommodated a large later sixteenth-century family and household – provided that such a family and household would have been prepared to live in the old medieval manner.

One of the reasons which has been offered for the changes seen in houses has been an increase in the desire for privacy and for material comfort. However, the 'rise of privacy' needs explaining. Why did people want to be more 'private'? What does the word 'private' mean, anyway? Why were the older patterns of living, deemed appropriate for centuries, now actively rejected?

Privacy is a social idea, and, as such, ideas of privacy are variable, rather than a 'desire for privacy' being a constant, normal or natural attribute of human life. People want to be private from other people, in some social contexts rather than others. It is an idea that varies between the worlds of women and the worlds of men, as feminists Shirley Ardener and Lidia Sciama have pointed out (Ardener 1993; Sciama 1993). The desire for privacy was also tied up with a growing preference for living inside, rather than participating in popular cultural traditions focused on outdoor activities. It can be argued that 'privacy' is a distinctively middle-class idea, and that the rise of a cultural preference for privacy is closely linked to the rise in the culture and self-confidence of the middling sort of people. The great historian Christopher Hill wrote of the early seventeenth century in terms which stressed indoor activities that were nevertheless group rather than solitary activities: 'middle-class talent and industry were creating houses of unprecedented comfort and privacy, thanks to glass windows, coal fires, upstairs bedrooms, chairs replacing benches. Middle-class houses became places to which friends could be invited, to sing, to play, to discuss' (Hill 1966, 488).

To understand why these changes were happening we need to look beyond the building of the houses, the raw statistics of population, and conditions of tenure, to wider changes in the material and cultural landscape – in the fields surrounding the house, and in the church along the road.

Enclosure and Reformation

The rural landscape in which the house was set was also being transformed. In the previous chapter, I looked at the beginnings of a process of enclosure across the landscape as a whole. Enclosure changed its nature during this period, and the way it was perceived by contemporaries also changed. Piecemeal enclosure involving the engrossing of strips and the building-up of farms and estates unfolded in many wood-pasture areas in the aftermath of the Black Death, for example, with the 'barton' farms of Devon (Turner 2007). Up until about 1550, much larger-scale

Figure 5.5 Brassington, Derbyshire: traces of the medieval patterns of furlongs are picked out in this aerial photograph by light snow. The enclosure 'by agreement' suggested by the piecemeal amalgamation of strips into hedged fields probably happened early, in the sixteenth and seventeenth centuries. (Copyright reserved Cambridge University Collection of Air Photographs, Unit for Landscape Modelling).

enclosure of the sort more characteristically found in the Midlands was held to be related to the forced depopulation of villages by contemporary commentators, and to the turning over of what had been arable land to pasturing cattle and particularly sheep – from 'corn' to 'horn'. As such, enclosure was perceived ideologically by Tudor administrators and moralists as threatening to the commonwealth. From the later sixteenth century onwards, the economic motives and rationale for enclosure was often rather different. Common fields could be 'engrossed' and enclosed, and strip fields merged by agreement between individual farmers, in a variety of ways. These forms of enclosure was held by many to be beneficial to the commonwealth, as they were believed to promote more efficient farming and, it was believed, higher productivity (Johnson 1996, 56–8; Figure 5.5).

Enclosure of the landscape, like the closure of the house, was one area where different ideas about how people should live were being performed. Individuals, families and communities were engaging in debate over these ideas, not simply through texts and tracts but through practical, everyday action. Where traditional and Puritan moralists agonised over profit and usury, and lawyers argued over the niceties of property law, some ordinary folk got out their spades and shovels, came together in angry groups and proceeded to level newly-erected hedges and ditches.

Houses in the English countryside were, in the main, working farms. Their builders and owners might sometimes have other professions such as carpenter or clothier listed in their wills and inventories, but a farm was generally maintained as part of household activity. The link between changes in the spheres of the domestic and of the agrarian, then, was part of the everyday, practical experience of ordinary people in the countryside; just as the house was becoming more segregated and privatised, so it was with the agrarian landscape as a whole.

The second transformation of the landscape was that of the Church. We have already seen that the parish church stood, as in most cases it continues to stand, at the physical and social heart of virtually every local community in the English countryside. The physical fabric of the church, as the observer sees it today, is not simply a record of changing religious belief: its form structured the lives of ordinary people, and it, in turn, was structured by their decisions. It is also, like the landscape, a complex record, a palimpsest of traces of succeeding generations of the changing social and cultural composition of the local community.

Towards the end of the Middle Ages, as with vernacular houses, many parish churches were extensively or completely rebuilt. The financing of such rebuilding did not exactly reflect the overall wealth of the community. Many of the famous 'wool churches' of East Anglia and the West Country, for example, were built from the profits from the wool and cloth trade of the landlords and wealthier peasants, and were far larger and grander than the local community really needed.

The internal fabric and texture of the church materialised the values of the community. Just as in the open fields, the space mapped out in churches represented a complex structuring of rights and responsibilities, with the chancel being the responsibility of the priest and the nave that of the parish, respectively. The walls of the church were covered with pictures. These were of Biblical scenes, and/or had moral and allegorical content that attempted to give guidance to people's everyday lives that reflected the construction of power in the medieval village – scenes of women 'gossips', portrayals of saints, a plough to be blessed at ploughing time, and so on. Frequently there would be graphic depictions of Purgatory and Hell, depicting precisely what fate awaited the sinful, an age before the concept of photographic reality. Such images were repeated in the stained glass in the windows, filling the church with coloured light (Duffy 1992; Marks 2004). Persons of prominence in the community were buried within the church, often with brightly coloured effigies; those of great means and status were especially marked out by their endowment and provision of chantry chapels. Beyond the walls of the church, the graveyard was segregated between north and south sides, and beyond that, the landscape was dotted with shrines, holy wells and other expressions of everyday religious faith.

In the sixteenth century, the majority of those dwelling in houses and going to church on Sundays were illiterate. Most labourers could not read or write, and neither could a large number of yeomen (Cressy 1980). More men than women could read and write. Consequently, the visual imagery of the church, and the performance of liturgy, played a pivotal role in giving meaning to people's lives, particularly for ordinary folk and for the women who managed the household. The performance of the Mass by the priest was only seen indistinctly by the congregation through the openings in the rood screen dividing nave and chancel; the words, spoken in Latin rather than the vernacular, added to this mysterious quality. Pam Graves has emphasised the power of this architecture and performance, and the richness of meaning it held for both priest and congregation; but she has also stressed how ordinary people had their own understanding of what was going on around them in church (Graves 2000 and Graves 2008). It was this immensely powerful configuration of religious and social authority and power that resonated so strongly with the configuration of the house and household.

It was this configuration that the English Reformation deconstructed and sought to reassemble. The immediate context of the reformation was a top-down process, driven by the character of the king, and later by the religious convictions of the wealthy and powerful, and enforced by the growing bureaucratic power and authority of the sixteenth-century state (Bernard 2006). Its impetus was the personality and dynastic ambitions of the monarch Henry VIII. However, once started, the power and impetus of reformation in many of its doctrinal aspects was gained from preceding and parallel developments in continental Europe, in particular the work and writings of Luther and Calvin. There were also pre-existing traditions of reformism in England, characterised by the authorities as heresy, such as Lollardy. Henry broke with Rome and declared himself Head of the Church of England, and proceeded to dissolve the great monasteries and seized their wealth. Rebellion and resistance, most notably by the Pilgrimage of Grace, were crushed by the brute force of an ever more bureaucratically organised and powerful Tudor state.

After Henry's death, the council set up in the name of his young son Edward proceeded to give the Reformation a distinctively Protestant character, and to extend reform beyond the monasteries into the parish church. In this way, the power of the English State was extended outwards and downwards into every single local community in the realm, even into what Puritans were later to call 'the dark corners of the land'. The death of Edward, the subsequent accession and death of the Catholic Queen Mary, and finally the accession of the Protestant Queen Elizabeth, saw a succession of sharp changes in religious preferences of the monarch, each of whom attempted to impose a new 'settlement' on the Church. And each new 'settlement' was felt in every parish church in the kingdom, with changes in church furnishings, layout and material culture.

The impact of religious reform on any local parish church was quite sudden (Figures 5.6 and 5.7). Changes in the church marked changes in the way people

Figure 5.6 Binham, Norfolk: the reformed interior of the parish church, formerly the nave of the abbey church. As was common practice, the nave was used as the local parish church, and so preserved when the abbey was dissolved in the 1530s; the blank east wall with its Tudor window seals off the church from the ruined crossing and chancel. The bare stone of the interior gives a similar impression to the freshly whitewashed appearance of post-Reformation churches in the 1560s. The font in the foreground has had the heads of its carved figures smashed at an uncertain date (cf. Graves 2008). (Photo author's own).

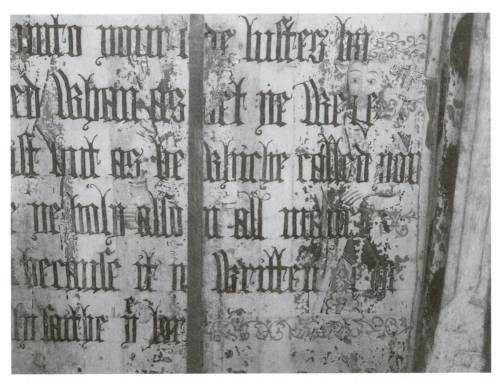

Figure 5.7 Binham, Norfolk: part of a screen whitewashed and covered in religious text in the 1560s; the figures of saints have re-emerged over the centuries. (Photo author's own).

understood the space within it, and fundamentally changed the performance and everyday experience of religious ritual and belief. As a result, changes in the fabric of the church resonated very directly with changes in the form, appearance and material textures of rebuilt houses: the rebuilding of houses and the reformation of churches went hand in hand.

The appearance of the internal space of the church was abruptly transformed, although the architectural fabric of the shell of the building was largely left. Chantry chapels and other fixtures and fittings were removed and destroyed. Images of the Virgin Mary and of other saints were seen by Protestant reformers as idolatrous and were therefore smashed. Stained glass was destroyed. The internal walls of the church had their pictures covered over; the entire church was whitewashed. After 1538, the burning of lights before saints' images was prohibited, and a Bible in English was placed in every church (Goldberg 2004, 240).

The perceptual transformation produced by these changes was intended to instil a new Protestant ideology that stressed the Word of God. Religious belief, and with it a spiritualised understanding of the world, was to be instilled in the populace not through images, which always carried the suspicion of idolatry, but through the written and spoken word. As a result, a new stress on text was introduced.

The whitewashed walls were covered with the words of the Ten Commandments and the Royal Coat of Arms set up at the upper end of the church; thus, when the congregation faced the altar, they faced the Royal Coat of Arms as well. In the official doctrinal view, the Word of God was to be disseminated into hearts and minds not through visual imagery but by the spoken word, through preaching. The liturgical mystery was reduced or abandoned – the rood screen with its pictures of saints cut down or dismantled, the view to the altar made clearer or the altar even moved forwards into the nave of the church, the orientation of the altar ('altar-wise' or 'table-wise' as it was termed in sixteenth-century records) changed according to religious preference.

These changes in their initial stages were top-down; they were enforced by the power of the State. Local officials were appointed by the central authority and given licences to go into every church in the land. Extensive written records are our best evidence for this transformation. Their survival, carefully archived in local record offices and faithfully reproduced in edited publications, is not just testimony to the changes they record, but testimony to the way that change was remorselessly driven through by the bureaucratic technologies of the Tudor state. Local priests were directed to comply and ensuing correspondence details enforcement where priests and communities were less than willing. It is no coincidence that 1538 also saw legislation to ensure parish registration of births, marriages and deaths. Local communities resisted passively or actively; Eamon Duffy paints a compelling portrait of one Devon community, Morebath, reacting wearily to change after State-sponsored change (Duffy 2001).

What were the reactions of ordinary people to these changes? An elderly yeoman in 1580 would have seen, looking back over the course of a sixty-year life, a cataclysmic change in the ordering and reordering of the most important element of his community: the Church. He would have seen, first, the dissolution of local monasteries; the destruction of chantry chapels; an assault on familiar elements of the landscape such as holy wells and wayside crosses; the destruction and remodelling of the interior of the church. And he would also have seen what were formerly accepted practices, rooted in memory and tradition, become an arena of contention and division, with the restoration of traditional practices under Mary and yet another new settlement under Elizabeth.

The inner thoughts of our elderly yeoman are hard to guess; after all, this was an age when overt expressions of religious or political disloyalty were habitually punished in harsh and graphic ways by the state, for example, whipping, physical mutilation or worse (Amussen 1995). What we can do is note a series of changes or processes that characterised the century during and after the later Reformation, and think about these changes in terms of the agency of ordinary people and the way that many of those ordinary people then turned to the rebuilding of houses.

First, there was an increased consciousness of the state and of nation. Ordinary people, after all, had seen an overt intrusion of the Tudor state into their everyday lives. One of the ideological implications of the late medieval corporate community was that order and authority at the level of the king and the lord was echoed by, and derived support from, authority at the household level. Each household was seen in the political and cultural thought of the time as 'a little commonwealth' (Demos 1999); offences against that commonwealth, for example, in what men considered to be overly assertive behaviour by wives, were matters of public concern and punishable as such. However, the changes of the sixteenth century left the middling sort with much greater willingness to intervene in another direction, both in terms of buttressing political authority through participation in local politics and in questioning it. The later fifteenth and sixteenth centuries saw a series of major and minor revolts with immediate political ends in mind; but in the view of many historians, the later sixteenth and seventeenth centuries saw the steady development of a wider political consciousness and a willingness to identify primarily with nation and with class, rather than with locality, in wider political debate (Hindle 2002). This increased consciousness fed into a changed understanding of the material world, and a specific change in how houses and material objects reflected ideas of status and national identity – a topic I will explore in the following chapter.

Second, there was a reluctance to put much more money into the Church. The rebuilding and adornment of the late medieval Church had been a matter of lay patronage, as we have seen. Walking around a medieval parish church today, in most cases the visitor will see relatively little rebuilding dating from the 1530s onwards. A typical church may well have a fine collection of individual funerary monuments from the sixteenth to eighteenth centuries, and there might well have been much sixteenth- and seventeenth-century expenditure on church furnishing that has subsequently been swept away by later generations of Victorian reformers intent on 'restoration' to a medievalist ideal. However, with notable exceptions (Howard 2007), the basic fabric of the parish church received very little investment after the Reformation. After 1600, the reforms introduced by Archbishop Laud and their material reorganisation of the Church doctrinally marked a return to ceremony, but were met with hostility by Puritans, and resulted in further controversy and division (Parry 2006). It may well be the case that Hoskins' case for a rebuilding of domestic architecture from 1560–1640 was overstated, but it is perhaps just as important and revealing that this same period saw little rebuilding of church fabric in comparison to the previous centuries. Not only did the middling sort have money to spend, but they chose not to spend it on the Church.

In part, the reluctance of the middling sort to finance further rebuilding of the Church was owing to the abolition of the doctrine of Purgatory. The late medieval sinner had been offered the prospect of a speedier passage to Heaven through the purchase of pardons (to Martin Luther's famous disgust) and through patronage of the Church. Nevertheless, a simpler and more basic motive for the reluctance of the middling sort to contribute to the Church may be found in their simple observation of what had happened since the 1530s – the repeated State-sponsored pillaging of the goods and furnishings, the removal of costly church plate, the requirement to finance yet another new set of religious regalia according to the religious preferences of a new monarch, preferences which (to the eyes of a jaundiced and cynical local community) seemed to be prone to rapid, abrupt and arbitrary change.

Third, there was a desire to understand the new emphasis on the Word of God, as it could be read in the Bible and as it could be seen in the texts now written on the whitewashed fabric of the church. Our illiterate yeoman could not read these texts, but he understood their power and authority only too well. The reaction of many socially middling families to the changes of the 1560s and 1570s was to send their sons to grammar school. Grammar schools, where boys could learn to read and write, had been known from the later Middle Ages, but flourished in size and numbers from the later sixteenth century onwards (Cressy 1976, 501–6). Many grammar schools survive from this period (Howard 2007). Huntingdon grammar school was housed within the walls of an old monastic establishment, so the young Oliver Cromwell, born into an obscure gentry family, gazed up at the medieval walls as he learnt his lessons there. Where an earlier generation put surplus funds into the community through its religious expression, in the hope of a better afterlife, a new generation took a more worldly approach and invested in the future through education.

After a fall in literacy in the mid-sixteenth century, possibly owing to the abolition of Church institutions that taught reading and writing, levels of literacy subsequently rose steadily. It has been argued that rising levels of literacy led to a rise in the practice of solitary reading, most obviously of the Bible (Sharpe 2000). The practice of solitary reading in turn led to a heightened sense of self, and was thus related to a rise in 'privacy' that we have noted architecturally. In the very long term, over the next two centuries, reading alone became a cultural practice of both the elite and the middling sort that I will return to in Chapter 8 on the Georgian Order.

Fourth, there was a new impetus in the rebuilding of houses, and to fill those houses with more and better movable goods and fittings. When the medieval peasant had a succession of good harvests, the money might well be donated to the Church, for the good of his soul; after the Reformation, the money might go in other directions, for example, towards the purchase or enclosure of land, or the construction of a new home. That new home was to be constructed in a new form. It still had a hall, and the hall still retained much of its power and meaning. However, the hall was now smaller, and had lost its centrality to the circulation pattern of the house.

Many of these houses were built, literally as well as metaphorically, on the ruins of the old religious order, in that they reused monastic stone in their fabric (Figure 5.8). It might be for some builders that the reuse of monastic stone was a conscious assertion of Protestantism, or for others an association with presumed magical properties (we will see in the following chapter how particular building materials took on symbolic or status associations). However, it might also be, following the views of Roger Martin, the recusant churchwarden of Long Melford

Figure 5.8 Binham, Norfolk: pieces of reused monastic stone can be picked out amidst the flint walling of local buildings. (Photo author's own).

who saw the transformation of the famous parish church, that builders saw the way the wind was blowing and took their opportunity (Dymond and Paine 1992; Duffy 1992, 496). As a recusant Catholic, Roger Martin held out against the new order, but he saw in his contemporaries a middle-class eagerness to take and turn to material benefit whatever opportunities changing times threw up.

Conclusion

In the century after 1540, three generations of farmers rebuilt their homes. Some were conversions, others were new houses; all marked an abandonment of the old open hall, though the variety of new forms adopted still retained many of the old arrangements, and with them elements of the old pattern of living. The pattern of these variations was different from region to region, and from household to household.

We have seen in this chapter that the reasons for this rebuilding were complex. In many instances, peasant farmers had new sources of wealth, and changing cultural values played their part. In particular, changes in houses went alongside changes in the landscape as a whole. The agrarian landscape was marked by a process of enclosure; farming was based less on values of community and more on a private, market-oriented business. Farming households, instead of spending money immediately, held funds back, which were then invested in enclosure of the landscape, in new houses, and in sending sons to grammar school – all forms of delayed gratification, in which the pleasures of immediate enjoyment were sacrificed to long-term profit. Historians have famously, if controversially, seen the influence of Protestantism in this wider stress on the individual, on hard work, and on the accumulation of wealth (Weber 1965; Tawney 1926). At the same time, the layout and appearance of the House of God were being transformed. Changes in ordinary houses were part of changes in the landscape as a whole, and part of a culture and mentality that was undergoing transformation in its turn.

However, whatever their immediate rationale and context, these countless individual acts of rebuilding produced a final pattern. The end result of these three generations of rebuilding was that across most of England a visitor would observe large numbers of solid, substantially built farmhouses, one room deep and from two to four rooms in length, built of local materials and in a style that bore the marks of distinctive regional variation. These farmhouses were dwelt in by families and households of yeoman and husbandman status, who employed labourers and a few servants, and who enjoyed some security of tenure. They framed the socially middling household that was part of the core of contemporary political and religious belief. Andrew McRae has commented how in later sixteenth-century sermons and other religious texts 'it is . . . the industrious husbandman or yeoman who is drawn to the moral centre of Protestant representations of rural life, his productivity claimed as tangible evidence of moral rectitude'. Solidly built vernacular farmhouses materialised that representation, and expressed an ethic of improvement that contemporary husbandry manuals emphasised with increasing vigour after 1600 (McRae 1996, 60 and 136–7).

These changes in the material form of farmhouses related in turn to changing ideas of status and social order. In the next chapter, I will look at how rebuilding and reformation did not simply involve changes in vernacular building. It was also tied in to a growing gap between the architecture and material life of the elite, and the architecture and material life of lesser folk. In other words, 'polite and rustic' forms of building and of household began to diverge, and a tension between traditional and early modern forms of cultural authority began to be opened up. It is this tension which different kinds of building and material culture sought to work through – for example, the Montacute frieze, with which I begin Chapter 6.

6
Polite and Rustic

One of the most astonishing and evocative artefacts of the culture of the English countryside is to be found not in a vernacular building but in a great Elizabethan house, at Montacute in Somerset. Walking into the hall at Montacute, the visitor is greeted by the sight of a large plaster frieze at the upper end, clearly intended to be gazed at above the heads of the lord and his immediate family and guests dining at high table (Figure 6.1).

The frieze is sited in a great house, but it is a fictional representation of a scene from the life of the ordinary members of the community. It depicts a custom well-known from references in documents and folk culture: a 'skimmington ride' (for example, Ewart Evans 1962; Thompson 1991: Underdown 1985a). To the left, we see a schematic representation of a house or roofed structure, within which is a man carrying a baby and helping himself to a drink from a hogshead; he has been discovered by a woman, presumably his wife, who is about to beat him around the head with a shoe or wooden clog. The scene is a familiar stereotype from the period: the 'henpecked husband'. It is interpreted as such by an observer standing to the left, who seems to reappear in a second scene to the right. In this second scene, a figure, possibly the henpecked husband or someone in his place, is being carried round the village on a pole by a group of men, with women looking on and with a church in the background. Women are placed at the back; after all, the ideological message of the skimmington ride is in part that they should stay indoors, just as in the words of the contemporary Puritan moralists Dod and Cleaver they should keep their tongues firmly locked inside their mouths (Luckyj 1993, 35). The rider appears to have a leader with a cloak; they do not have pots and pans but they do have pipe and drum. Houses in the frieze, grouped around the church, are represented schematically, with low-pitched roofs and only one storey.

The Montacute frieze is not an artefact with one simple, single meaning or interpretation. The scholarly expert cannot say with certainty, 'it meant this one thing'. Rather, like any Shakespeare play written around the same time that the frieze was created, its power and genius, and its fascination for us as modern observers, lies in its openness to different readings. It tells a complex story about household relations, women and men, the local community, and also about relations of status between the great and the middling and lower orders of the community. The social historian Anthony Fletcher writes, 'This community shaming ritual – the rough music of pots,

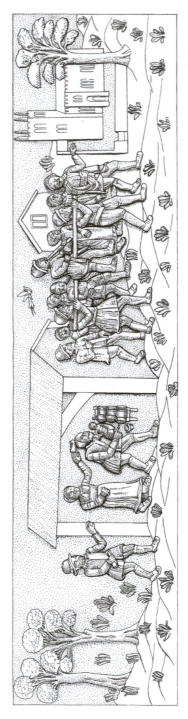

Figure 6.1 The Skimmington frieze. The frieze stretches across the whole of the upper end of the hall at Montacute, behind the high table. (Illustration by Penny Copeland).

pans, effigies and rhymes – was for centuries the authentic voice of the English people about what is tolerable and what intolerable in marital relations'. For Fletcher, the Montacute frieze represents 'an affirmation by Sir Edward Phelips . . . that everyone knew about patriarchy having to have its final sanctions' (Fletcher 1995, 201 and 273). It raises a host of questions about what it represents: what is such a 'vernacular' portrayal of an ordinary scene and of a 'folk custom' doing in a great house such as this one? Who would have seen the frieze, and how would they have interpreted it – as a piece of rampant misogyny, or as an expression of 'what everybody knew' about how household order should be kept? As such, the frieze can be 'read' or interpreted in many different ways.

I want to start with the frieze as an entry-point into thinking about the relationship between great houses and small houses, and the elite and humble households that they contained. So far, this book has discussed 'vernacular' or 'traditional' architecture, houses that have been held to be of the 'middling sort' or 'ordinary folk', but we have not looked in great detail at what these terms actually mean. How did houses great and small, magnificent and humble, 'polite' or 'vernacular' relate to ideas of social status, and how did this relationship change over the centuries?

The setting of the screen, Montacute House, is itself an artefact of profound social transformation. It was built by an Elizabethan 'new man', Sir Edward Phelips, an upwardly mobile, successful lawyer, who went on to be Speaker of the House of Commons in 1604 and Master of the Rolls in 1611. Phelips built himself a house which, in terms of scale, was anything but vernacular (Plate 10); it ranks with the greatest houses of the time, smaller in scale only to great royal and aristocratic palaces such as Whitehall and Hampton Court. The exterior of the house was carefully composed, with Classical figures on the east façade (nine 'worthies' in Roman armour). The west front has not survived. (The west front of Montacute observed today is made up in part from architectural elements from Clifton House near Yeovil, which was pulled down and the stone transferred to Montacute in 1786.)

However, like many such Elizabethan 'prodigy houses' in terms of its plan, Montacute House can be seen as a particularly large and complex version of a layout that would have been familiar to a yeoman farmer from the locality. The plan is in the form of an H, with hall in the middle, screens passage at one end and service range beyond, and parlours and chambers at the upper end beyond the hall (Figure 6.2).

If socially middling visitors found the layout of the house to refer to familiar ideas, so the references of the frieze would also be familiar to them. The portrayal is done in uncompromisingly vernacular style. Elsewhere in the house there are other plaster friezes, but none so graphic in their representation and none so assertively vernacular. This does not mean that it is crude; pamphlet illustrations of this kind, which the frieze resembles in many respects, had a whole series of sophisticated allusions (cf. Williams 1990). The location and context of the frieze also militates against an easy reading. Grotesque figures are well known at the lower end of halls

Figure 6.2 Exterior of Montacute House. Nine Roman worthies adorn the upper storey. (© NTPL/Robert Morris).

of great buildings, where it is appropriate to put such scenes: disorder and social mayhem are thus represented, but put literally and metaphorically in their proper place, down at the bottom of the hall, well away from the gentle classes. With grotesques, disorder is simultaneously acknowledged and marginalised, as it is in the 'comic' or 'rustic' scenes of Shakespeare's plays. It might be logical, then, to place such a frieze above the screens at the lower end. But it is in fact above the door to the parlour at the upper end.

This choice of position for the frieze can be explained in part by remembering the changing use of the hall in polite buildings of this kind during this period. There is a separate dining room at Montacute, where Phelips presumably dined on an everyday basis. So the hall would have been used for ceremonial, reception of the 'local community', or more accurately reception of those men who headed households within that community, whether for feasts, the enactment of justice, or for other rituals. We can picture the scene at the opening of a great feast or banquet: the guests have arrived, but Phelips himself has yet to make an appearance. As they wait to greet and show deference to their master, before he appeared through the door at the upper end, the gaze of the guests would be drawn to the frieze: the place of Phelips as lord would be metaphorically taken and reinforced by the frieze itself, alongside the heraldic motifs in the stained glass in the windows of the hall. But Phelips' guests, who were also his social inferiors, would *not* see other spaces within the house, such as the dining room and the long gallery upstairs. These other spaces were just as important in the negotiation of power, for example, between Phelips and visitors of similar or near social rank to him, but for the audience in the hall they would remain hidden and implicit, would be written out of the picture by the way the interior spaces of Montacute are organised.

A few years later, Ben Jonson wrote elements of the great house out of the picture, using written language rather than space, in his country-house poem 'To Penshurst'. Jonson's poem presents Penshurst, the residence of the Sidneys in Kent, as a great house, whose elevated status as a centre of lordly consumption is so natural that the fish leap out of the water into the serving-dishes of the household; he portrays a happy, organic community where there is a place for everyone and everyone knows their place. But while the poem resonates with the traditional medieval core of the house at Penshurst, in particular with the great fourteenth-century hall, the new elements of Penshurst that were added in the sixteenth century – the long gallery and private apartments – are not mentioned; they are 'written out' from his text, just as the organisation of the house writes them out of ordinary folks' experience (Johnson 1996, 119–20).

However, for all its assertion of a fixed social order, there is an undertone of anxiety about the composition of the frieze. If the frieze expressed 'what everybody knew', why spend a great deal of money and effort creating it in the first place? Why did people need a permanent, constant and insistent reminder of the values it expressed? Why did Phelips wish to insist so stridently and overtly on the links between household and wider social order? Why were these links not accepted and therefore left implicit, as I have argued late medieval relations had been? The skimmington ride could be seen as threatening the social order as much as reinforcing it. In succeeding decades, perhaps as the gulf between the elite and ordinary folk widened, gentry families might perceive it as a threat; King's Bench judgments of 1676 and 1693 decreed that riding skimmington constituted riot. However, when Puritan clerics objected to its practice, local gentry would reply mildly that it was only a harmless pastime (Fletcher 1995, 202). The double nature of skimmington, at once an assertion of a fixed moral order and yet an aggressive, abusive and frightening piece of carnival, at once both wildly anarchic and aggressively authoritarian, is most famously captured in the account from Thomas Hardy's *Mayor of Casterbridge* (Underdown 1993, 264–5).

The 'audience' for the frieze was predominantly male. Phelips' guests were expected to be male heads of household, while Montacute House as a whole would have had a preponderance of male over female members. In one sense, then, the frieze was about how values of masculinity were materialised and performed, by men and for men. Judith Butler (1993) has commented on the early modern theatre as a whole that it is inherently subversive. When Elizabethan audiences saw the roles of men and women being played out on stage, they were acutely aware that these roles were not normal or natural, but were in fact being performed, women's roles being taken on by young boys. Therefore, the more overtly the early modern theatre paraded the values of patriarchy, the more those very values were shown to be staged and artificial. A play such as *The Taming of the Shrew*, then, had a double nature, like the frieze itself. I would extend Butler's comments to other forms of theatricality such as the ceremonial of the hall and its trappings, where theatre might be played out less overtly but was nevertheless there on an everyday level. The frieze presents the values of patriarchy, but in presenting them so stridently and overtly, invites the possibility of opening them up to questioning by other elements of the household, and those beyond.

Emulation and Resistance

The pre-industrial English countryside housed and structured a society that was deeply conscious of social status, and was deeply concerned with the way social roles had to be acted out. We have seen how relative status and household order was reflected within the form of the traditional house, and we shall see in the next chapter how the different roles of women, men and children found expression in the form of the seventeenth-century house. Houses before the eighteenth century certainly expressed ideas of status in their form and decoration. However, this simple statement conceals a great deal of diversity and complexity. People were conscious of status, but this does not necessarily mean that they accepted it as normal and natural. After all, it had to be performed and re-performed over and over again, and it was open to constant subversion. There was constant worry about people dressing above their status (Hinton 2005, 17–19).

There are two stereotypical interpretations of social status in England before the eighteenth century: social emulation, and class conflict. For many historians and archaeologists, ordinary people were engaged in a constant attempt to emulate their social superiors. The term 'emulation' covers a number of different presumed processes, but it includes the notion that different social classes were engaged in an attempt to 'ape' the manners of the elite and imitate their lifestyles. Everyone in this view was trying to move up the social ladder. For other scholars, the reverse was the case. English society was a seething mass of class conflict, with rich and poor locked in a violent struggle for who was to be master. This class conflict broke out into the open with the 'bourgeois revolution' of the English Civil War before once more being quickly repressed in the aftermath of the Restoration.

Both these views derive less from the evidence itself than from later stereotypical depictions, specifically the political and cultural literature of the eighteenth and the nineteenth centuries, respectively. Eighteenth-century writers were very fond of condemning the lower social orders for 'aping' their superiors, and the fears and complaints of these elite writers that their exclusive social position was being eroded by the vulgarity and brashness of their social inferiors were commonplace. These

Plate 1 Houses in an English landscape: Monks Eleigh, south-western Suffolk. A cluster of mostly fifteenth- to seventeenth-century houses around a small triangular green, with a church at its head. The fabric of the church is late medieval, but the site is of pre-Conquest origins. (Photo author's own).

Plate 2 Houses in an English landscape: Eardisland, Herefordshire. Square-framed and Georgian houses along the banks of the River Arrow, thirteen kilometres from Offa's Dyke and the border with Wales. The bridge in the foreground has a datestone of 1800. (Photo author's own).

Plate 3 Houses in an English landscape: Bosham, on the coast of west Sussex. Bosham Channel leads into Chichester Harbour and thence into the English Channel; this has been a central place for millennia, with Fishbourne Roman Palace less than three kilometres away. The church has a 'broached' spire typical of the area; it has a Saxon tower and was at the centre of an important pre-Conquest estate. Brook House, to the right, was built in 1743; it was originally symmetrical, but has had an extra bay added to the right of the picture. (Photo author's own).

Plate 4 Houses in an English landscape: near Reeth, Swaledale. Isolated farmhouses stand on the shoulders of the dale, surrounded by the distinctive pattern of stone walls and field barns distinctive to the Yorkshire Dales. In this most northerly of the Yorkshire Dales, the houses are often of relatively late date, but stand on earlier sites. (Photo author's own).

Plate 5 William 'Strata' Smith's geological map of the British Isles, with different shades indicating different strata. Taken as a whole, the softer and younger rocks are on the surface in the south and east of the country, with harder and older rocks to the north and west. Smith's map remains broadly accurate 200 years after its first printing.

Plate 6 Two attached houses of the seventeenth century in Kelmscott, Oxfordshire. That on the right has alternate bands of Jurassic limestone. The roofs are of stone slates. (Photo author's own).

Plate 7 Grinton parish church, Swaledale, North Yorkshire. The fabric of the church dates from the twelfth century onwards; the different window styles are testament to piecemeal rebuilding and additions, the church as a whole an expression of the life of the community though the ages. The gravestones are largely of the eighteenth century onwards. To the right is Blackburn Hall, probably a residence for canons of Bridlington Priory who administered the church before the Reformation; it was acquired and extended around 1635 by Elizabeth Hutton, whose initials appear with the date of 1635 on the fabric, and who married into the Blackburn family. (Photo author's own).

Plate 8 Bayleaf, Chiddingstone, Kent: a 'Wealden' house, re-erected and reconstructed at the Weald and Downland Museum (Weald and Downland Open Air Museum).

Plate 9 Bayleaf: the interior of the open hall, looking from the lower end towards the table at the upper end. The hall has been furnished with typical items of the period, including wall hangings; to the right, the chamber beyond can be seen (Weald and Downland Open Air Museum).

Plate 10 Sanders, Lettaford, Devon: a late fifteenth/early sixteenth-century Dartmoor longhouse. The shippon to the right drains down the slope. The hall was floored over in the early seventeenth century, and the external projection to the left of the door, possibly originating as an external chimney-stack but now housing a staircase, added at that point. (Photo author's own).

Plate 11 Blackmanston Farmhouse, Moreton, Dorset. This is a late sixteenth-century house with the right-hand, kitchen end rebuilt in the early seventeenth century. The position of the door, with its impressive gabled porch, relative to the central chimney-stack, indicated that it gives entry on to a cross-passage behind the stack. (Photo author's own).

Plate 12 Bastle, Tarset, Tynedale, Northumberland. The classic arrangement, with stairs to a first-floor doorway, and a ground-floor doorway in the far gable end with recesses for drawbars, has been preserved. The walls are about 1.5 metres (5 foot) thick. The nineteenth-century roof is of Welsh slate. (Photo author's own).

Plate 13 Two painted schemes, of different phases, from No. 1 Gracechurch Street, Debenham, Suffolk. 'A richly patterned imitation textile is overpainted with a plainer scheme of green columns in the seventeenth century. The two schemes would not be visible in this way originally. The earlier scheme was obliterated with white then the green columns applied to the white background. The use of green suggests this was the best chamber'. (Photo and caption courtesy of Andrea Kirkham).

Plate 14 Springwell, North Warnborough, Hampshire: the symmetrical front of this eighteenth-century house is the result of a piecemeal process. The left-hand side of the building is clearly earlier, with lozenge and zig-zag patterns in the brickwork, into which the sash windows have been inserted. (Photo author's own).

Plate 15 A house in Grinton, Swaledale, dated 1831. At first sight it appears to be a typical smaller house of symmetrical design, with a central door and gable-end chimney-stacks. However, the small window to the left of the picture disturbs the symmetry and hints at a more traditional internal arrangement to the building. The byre on the right has been added at a later date. (Photo author's own).

fears and complaints have often been taken at face value by historians. Conversely, the nineteenth century is famous for the industrial conditions, urban misery and conflict that gave birth to the thought of Karl Marx, and for creating and exemplifying a potent model of very sharp and bitter class conflict.

The meanings of traditional houses do not, in my view, fit either of these stereotypes. Houses are, among other things, material engagements with the social status of those who built and dwelt in them, but not in a simple or straightforward way. Vernacular houses, their owners and ornaments, such as the Montacute frieze, can be 'read' or interpreted in several different, complex ways. Picture the scene again at Elizabethan Montacute, this time after a night of drunken excess at Phelips' table of hospitality. It is unlikely that the socially middling guests of Phelips, tottering back to their farmhouses, were forming immediate plans to cut his throat in an action of class struggle. Equally, it is unlikely that their first intoxicated intention was to recreate at home the visible markers of a culture and lifestyle that they hoped would cause their neighbours to think of them in the same social bracket as Phelips.

The one certainty is that the thoughts of Phelips' guests and social inferiors were more complex – and probably less coherent – than either of these two attitudes. The houses that were built and dwelt in, then, reflect a diversity and complexity of attitudes towards social class and status that are not easily summarised or explored. Montacute House and the lesser houses around it mark a critical point in the development of different forms of architecture. This development was away from a unified medieval system of architectural order, and towards the differentiation of distinctively 'polite' and 'rustic' forms.

Medieval Houses and Social Status

Late medieval houses were of higher and lower social status, and of different gradations along that line, expressed in terms of relative size, choice of building material, and level of decoration. However, it is difficult to draw a sharp or meaningful distinction between two independent 'vernacular' and 'polite' modes of building in terms of distinctive ways of conceiving or planning the house, or in terms of the manner of living in it.

In Chapter 4 we saw how later medieval houses could be very elaborate, but at their heart had a relatively simple architectural vocabulary, centred round the hall. The hall was a leitmotif of medieval society at all social levels. The great halls of Westminster and Kenilworth were on a much larger scale than that of Bayleaf, and in turn Bayleaf's hall was much larger than the hall of a husbandman's dwelling or labourer's cottage, but they possessed a common structuring. This common structuring expressed a common social ordering, based on the values of patriarchy and corporate community. In other words, the husbandman was master in his household just as the lord was in his, and both derived their authority from a common model of lordship. This common structuring was also reinforced by common elements of the craft tradition, where the building techniques and patterns at one social level were echoed in the next. Builders worked on projects of different social status, while using a common grammar of form and ornament. This was also reinforced by strong links between households, younger members of the family being sent off to serve in households of higher status, where they learnt how to behave as adults in these larger households (McCracken 1983).

The presence of this common architectural structuring has implications for the term 'vernacular'. It means that it is very difficult to talk of a distinctive 'vernacular' architectural tradition in later medieval England. There is no obvious or simple dividing-line between respective groups of smaller houses, socially middling houses such as Bayleaf, manorial structures, the houses of the late medieval gentry, and great houses and castles of the aristocracy and royalty. Many of the features found at higher social levels, such as the battlements and moat of the great castle, can also be found in lower ones, for example, ornamental battlements and the moats of gentry and even yeoman houses. Often the use of these features at lower social levels has been termed 'emulation', but a simpler and more convincing explanation is that of a common architectural vocabulary expressing a common set of social ideas. Indeed, one of the common elements of late medieval buildings at a higher social level is the presence of suites of lodgings for 'retainers', in other words, men further down the social scale who owed their allegiance to the lord and were required to attend his house. They had smaller houses of lesser status of their own, run in their absence by their wives. Such suites can be found, for example, at Dartington Hall in Devon, and at South Wingfield, Derbyshire, where they are 'stacked' one on top of another, in a tower (Emery 1985).

Where there was increasing architectural complexity in the later Middle Ages, it was in the spaces around and on either side of the halls (King 2003). There was a marked divergence in terms of building material, and this divergence carried a diversity of social messages (Howard 1987, 164). Stone was often seen as being of highest status, particularly when finished as coursed, finely cut and squared ashlar. Increasing numbers of high-status and urban brick buildings can be found in later medieval England, particularly on the east coast, though brick was not used widely for walling at lower social levels until the seventeenth century.

The common ordering of the architecture of different degrees of social status came under threat in the sixteenth century. We have seen how the sixteenth century was a critical moment in terms of the development of vernacular building, with the end of the open hall. It was also a critical moment in the development of the relationship between the houses of the elite and those of lesser folk.

Polite and Rustic in the Renaissance

The form and style of great houses changed markedly in the century after c.1500. These changes have often been explained in terms of 'the influence of the Renaissance', in other words the rediscovery of Classical art and architecture in fifteenth- and sixteenth-century Italy, and the diffusion of these ideas and architectural forms to England and northern Europe. However, the motives and factors behind these changes were much more complex than a single set of ideas (Johnson 2002, 121–35). These factors included a loss of architectural cross-referencing between different classes of structures; a new wave of building of Royal palaces; new kinds of architectural style and practice; a new architectural self-consciousness; and new patterns in the ways that great men of the Renaissance chose to fashion themselves.

First, a loss of architectural cross-referencing. We have seen that domestic buildings derived much of their meaning from cross-referencing, both to military and religious structures, for example, through the use of battlements and moats, and a common late Gothic style. This cross-referencing was lost, or at least very severely eroded, by c.1600. The dissolution of the monasteries had resulted in the ruination of many of the great religious buildings, or more commonly their very visible cannibalisation and conversion into secular houses. At the same time, the improvement and more widespread use of cannon in siege warfare meant that the architecture of great mansions and 'military' purpose diverged. Where a medieval house could be studded with towers and battlements, no Renaissance mansion could be confused with the new flat, angular bastions of the artillery fort.

In addition to dissolving the great monasteries, Henry VIII also constructed a new series of royal palaces on a hitherto unprecedented scale. The most famous surviving palace is Hampton Court, where Henry continued and extended the work by Cardinal Wolsey. Nonsuch, Whitehall and others were built or rebuilt by Henry. The architectural form of these palaces was still that of the late medieval courtyard house; indeed, Hampton Court has one of the largest and loftiest open halls ever built. Renaissance details appeared in Classical roundels and decoration. William Harrison wrote less than fifty years later:

> Those [palaces] that were builded before the time of Henry the eight, reteine to these daies the shew and image of the ancient workemanship vsed in this land: but such as he erected (after his owne deuise (for he was nothing inferiour in this trade to Adrian the emperour and Justinian the lawgiuer)) doo represent another maner or paterne, which, as they are supposed to excel all the rest that he found standing in this realme, so they are and shall be a perpetuall president vnto those that doo come after, to follow in their workes and buildings of importance. Certes masonarie did neuer better flourish in England than in his time.
>
> (Furnivall ed., 1877, 268)

This new 'maner or paterne' can be seen more visibly in the architecture of great houses from the middle of the sixteenth century onwards. These involved a number of related features. First, symmetry was used explicitly. While great medieval castles like Bodiam, and indeed houses such as Bayleaf, had deployed elements of symmetry, symmetry was now to be used down to the last detail of fenestration. At Montacute and other houses, the hall is placed carefully to one side of the main

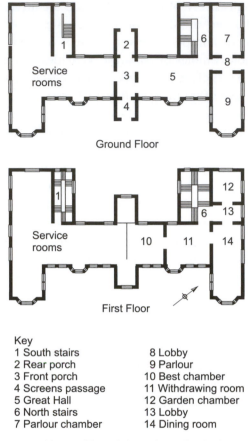

Ground Floor

First Floor

Key
1 South stairs
2 Rear porch
3 Front porch
4 Screens passage
5 Great Hall
6 North stairs
7 Parlour chamber

8 Lobby
9 Parlour
10 Best chamber
11 Withdrawing room
12 Garden chamber
13 Lobby
14 Dining room

Figure 6.3 Plan of Montacute House. Though large in scale, the house is still based on an H-plan with central hall and traditional arrangement of upper and service/lower ends. Like many larger houses of the period, the design goes to great lengths to give a symmetrical appearance to the outside world (see Figure 6.2) but retains a traditional plan oriented around the hall internally.

façade so as to retain the old screens passage, but behind a façade that is now symmetrical (Figure 6.3). Second, Classical ornament was deployed, in sculpture, plasterwork and other media. Third, while the great hall was retained, it was no longer open to the roof; at Hardwick, it was turned by 90 degrees and while still important became, as at Montacute, more and more of a ceremonial and reception area rather than the hub of everyday life. Fourth, the house as a whole was turned from an inward-facing plan, in which the main rooms were accessed from a courtyard or series of courtyards, to an outward-facing plan in which great windows looked out on to distant prospects. Fifth, new architectural forms were introduced, such as the loggia and long gallery. The great house at Longleat, for example, was reconstructed after a fire in 1567; the facades show a symmetry, regularity and rhythm. The great 'prodigy houses' of the later sixteenth century, of which Montacute is one, combine external symmetry with the retention of many of the features of the late medieval plan such as the screens passage and central hall.

However, there was a more subtle but more profound aspect to Renaissance ideas, as they were received and played out in sixteenth-century England. The Renaissance 'rediscovery' of Classical texts led to a new consciousness of architecture and meanings of buildings. The building of great houses had always been a major item of aristocratic expenditure, but now it was the subject of much more conscious reflection. In particular, those of aristocratic and gentry status reflected overtly rather than implicitly on the form and appearance of a building, and published these reflections in printed books. As a result, a building could be 'medieval' in appearance to our eyes, for example, the turrets and pinnacles of the later sixteenth-century Gothic pile of Burghley House near Stamford; but it reflected in the self-conscious manner of that 'medievalism' a very new way of thinking (Johnson 2002, 132–3; Howard 2007).

What this meant was, at the level of the elite, the layout and appearance of buildings was overtly discussed in a very new way. In other words, elite men did not simply build new kinds of great house; they also discussed the meanings of architecture very explicitly and in detail, using a language derived in part from the key texts of the Renaissance, most obviously the works of Vitruvius and Palladio. These elite men also rethought the landscapes around them, so that landscapes and buildings that had survived from preceding centuries – old monasteries, ruined castles – were now thought of as 'antique', using images and symbolic devices derived from the Classical world. Again, old words like 'nobility', 'honour' and 'chivalry' were reused, but in very new ways.

This new way of thinking created a distance between the elite observer and the everyday landscape around him. Elite men in the Renaissance now looked down, literally as well as metaphorically, on the everyday landscapes around them and found them 'rustic' or 'pastoral', and in the process distanced themselves from those landscapes. It is striking that where women had the opportunity to build, they did so in particularly distinctive and original ways, for example, Bess of Hardwick and Hardwick Hall (Friedman 1997).

As a result, 'sixteenth century social identities are constructed around *the way buildings are viewed*, rather than simply changing architectural styles (Perpendicular, Renaissance)' (Johnson 1999, 122; see also Hines 2004, 137–41, and Howard 2007). This very careful and complex architectural construction materialised Renaissance values and practices. These included civility, politeness and learning as markers of social status for elite men in particular, and more subtly a growing set of mental distinctions that is so familiar today that we often take it for granted: for example, between the material world and the ideal, the world of things and the world of language, the world of practical utility and the world of aesthetics and taste.

All these distinctions (material/ideal, things/language, utility/taste) were either actively created or given a new twist in the sixteenth century, and all were elements in constituting a new architecture for the elite. Nicholas Cooper has shown how sixteenth-century literate thought drew on the Classical models of Aristotle and Vitruvius and Renaissance writers on personal conduct like Castiglione to construct a new picture of how a 'gentleman' should live (Cooper 1999, 19–51). The medieval emphasis on magnificence and display were still there, but was deployed with the new element of 'taste' and a set of rules, the knowledge of which defined a gentleman and separated him from the vulgar masses.

Evidence of 'taste' might be seen in the final product of a formal façade of a house, but taste also marked a change in attitude towards the whole process of architectural design. By 1600 a distinct idea of 'architecture' had emerged that was held by the literate classes to be distinct from the practical skills of the artisan. The distinction between polite architectural knowledge and that of the common craftsman had an explicitly social dimension. Architectural knowledge was considered to be the preserve of the gentleman, and should be deployed quite explicitly to direct, control and delimit the activities of the mere artisan. The Elizabethan writer and magician John Dee wrote that 'the true Architect is [able] to teach, Demonstrate, distribute, describe, and Judge all workes wrought, And he, onely, searches out the causes and reasons of all things'. Henry Wotton added for good measure that 'speculation [on rules of proportion] may appear to vulgar Artizans . . . too subtile, and too sublime' (cited in Cooper 1999, 13–14 and 27). Comments such as Dee's and Wotton's were not straight-forward descriptions of reality: like Jonson at Penshurst, and like the Skimmington frieze, they were assertions that negotiated new ideas and discourses.

The implication of such changes was that the distinction architect/artisan was added to the others. A gulf was being actively created between the rules and discourses that marked what came to be known as 'polite' architecture, and the architecture of everybody else; and between the governing mind of the architect, and what were being classified as the lesser, practical skills of the craftsman. It was not until two centuries later that a single architectural system – that of 'Georgian', from the later eighteenth century onwards – could lay claim to govern the rules of building for both the upper classes and lesser folk.

The housing of early modern culture, then, was marked by an emergent con-tradiction. This contradiction was implicit but quite profound, and it threatened to destabilise the very foundations of the early modern social order. On the one hand, political ideology, descending directly from late medieval social models and still holding immense vitality through into the seventeenth century, loudly proclaimed that 'every man's house' was, literally and metaphorically, the basic building block of the social order. One the other hand, Renaissance ideas of civility meant that the upper social orders were attempting to disengage from the common set of cultural markers, such as the layout of the house and the craft tradition that underlay it, that cemented these building blocks together.

Such contradictions and tensions were worked through by writers and com-mentators in a number of ways. In the first place, there was the genre of 'country house poetry' of which Jonson's poem 'To Penshurst' is the classic example. In the early seventeenth century, poets wrote of the greatness of their patrons' houses, therefore implying the greatness of their patrons. In the process, country house poets praised the values of hospitality and lordship that were held to be characteristic of traditional great houses – and which were held by contemporaries to be under grave threat. Country house poetry, then, is a marker of anxiety about the decline of the traditional great house and the values it represented. Penshurst, described by Jonson as a great organic house, is contrasted to the new forms of houses and starts with a telling, accusing negative: 'thou art not, Penshurst built to envious show . . .'

A second way of addressing these tensions was a series of idealised statements written by male members of the gentry classes, seeking to offer advice to the middling sort of people on how to lead their lives. These books and pamphlets were made possible by the printing press, and their marketing was made feasible by the rise in literacy described in previous chapters. These advice books covered all aspects of 'husbandry', including farming techniques, household organisation, and relations between husband and wife (two of the most famous and successful books were Gervase Markham's *The English Husbandman* and *The English Housewife*: Figure 6.4).

The genres of country house poetry, and of advice books and pamphlets, are often nostalgic and celebratory in tone, and traditional in scope. They have been cited by many scholars as evidence of nostalgia for the old ways, and the continuing vitality of them. However, nostalgia should never be taken at face value. What is interesting about these new forms is that they feel they must articulate stridently, explicitly and at length what, for earlier generations of medieval communities, had been taken for granted. They can be read therefore as symptoms of anxiety, anxiety that these social

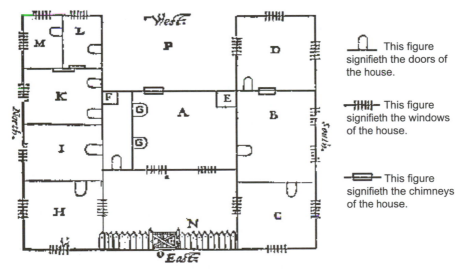

Figure 6.4 Idealised plan of a house, from Gervase Markham, *The English Husbandman*. This was intended as an ideal scheme for a husbandman's house, with the letters indicating the names of the different rooms (A is the hall, K the kitchen, and so on). However, Markham's mental image seems to be more of a manorial centre; compare with Figure 6.3.

relations are under threat and that unless they are constantly reasserted, the social world really will disintegrate. The issue of how to use these 'sources' is therefore much deeper than one of simple bias.

When these elite writers and builders turned to the discussion of more humble houses, the image created by the elite was neither neutral nor objective. In seeking to create their image of the 'polite' and the 'civilised', Renaissance writers created a parallel image of ordinary folk – the 'rustic'. In so doing, they were not writing innocently about rural reality. Rather, they drew on idealised images and preconceptions – on Classical models of the pastoral and of Arcadia, of the martial hero Cincinnatus' return to his farm, of Cicero's hankering after the simpler country life away from the metropolitan intrigues of Rome. Classical imagery celebrated rustic simplicity and self-sufficiency, and the values of a (supposedly) simpler way of life – values which continue to hold a powerful grip on the modern imagination. Such Classical texts were increasingly influential in the second half of the sixteenth century as they were printed and circulated among gentry farmers (Thirsk 1992).

Ultimately, when I look at the Montacute frieze, I see a pictorial counterpart of one of these literary forms that seek to work through the widening space between polite and rustic. Phelips sought to stress his position at the apex of the local community. But he was himself a 'new man'; his own career was exemplary of some of the new forces shaping Elizabethan society. The frieze is a strident, even shrill, assertion of the traditional values of the house and household at a moment when they are coming under threat, an assertion that the great house of Montacute and the ordinary houses around it are smaller and larger versions of the same thing – though they clearly, by 1600, are not. The Montacute frieze is a symptom of anxiety. It 'frames' a rustic image of rural life, and by placing a frame around it, stops the violence and disorder of that life from leaking into the world around it. Like the rustic knockabout of Shakespeare's comedies, it makes the violence and disorder bubbling under the surface of early modern life safe by making it comical, turning it into a visual story or parable rather than an historical record.

Such an elite framing of the 'rustic' occurs in other contexts also. The great castle of Kenilworth in Warwickshire was remodelled and partly rebuilt by the Earl of Leicester, in part to receive Queen Elizabeth as a guest in the 1570s. One of its most interesting features is an Italian Renaissance garden, viewed from above from a long terrace and the medieval donjon, which itself had its appearance transformed into a Renaissance house by the addition of great windows (Johnson 2002, 149). But the elite viewer, standing at the windows of the donjon or perhaps on the terrace below, would have looked across the garden and beyond the outer castle wall to the green, lined with thatched cottages, beyond. The thatched roofs and rustic forms of the ordinary houses formed, from the viewpoint of the owner of the castle or an elite guest standing on the terrace, a perfect backdrop to the civility and formality of the Renaissance garden (Figure 6.5). Elite visitors to Kenilworth would have seen the rustic village green and houses beyond the castle walls – but

Figure 6.5 'Rustic' houses at Kenilworth, viewed from the castle above the reconstructed terrace and Elizabethan garden. (Photo author's own).

their view of 'rusticity' would have been harmonious, carefully framed in its 'proper' physical and social place, outside the carefully placed physical, social and cultural bounds of the castle.

What this means is that when we read documentary evidence about the solid sufficiency of the yeoman way of life, and of rural houses as representing this sufficiency, the images invoked by such documentary accounts should not be taken at face value. A large part of their substance comes not from 'reality' but from documentary sources that have been generated by an elite stereotype that owes more to a reading of the Classics than actual experience of 'reality'. This does not mean that such images were necessarily false or fraudulent. Some of these images and values may well have been held by yeoman and husbandman farmers; many of them, particularly the increasing number of men who were literate, would have read some of the Classics at grammar school.

Rusticity and associated images of Arcadia is a stereotype that, in the twenty-first century, is met most often in the context of a Shakespeare play. Many of Shakespeare's characters engage in debates over social identity and status; we must remember that even in his history plays, Shakespeare's men and women display mentalities and attitudes that are revealing not of the historical events being narrated, but rather of when he was writing, and when Montacute was being built, in the years and decades around 1600. The Kentish yeoman Alexander Iden, who turns up in *Henry VI Part Two*, is one example of many. Iden extemporises on the self-sufficiency of his fine brick-walled garden which for him is 'worth a monarchy' and the hospitality of his house (Siemon 1994, 26). Iden's lines were written by Shakespeare to fit in with a London, metropolitan audience's view of the stereotypical rural yeoman, content with his allotted place in society, and he draws on genres of pastoral poetry from Classical models rather than reflecting an unvarnished reality:

> I seek not to wax great by others' waning,
> Or gather wealth I care not with what envy;
> Sufficeth, that I have maintains my state,
> And sends the poor well pleased from my gate.

(*Henry VI Part Two*, 4.10.16–23; though the scene ends with Iden, in apparent contradiction to this sentiment, declaring a desire to become a gent and attend at Court.)

State Formation

At the same time as the later sixteenth- and early seventeenth-century houses and households of the countryside were being idealised in different ways, they were also being described, mapped, classified, listed, ordered and taxed in new ways. Where the values of Renaissance civility demanded that yeomen and husbandmen exemplified an idealised rural existence, the emerging bureaucracy of the Renaissance State ensured that their documents were in order.

Part of the reason for the existence of these new documents was new forms of state power and organisation. Documents such as inventories were drawn up for bureaucratic and financial purposes: in other words, the State had (and has) an interest in ordering and documenting people's lives, in part to extend and maintain political order, in part to better extract tax from them. The sixteenth century is famous for seeing a 'Tudor revolution in government', most famously described by the celebrated historian Sir Geoffrey Elton (1953). More recently, historians have talked of 'state formation' (Braddick 2000; Hindle 2002).

The growing power of the state was not necessarily the same thing as the personal power of the monarch. Indeed, a key change in this period was a growing distinction between these two elements. In the Middle Ages, loyalty to the King was indivisible from loyalty to the nation; it was this identification of loyalty in the personal body of one's lord and master that made the medieval hall and its placing of the lord's body at the upper end so full of authority. However, in the 1640s many householders went to war with their fellow countrymen, and many lost their lives. The English Civil War was a quarrel that was in part about what the monarchy and the commonwealth should look like, and it was a conflict that ended in the judicial murder of the king in the name of the commonwealth.

The sixteenth century onwards saw an upsurge in the production and survival through archiving of a range of documentary forms. The proliferation of these new kinds of document is surely telling us something. Documentary sources are habitually treated as 'evidence', evidence that scholars of vernacular architecture have not always used as fully as they might. (Currie 2004 has explored the many ways in which the potential of the documentary sources in this respect remains unfulfilled in the study of vernacular architecture.) However, it is equally important to think about what the presence or absence of such sources means. In other words, *why* were people drawing up new kinds of document, or why were they being instructed to do so by their political masters? What does that urge to describe, document, classify, order, tell us? Might it be related to other social changes, such as 'the rise of the State', the 'growth of literacy' (Ferguson 2003) and the 'rise of the middling sort'?

And might these changes, in turn, tell us more about why people were building and living in new and different forms of house? Most broadly, what does the explosion in the nature, types and range of documents after the earlier sixteenth century mean? Might this explosion in documents relating to *households*, particularly in forms of document such as probate records and inventories, have something to do with the physical rebuilding of *houses*?

As someone trained as an archaeologist, trained to look for patterns in material things and to make connections across different classes of artefacts, what interests me about these new forms of document is not just the evidence they offer for new patterns of building. It is also the presence of the documents themselves. Many standard documentary histories of social, economic and cultural life are dated from 1500 onwards, and for a reason. It is from 1500 onwards that we have a set of certain kinds of records. None of these records are 'neutral' sources that can be taken at face value. Hoskins himself noted that legal records 'are by their very nature a pathological source' and that 'one could with equal facility compile a study of sexual life in the twentieth century from the columns of the *News of the World*' (Hoskins 1955, 52). However, the issue is much deeper than one of simple bias. It is about the way these 'sources' are artefacts or technologies of power.

These documents are of many and various forms. They include parish registers, giving details of births, marriages and deaths, and 'surveys' such as Richard Carew in Cornwall. 'Descriptions' of the nation appear: William Harrison's description of rebuilding cited in the last chapter is not important simply for the informative details it provides on housing and furnishing standards: it also tells us of a new consciousness of nation, a sense that Harrison is addressing a national audience. Manorial court records had always existed and been used; inventories, which will be discussed in the next chapter, were required by church courts. Printed materials proliferated: books, pamphlets, newsletters, advice books.

The last but by no means least new form of document was diaries. Socially middling men, frequently driven by the inward-looking emphasis of Puritan belief, kept diaries in increasing numbers. Shut away in a closet or chamber, these men (and occasionally women) withdrew from the bustle of the hall and the outside of the house to write down their innermost thoughts. In many ways, the physical action of keeping a diary tells us as much about the changing use and perception of space in a house as do the events and sentiments recorded in the diary itself (Sharpe 2000a, 339).

Houses of the Middling Sort?

The community of Montacute saw a steady rebuilding of houses by the middling sort in this period (Figure 6.6). These houses were of traditional plan. Many reused elements of the old monastery; like many houses built and rebuilt in this period, their fabric bore visible testament to the changing times, and specifically to the loss of the old religious and cultural order.

The houses discussed in the last two chapters were built, rebuilt and inhabited in a rapidly changing context. The appearance and layout of an open-hall house of c.1500 referred implicitly to a wider corporate community, to the lord's manor up the road and the castle beyond, and to the smaller husbandmans' and labourers' cottages down the road. A yeoman's house of c.1650, however, was placed in a rather different social and cultural setting. Further, the yeoman's consciousness of that world would have been very different. The head of household was now much more

Figure 6.6 Houses at Montacute, dating from the sixteenth century onwards. (Photo author's own).

likely to have read popular pamphlets and booklets along with the Bible. He was also much more likely to have travelled, for example, to London, or more frequently to county towns or other provincial capitals. And he was thus more likely to be conscious of what he had in common with yeomen from other regions of England, men of similar social class with common economic interests that cut across their regional affiliations and ties.

The rebuilding of houses in regional style, then, was in part an active choice on the part of the builder and owner. It represented neither complete acceptance of the social authorities, nor complete rejection. The farmers of Montacute, nursing a slight hangover the night after their visit to the great house, might have sat in their parlours reading Gervase Markham's *The English Husbandman* by rushlight or candlelight, and digested his idealised picture of 'the honest plaine English Husbandman' (cited in McRae 1996, 145). There they would have carefully noted the graphic layout of an idealised farmhouse that Markham included in that text (Figure 6.4 see p. 125). They then would have chosen to build houses that contained some elements of Markham's plan, but differed in other respects (Figure 6.6 see p. 130). Markham proposed an H-plan dwelling with a traditional hall at its heart; it is clear that he really had in mind a structure of the size and scale of a manorial centre. (Penoyre 2005, 112, shows a range of manorial plans of a similar size to Markham's scheme, alongside Montacute House, which is much larger but similar in plan.) As we saw in the last two chapters, farmers possessed the wealth to build substantial houses, but they often elected to retain a hall that was reduced in scale, and chose more compact forms for their dwellings. The style of those dwellings remained assertively vernacular, as I will discuss in the next chapter. Builders of ordinary houses chose to make their own histories, then, in the face of authorities trying to control their destinies, and this choice was neither a wholesale acceptance nor a wholesale rejection of elite conceptions of the house and household.

Vernacular builders have often been characterised as the middle classes, or the 'middling sort'. This statement contains some truth, but the full picture is more complex. In late medieval England, and in the formal political schema of the early seventeenth century, there was no such thing as an explicitly defined middle class, though references to yeomen and husbandmen were common. The famous social hierarchy of Gregory King worked downwards from 'lords' and others to 'gentlemen' to 'persons in Offices' to 'Merchants and Traders by Sea' to 'persons in the law' 'clergymen', 'freeholders' and 'farmers' down to the labouring classes, with no clear distinction of the middling sort of people.

Many historians have traced the middle ranks of this hierarchy as growing in numbers, wealth and political influence in the sixteenth and seventeenth centuries. Richard Tawney was famous for his essay 'The Rise of the Gentry' (1941). A generation of Marxist historians saw the period before 1640 as that of the rise of the middle classes. This rise was linked by these scholars to Hoskins' idea of the Great Rebuilding (Hill 1966, 488). In this view, most clearly held by Marxists, the ordinary houses that were the product of rebuilding at a socially middling level were one symptom of the rise of the middle classes, and the English Civil War, which they termed the English Revolution, was another symptom. The view linking rebuilding of ordinary houses with a class-based view of the early modern period has been hugely controversial. With the decline of a Marxist politics has come a growing doubt that the period before 1640 really did see a 'rise' in 'the middling sort of people', and a growing uncertainty about how to define those terms.

There is little evidence that before the middle of the seventeenth century 'socially middling' people saw themselves implicitly as part of a self-conscious middle class. A prosperous farmer in, say, Northamptonshire in the early seventeenth century might have classified himself as a yeoman, and been very conscious of a social position above that of the husbandmen and labourers in the community while being below that of the local gent; and his wife would have taken her status in this scheme from her husband. It is also possible that such a yeoman might have expressed a view of the world not dissimilar to that of Shakespeare's Alexander Iden, in terms of a kind of sufficiency and lack of pretension. He might also have referred to the idea of being 'in good credit', a concept that combined financial, social and cultural elements. A man of good credit was literally creditworthy, an important attribute in a village economy that depended on written notes of credit rather than coined money, and of good and reliable reputation (Muldrew 1998). Probate inventories were drawn up and signed off by men of good credit, whether or not they were literate.

This does not mean that we cannot talk of socially middling houses and households before this point, any more than it means that we cannot apply the term 'peasant' to medieval households because they themselves did not use that term (French 2000). The insight of Karl Marx remains valid: that we should not judge an historical period by its evaluation of itself, any more than we would judge an individual by their own perception of themselves. However, the phrase 'middling sort' did not come into currency until the later seventeenth century, and it is at that point that the origin of an idea that we might term 'the vernacular' can first be applied to rural building.

The Later Seventeenth Century and the Creation of 'Rustic'

The word 'vernacular' itself is not used about architecture until the late nineteenth century. The term is first recorded in 1691, its derivation being from the Latin *verna* or home-born slave. It is applied both to language, specifically regional dialect, and also to the 'native language' of a particular country in the seventeenth century. Its first recorded use pertaining to material things ('the arts') is 1857.

As Adrian Green has carefully noted (Green 2007), what does emerge in the later seventeenth century is a new kind of consciousness of status and class, in which rural folk are seen, particularly by urban and elite writers, as having a very different culture to that of urbane and polite society. (Ironically enough, one of the pieces of evidence Christopher Hill cited to demonstrate the existence of the 'middling sort' is the retrospective and snobbish commentaries of Royalist commentators on the Civil War, writing after the 1660s.) These changes actively created a regional culture that could be studied by men such as the antiquarian John Aubrey, cited in Chapter 3. For Aubrey, this culture was literally rooted in the soil (a metaphor that has proved of enduring power); the study of soil would reveal the nature of human society and variations between local communities.

At the same time, then, as 'polite' and 'rustic' architecture was becoming more clearly differentiated, and the houses of the gentry were becoming less and less similar to those built by people further down the social scale, so the lower orders were being described, mapped and classified as objects sprung from the soil, and thus objects fit for study in terms of regional variation and local character. Without this description and classification there could have been no objective study of the 'vernacular': the separate sphere of vernacular architecture, then, was in part *created* by this process.

The seventeenth century saw class polarisation and centralisation (Fletcher and Stevenson 1985, 10), and changes in the self-perception and confidence of the middling sort (Brooks and Barry 1994). The result was a divergence between different ways of building houses, and the emergence of distinctive styles that would come to be called 'polite' and 'vernacular'. J.T. Smith comments for Hertfordshire that 'not until after the Civil War did a distinctive vernacular aesthetic come into being . . . two elements in particular stand out, the continuous gabled elevation and the decorative chimney-stack' (Smith 1992, 111). The origins of this divergence have been traced back to the sixteenth century, and the Montacute frieze was seen as working through emerging tensions that were associated with it.

Conclusion

This chapter set out to explore the way houses related to social status, and specifically how 'polite' architecture related to the houses of lesser folk. What I have tried to show is that social categories were actively created by people and materialised by houses in this period. Houses reflected social status, but they did much more than this. Houses were and are material statements about how the social order was and is constituted, how it works, and how it places individuals, families and households within a grid of expectations and obligations. This grid was a cultural and moral one, linking the social world on the one hand to the natural and God-given universe on the other. Moving through the English countryside, people of all social classes, from landless labourers to commentators of gentry and aristocratic levels, would have known how to understand a house's social position from its outward appearance, and would have made quite nuanced judgments about the occupants of the house from the evidence of what they saw.

The enduring power of regional style in this context was not just 'innate conservatism'; it was an active statement on how to live. We have seen how ordinary houses can be read as active commentaries and responses to the values and meanings of great palaces; in the next chapter we shall see how this also worked at a level within as well as between households – how the seventeenth-century vernacular house expressed and embodied a conception of life as complex and as profound as any piece of elite architecture and culture.

7

Everyday Life in the Traditional House

A spring afternoon in the small village of Chetnole, near Yetminster in Dorset. The date is 17 April 1665.

The farmhouse of Chetnole Farm is a medium-sized house, of six rooms. Its hall has a fine moulded ceiling, but otherwise it is not exceptional: it is both a family home and a working farmhouse, the centre of a farm concentrating on dairy products, as indicated by the names of its rooms: buttery, cheese loft, milk house, and kitchen. It is deathly quiet, disturbed only by the suppressed weeping of the grieving widow, and the low murmuring of a group of men.

'. . . in the hall . . . one cupboard and one chest . . . six joint stools . . .'

The men move from room to room in the house. In each, one of them intones the names and value of things: beds, bolsters, a chest, tables, kitchen items, hearth furniture. Another carefully writes down each item as it is named.

'in the hall chamber . . . one standing bedstead, one feather bed . . .'

'in the kitchen . . . one table board and a side board . . . one brewing pan, three brass pans . . . skillets and kettles . . .'

Occasionally the group pauses to debate the value of a particular item, and at the end of their task are careful to add a little disclaimer:

'for forgotten goods . . . one shilling . . .'

Finally they finish. The writer checks that he has taken down the correct legal form of the document, and they all sign before repairing to the alehouse.

The cold body of Thomas Downton lies in the parlour; in life, he was the social equal of the men now inspecting and valuing his every worldly possession, and who in their precise inventory are careful to describe him as 'yeoman'. Previously he had sat with them in the alehouse, where they had formed a group of men of good credit; they and their respective families and households had sat in serried ranks in the church, their seating locations in the pews carefully differentiated from front to back of the assembled congregation by subtle but all-defining ideas of status, with gentry families in front of them and husbandmen and labourers behind. The Downtons were an affluent family; the total goods listed in the inventory amounted to the very large sum of £468. This wealth was derived in part from Thomas' marriage to Elizabeth Keate, who came from a prosperous family of farmers in neighbouring Leigh, which meant that the Downtons were described in court records as of gentry status. Now these same men, who had once sat with him in the alehouse and church, are going through his personal belongings, his 'personal stuffe', and are describing him as a yeoman when court records in 1656 call him a gentleman (Machin 1978, 36–9).

In moving solemnly around the house and carefully writing down the goods and furnishings that they see, the men are fulfilling a duty required of them by the church courts of England, a duty that had been imposed as part of the practices of a newly assertive, bureaucratic State discussed in earlier chapters. If a man died with a certain level of goods of a certain value, before his will could be approved, the courts took an interest in what he owned. They directed that an inventory of his goods be drawn up in proper legal fashion. This inventory had to be written, approved and signed by a group of men of 'good credit', a term which implied a social, as well as economic, standing within the village community (Muldrew 1998). 'Probate' could then be granted.

Such inventories survive in their thousands from the middle of the sixteenth century onwards. They have been used as evidence of interior furnishing of houses, and of household economies. Probate inventories are not as reliable as they seem at first sight – careful comparison with wills and probate records may show that items 'disappear' between the death of the individual and the drawing-up of the inventory, while many inventories are simply not drawn up very carefully (Weatherill 1988). Most inventories cannot be tied securely to a particular house, but this one can. The careful scholarship of Robert Machin and his extramural students, who transcribed and published the inventory, linked it to Chetnole Farm (Machin 1978, 160–1. I have modernised the spelling above).

The scene I have portrayed is one very small tableau that can be grasped in immediate and human terms. It is one particular instance that, like all such instances, is unique in some ways, but which offers tangible insight into the early modern house and household. The house of Chetnole Farm still stands (Figure 7.1): it is a solidly built house of three or four ground floor rooms in line, one room deep, and with an attached farmstead. Chetnole Farmhouse was built in 'regional' style, but variants of this form could be found across much of England. Vernacular houses from the mid-seventeenth century or earlier survive from most areas of the English lowlands.

In the previous three chapters, we have seen how vernacular houses were built and rebuilt in the later Middle Ages, and how these houses were transformed in the period up to 1640. As a result of the processes outlined in those chapters, most areas of the English countryside today have a number of vernacular houses that survive from at least the later seventeenth century. The only major exceptions to this rule are areas of the north, but even the most northerly of the Yorkshire Dales, the beautiful but relatively poor Swaledale, features groups of well-built stone

Figure 7.1 Chetnole Farm, Chetnole, near Yestminster. Formerly a cross-passage house, Chetnole Farm was substantially altered at the end of the seventeenth century (a former datestone reads 'TD 1689'). (Photo author's own).

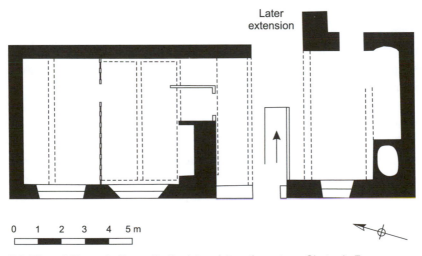

Figure 7.2 Plan of Chetnole Farm. 'In the later sixteenth century, Chetnole Farm was a long-house with a particularly fine hall and inner room-cum-buttery' (Machin 1978, 38), with a plank-and-muntin partition between hall and inner room. There is a large kitchen with fireplace and bread oven to the right.

farmhouses dating from before 1700 (Harrison and Hutton 1984; Plate 4). North of Yorkshire, in County Durham and Northumberland and the counties of Cumbria, numbers of 'bastles' survive (Plate 12; Ramm et al. 1970; Dixon 1979; Ryder 1990), and numbers of longhouses and other traditional forms have survived from before the eighteenth century.

Well-built vernacular houses, then, could be found across most of the country by 1700. They were nevertheless strongly differentiated from one region to another. Farmhouses continued to be built of local building materials, with structural and decorative details that spoke strongly of region and locality. Further, a visitor travelling from county to county and entering a selection of these houses would be immediately aware of differences in house plan, circulation pattern, number and quality of furnishings, and the different ways in which the spaces of the house were used by different households. The visitor might further note that while individual variation was important, much of this variation reflected a regional preponderance: for example, numbers of longhouses in this area but not in that, houses with lobby entries more common here than there, more granaries in this region and more detached dairies in another.

Nevertheless, despite this regional diversity and individual variation between households, early modern houses, like their medieval antecedents, had one thing in common: the house was a material representation of a distinctive view of the world. Houses embodied and expressed a very strong set of ideas about household and family life, and the relationship of the household and family to the social and natural world around it. The house, then, was much more than timber, lime, stone, bricks and mortar. In its appearance, its division and structuring of space, its decoration and textures, and in the qualities of the movable goods that it housed, it represented a way of living and a way of understanding the world. If the house was built and lived in by humans, it also built and structured patterns of human life.

In this chapter I will first of all explore what those ideas about the world were in the sixteenth and seventeenth centuries, and look at the early modern household's place in a wider political, moral and cultural order. I will then look at how the fabric of the house and its furnishing expressed and reinforced those ideas, gave a material form to a world-view, and how the house taught people how to understand their surroundings and how to live out their lives; and how different groups – men and women, masters and servants – took up different positions within this material and cultural matrix. Where previous chapters have concentrated on the *building* of houses, this chapter will shift the focus to the lived experience of *dwelling* in the house, and the everyday activities involved in living and working in the early modern household.

The Ordering of the House

The writings of political commentaries and advice books proffered formal guidance and commentary on the house as constituent of political and moral order. The vast majority of this written output was produced by male members of the gentry classes. Women, yeomen and husbandmen did not solicit this advice, but they did consume it; many successful books of advice ran into many editions and could be plagiarised. Ordinary people read advice books carefully, but as discussed in the last chapter, came to their own readings of them, in part through the everyday actions of building and dwelling in houses. The houses of the middling sort expressed their own distinctive view of political and moral order in very powerful ways, but in ways that were less overtly stated. Rather, the expression of household order was characteristically implicit, taken-for-granted, and mediated through the structures and rhythms of everyday life: through the practical and quotidian actions of eating, working, resting and sleeping.

The way people choose to live their lives has never been an abstract affair, a matter of taking a blank sheet of paper and sketching out a model existence. That might be the intellectual origin of certain utopian communities, and the idea of conscious, extended reflection upon the manner and mode of one's life was certainly taking hold of the minds of larger numbers of Puritans, Shakers, Quakers and other religious radicals as the seventeenth century progressed. However, it is not the way most early modern people lived, nor is it the way that most people live today. Rather, people learnt how to live through the practical example and pace of the everyday. Children playing in rooms and gardens learnt as they do now 'how to behave', a set of learnt understandings that they then applied in adolescence as they moved to other households as part of a pattern of adolescent service; they then set up households of their own, in a repeating pattern that consolidated this learnt behaviour. These repeated patterns were framed and structured by their surroundings – the layout of the house, its textures and spatial patterns, and how it stood within the wider landscape.

As I suggested in relation to the late medieval houses discussed in Chapter 4, the values thus learnt were all the more powerful precisely because they were unspoken and taken for granted – and, therefore, expressed most powerfully in material forms. The physical fabric of the house did not speak like a strident religious or political pamphlet, but it was all the more powerful in its implicit nature. It embodied and moulded the way people lived precisely because it presented those patterns of living as taken for granted in nature.

The most obvious way the vernacular house materialised the household is that it stood alone. Outside densely nucleated villages and towns, rural houses stood separately from one another, in contrast to other cultures where peasant houses are often built in agglomerated units. There are very few exceptions to this rule: these include houses on the 'unit system', such as Rock House Farm, Great Haywood in Staffordshire, which seems to have been designed as two contiguous dwellings (Hislop 2003), and there is documentary reference to a house at Rainow in Cheshire where in 1611 Thomas Clarke lived in a four-bay house next to where 'his son dwelleth being sometime the kitchen to the said messuage' (cited in Reed 1986, 153;

see also Smith 1993, 106–10, for examples from Hertfordshire). Most arrangements of the 'unit system' seem to have had their origins in the subdivision of an original house on the death of the owner (RCHME 1987, 88–90), and may well not have lasted longer than the succeeding generation. Rows of cottages or other houses designed deliberately to adjoin were rare: there is a continuous terrace of this kind at North Warnborough, Hampshire, but this has the appearance of an urban row (Roberts 2003, Plate 7), while one at Stoneleigh appears to be the result of piecemeal additions before and after 1700 to an earlier house (Alcock 1993, 128). Much more frequent are rows of cottages carved out from older farmhouses, where partitions have been inserted into the old building dividing it into two or more dwellings. Physical evidence of such subdivision is abundant in later centuries, but documentary evidence suggests subdivision may have been common as early as the later sixteenth century (Taylor 1992). Division of houses in this way is also attested by the evidence of wills, many of which specify division of houses between the son's household and the widow. A typical example is that of John Raneham of Brettenham in Suffolk, who gave his son Lawrence his house in nearby Bildeston 'on condition that he allows my daughter Margaret Osborne widow to have the only habitation of the east end of this tenement. The house is to be divided at the backside of the chimney over the east end and the entry now there' (cited in Evans 1986, 323). Inventories sometimes record instances of widows lodging with relations, for example, at Stoneleigh, where Bridget Osborne probably lodged with her cousin (Alcock 1993, 164–5). Very small houses are rare in inventories, for example, at Yetminster (Machin 1978, 7). Of course, the inhabitants of smaller houses may well have been too poor to require granting of probate and therefore the return of an inventory to the church court.

Around the vernacular house, the plot of the farmstead was very clearly bounded, with brick or stone wall, wooden fence or hawthorn hedge. Hawthorn made a particularly good organic barbed wire in this respect (Blomley 2007). In clayland areas, drainage ditches might emphasise the standing and independence of the 'messuage' or tenement. A popular saying of the time was that 'good fences make good neighbours', thus emphasising both the independence and the interdependence of households within the local community (Cormack 1991). Many villages, particularly in the Midlands and the north, had a marked division between the 'front space' of the tenement, with the house often directly facing on to the street, and the 'back space' of the tenement or messuage behind.

The vernacular house also stood at the centre of a working farm, whose primary purpose was to engage in 'husbandry'. Husbandry was more than simply farming: it was an engagement with nature, with the landscape, with animals and with other human beings in the broadest sense. The farm, with the husbandman and head of household at its centre, was engaged in a constant struggle with nature to tame its wildness and render the land productive (Johnson 1996). In this way, the daily, weekly and seasonal rhythms of farm management, the tending of cattle, threshing of corn, even the mucking-out of byres and stables, as well as the ploughing and harvesting of the fields beyond, were not simply or solely menial labour, however back-breaking the tasks and however hard the taskmaster. They were also ways in which humans created and recreated a landscape of cultural and moral order. In church on Sundays and in solitary reading of the Bible during the week, the early modern farmer learnt that God had condemned Adam to live by the sweat of his brow; it was by the sweat of his own brow that the early modern farmer came to understand the world around him. The husbandman was surrounded by visible signs of his own inevitable end, and not just from the tolling of the church bell: at Langton House, Great Ayton, North Yorkshire, the south-west gable had a sandstone finial probably taken from a medieval tomb: the 'grim reaper', a skeleton with a sickle was on one side and a Biblical serpent on another (Deadman 2004).

The layout and form of the farm buildings and courtyard also reflected this cultural ordering. Stable lads, male servants and others would be accommodated over the animals' quarters, a former arrangement that can often still be traced in the layout of the farm buildings (Rose 1998; see also Giles and Giles 2007 on the graffiti left by East Yorkshire 'horselads' in later centuries). The layout of the farmstead reflected an orderly flow of processes and agricultural products, for example, from the stack-yard through the barn to the granary and on to the stables, a flow that was both managed efficiently and represented the processing of natural into cultural products (for example, Barnwell and Giles 1997, 17). Beyond the farm, the ordered, rolling landscape of hedged, cultivated fields and maintained woodlands that covered much of lowland England by the end of the seventeenth century provided a visible metaphor of cultural order. The craggy hills and mountains beyond were anything but beautiful to the farmer before the age of Romanticism: they had been thrown up after Adam's fall, as visible proof of God's displeasure with Man. When seventeenth-century commentators referred to areas of the highland zone, then, as the 'dark corners of the land' (Hill 1962, 101), they had in mind a seamless fusion of its untamed physical state and the moral and spiritual state of its inhabitants.

The dominant and ubiquitous farm building in many areas, particularly and obviously that of arable cultivation, was the barn. At Ingatestone in rural Essex, 'nearly all properties with more than 6 acres had a barn' (Ryan 2000, 17). The barn was as well-built and as demonstrative a building as the house itself. Where it was of three bays, one bay would be for storing threshed straw, the bay opposite for tied-up corn sheaves, and the bay in between for the strenuous activity of threshing. This central bay had doors at both sides to facilitate the cross-draught needed for threshing and winnowing. In dairying areas, the barn could be combined with an ox-stall or shippon (for example, at Higher Farm, Stockland, Devon: Alcock and Carson 2007, 46). The massive structure of the barn was also an object of display, particularly in areas with a strong Puritan presence such as East Anglia, but in other areas as well (Figure 7.3); the framing could even be infilled with brick nogging, as at New Hall, High Roothing, Essex (McCann 1987, 113). For Puritans, wealth in the form of stored-up agricultural produce was also a visible sign of God's providence,

Figure 7.3 Comberton Farmhouse, Orleton, Herefordshire. The house is of several phases, including the later sixteenth and early seventeenth centuries. The weatherboarded seventeenth-century barn in front of the house, fronting the road, was extended in the early nineteenth century. (Photo author's own).

and the well-ordered and productive household and farmstead a visible manifestation of divine order on earth.

Farmhouses often also had a granary. Grain was often stored in the upper storeys of houses, according to the evidence of inventories, but specialised granaries increased in number from the sixteenth century onwards as the importance of producing corn grew. Many of those surviving date from after the introduction of mechanised threshing in the nineteenth century. The granary, usually of a square form, was placed either on staddle stones or above a cart shelter, in order to inhibit the ingress and depredations of rats and mice (Figure 3.3). The mushroom-shaped staddle stones of vanished granaries can often be seen even where the granary has been destroyed. There were also linhays or open cattle-sheds (Alcock and Carson 2007, 47), a cow-house or byre, and in some cases stables, tables, pigsties and piggeries (Figure 7.4), hen houses, bee boles, cart sheds, and ash houses. Dovecotes were often added after their restriction to manorial houses broke down in the early to mid-seventeenth century (Thirsk 2000, 54). Farm buildings were generally placed around the edges of the farmstead courtyard, with the great, steaming mass of fertility of the dung heap in the middle of it.

Figure 7.4 Piggery, probably eighteenth century, at Dyves Farm, Egton, North Yorkshire. After enclosure, pigs no longer had free range, so accommodation for pigs became more common. The large stone slabs were used to resist the gnawing habits of pigs (Penoyre 2005, 145). Chickens were often kept above the pigs, as 'the pigs were said to frighten off foxes while the chickens kept the pigs warm' (Wade Martins 2000, 23). (Photo author's own).

Particular regional economies featured specific types of farm building, for example, cider houses and large circular stones used for scrunching the apples in Devon (Beacham 1990), or malt kilns, hop houses and oast houses in Kent. Most featured a combination of barn, stable, and provision for cattle (N. Harvey 1984, 47). Work by English Heritage looking at the regional characteristics of landscapes has shown how different farmstead plans and farm buildings have close links to different kinds of regional economy and tenurial structure. For example, in Hampshire, 'courtyard' farms seem to relate to a particular class of tenant farmer; in the North, longhouses and farmsteads with buildings in-line again relate to regional patterns (Lake and Edwards 2006). Cheese rooms, with shelves on racks either in attics or in ancillary areas of the house, were common in dairying areas (Hall 1982, 172); a service room with a large trough at Hartland, Devon, has been interpreted as a salting room (Alcock 1994, 210). In East Anglia, baking, malting and brewing vessels were kept in a service room called the 'backhouse' (Barley 1961, 76). Bee boles and shelters are found across the country – recesses for skeps of different forms survive, for example, at the Lifeboat public house, Hunstanton, in Norfolk, or at Charity Farm, Lovington, Somerset (Penoyre 2005, 148). Duck nesting boxes and duck islands are more rare (Peachey 1990).

In many northern and western areas of England farm buildings were kept rather closer together than in lowland areas. Builders of the well-known form of the 'longhouse' placed a byre for cattle in line with the human dwelling, the whole under one continuous roof. The longhouse form was popular in Highland Zone areas, for example, Devon, the Welsh Borders such as Herefordshire, and the North York Moors (RCHME 1987, 62–71) among other areas, as well as in Wales and Scotland where the pastoral economy was important. It is also possible that it was deemed important to keep livestock close to the house-part in areas of the 'dark corners of the land' where there was a threat of cattle rustling. Longhouses are often very difficult to detect in their original form, as one or other end of the building has almost always been rebuilt. However, many examples have now been found, more often than not running up and down the slope of the hill, utilising the slope to assist the drainage and flow of manure away from the byre through a channel at its lower end (Plate 10).

One reason for placing house and farm buildings well away from one another was fire risk. If a fire started in the thatched roof of one of the buildings, the distance reduced the risk of it spreading to another part of the farmstead. It is unsurprising therefore to find longhouse and other forms of house where farm buildings are contiguous in the North, where stone slates rather than thatch were often (though not always) used for roofing and the fire risk was commensurately less. More broadly, placing the house away from farm buildings was a sign of household order, and came with the Georgian farmhouses of the eighteenth century to be seen as a mark of gentility and refinement.

Most farmhouses had small gardens. Gardens are less well recorded than other areas of the farmstead as they did not impinge either on inventories or on tax records, in part because gardens were considered to be the domain of the housewife and were not subject to tax or other assessments. Gardens were sources of vegetables and herbs, many used for medicinal purposes. On 28 July 1658, for example, the neighbour of Goodwife Cantrey, the wife of a Northamptonshire yeoman, made a list of the flowers in bloom in the garden next door: these included larkspurs, sweet williams, spiderwort, four colours of lupin, scabious, marigolds, life everlasting, London pride, hollyhocks and many others; and the medicinal herbs fennel, camomile, white lilies, goats rue, and 'double fetherfewle' (Campbell 1942, 241–2).

The exterior of the house itself was an expression of social order. Houses were placed in part to be end-on to the prevailing winds, but were also habitually placed broadside on to the street or track, as Duncan James found in Herefordshire (2003): thus the upper–lower orientation, marked by the door position and windows of the service and parlour ends of the house, could be discerned from the outside. As the passer-by or visitor walked the country lanes of England, the ordering of the commonwealth was therefore immediately visible (Plates 8, 10 and 11), repeated over and over by the facades of even the most humble dwelling.

Interiors

> The lack of interest in interiors is part of an art-historical orientation to architecture as a sort of sculpture that can be adequately represented by slides of elevations projected in dark classrooms. . . . The house is reduced to a shelter and a sign of status and public order that can be accommodated easily by histories that serve economic and political interests. If the intimate ordering of common life mattered in history as much as it does in reality, then the interior would matter, families would matter, communities would matter, and women would be in the story. Architecture would be defined correctly, and buildings would assume the powerful role they deserve in history.
>
> (Glassie 2000, 67)

If the passer-by or visitor had paused by a dwelling and entered the front door, he or she would have found that the sense of order materialised in the façade of the house continued through the ordering of its interior spaces. As vernacular houses before the Georgian period were generally only one room deep, there was a relative absence in the house of spaces of circulation such as corridors or a hall in the modern sense, apart from the screens passage or the lobby. Some houses had staircases, often housed in a separate turret or projection (Plate 10), but larger staircases were not common before the eighteenth century. Separate access to the upper end of the house, for example, through a separate parlour door, can be found, but this was rare before the more segregated houses of the later seventeenth century.

As a result, everyday movement through the house was less about movement along communicating corridors than it was from one room to another. Further, such movement was characteristically at ground floor level, before changes in room use in the course of the seventeenth century led to increased use of the upper floors. Consequently, one could not help but progress from one end of the house to another, and in this way everyday movement through the house was always a sequential, social progression along a single axis, from upper to lower end or vice versa.

If houses stood alone and independent, the internal spaces of the house also replicated each other to a relatively simple pattern, particularly within a given region and where the owners were of similar social standing. As a result, one house could readily be understood from the experience of another. Before the later seventeenth century, the vocabulary used for the naming of rooms was quite limited, with only seven or eight names for rooms predominating. In Yetminster there were halls, kitchens, butteries or cellars, milkhouses, chambers or parlours, and a few others.

Sound travelled easily in such houses. Oak or pine panelling or wainscotting was not common at the vernacular level before the eighteenth century; where it was known, it was characteristically found in the parlour, and treated as an expensive commodity that was movable, often being specifically bequested in wills (Campbell 1942, 233). Often, wainscotting has clearly been removed from another house and bears the marks of having been cut to fit the present one. A working farmhouse, then, was full of noise and clatter, full of the creak of timber-framed floors and joists, the commands given to servants, the clattering of pots and pans. Even where the outer walls were built of stone, internal partitions of timber and wattle panelling would block relatively little noise. As privacy and segregation became more important, and as the house became seen much more as a domestic retreat, the spaces between joists were packed with walnut shells or other materials to deaden the noise (Ewart Evans 1966, 43–5).

The only time of relative quiet was Sundays, particularly in Puritan households where the Sabbath was interpreted and enforced as a day of quiet contemplation. Puritan commentators enjoined the masters of household to keep their people indoors, perhaps in discussion of the Sunday sermon or reading of the Bible in the hall or parlour. Conversely, servants, many of them adolescents, took every opportunity to get away from the house. References in court records to illicit activity are habitually located in marginal areas of the farmstead – the stables or the barn (see the examples in Ingram 1987, 219–37).

The house would appear far more sparsely furnished than it does today, although it was more comfortably furnished than earlier medieval houses. There is little physical evidence for furniture below the level of the gentry household before the eighteenth century; where furniture does survive, it does so from the eighteenth century onwards. What items such as chairs, tables and chests do survive at a vernacular level from earlier dates, they often appear massive and crude to our eyes. Their solid build meant that they had a long life-span, and much of the furniture would be acquired from previous generations of house-dwellers. Objects, however, could be far more significant than the easily acquired and easily disposed-of items that furnish modern interiors. Before the Industrial and Consumer Revolutions, objects were often inherited rather than bought and sold, and had far longer lives of use.

Furniture and other objects also lasted longer, and were handed down from generation to generation. As result, they acquired patina, or a worn surface that denoted antiquity and hence ancient status: there was not the same premium on new things, or the assumption that new was necessarily better. Rather, old objects acquired patinas that linked to ideas of social status and perceptions of antiquity. The great thinker Walter Benjamin (1936) argued that objects of this kind have 'aura', an aura increased by the fact that they are not mass-produced or standardised, and each object is therefore slightly different from the next one. The notion that the family had farmed the land for countless generations, since 'time out of mind', was often a myth, but it was a powerful myth; and the patina of family heirlooms and the stories that would have been told around them reinforced that myth.

Though interiors were bare, they could carry a great deal of decoration and rich visual imagery. The more ornate and grander items of traditional furniture had carved scenes, often Biblical (Bebb 2007), with a large example from Cotehele, Cornwall (Riall and Hunt 2001). Religious themes were carried through to decorate ordinary household items: for example, housewives and servants bustling around the kitchen may have wielded a decorated skillet bearing the message 'Y[e] Wages of Sin is Death' (Pennell 1999b, 42). Painted cloths and textiles were common in the fifteenth and sixteenth centuries; by the seventeenth century, wall paintings had become more popular. Wall paintings from many vernacular houses are well known, and many more await discovery: there are a hundred known in Hertfordshire, and two hundred in Essex, though their distribution varies greatly from region to region (Baird 2003). While the majority of known wall painting comes from urban contexts, or from the houses of the gentry classes, rural farmhouses often had painted walls. The design and style of wall painting varied. The majority of the designs were probably very simple and repetitive, and it should be remembered that these plain schemes were much more common than more complex designs (Kirkham 2007). More complex schemes ranged from simple imitation panelling or imitation timber framing, to heavily stylised Classical motifs, heraldic emblems, depictions of seasonal tasks, to seasonal portraits. Depictions of the Nine Worthies and of hunting scenes were popular in gentry houses (Moran 2003, 327 and 345–7). In many houses, simple portraits of a man and a woman, often paired, may be portraits of the owners (for example, Davies 2008, 9–10, and 202; see Plate 13).

Where writing is found surviving on the walls of vernacular houses, it is most frequently of religious mottoes or texts; an inscription in a new early seventeenth-century house in Montgomeryshire relates to values of hospitality (Britnell and Suggett 2002, 161). Groups of overtly Christian symbols could be seen on the interior walls of many houses: V (for Virgo Virginum or Virgin of Virgins), M (Mary), MR (Maria Regina), or P (Pax), crosses and ladders, or at Yew Tree House, Ombersley, in Worcestershire, a pelican pecking her breast to feed her children with her blood (Davies 2008, 185); the latter is a familiar religious symbol, but in a domestic context may also be construed as a reference to the values of child-rearing. Depictions such as these are known even from the seventeenth century, some generations after the Reformation discouraged or formally banned such overt expressions of devotion (Meeson 2005, 46); religious texts such as passages from the Bible were more popular thereafter. For example, at Moxhayes, Membury, Devon, dated 1683, a text in the best chamber appears to be a text to focus the couple's thoughts on God directly upon waking: 'in the morning will I direct my prayer unto thee' (Alcock and Carson 2007, plate Vb; see also Fleming 2001).

In areas of the West Country, particularly Somerset, there was a vibrant tradition of decorative plasterwork (Penoyre and Penoyre 1993). The most ornate examples come from 'polite' contexts and great houses (the famous Skimmington frieze from Montacute House was discussed in the previous chapter: Figure 6.1), and decorative plasterwork is frequently found in the houses of the urban middle classes, for example, at the Butterwalk in Dartmouth, an early seventeenth-century house with a fine Tree of Jesse in plaster (Hamling 2007, 176–8). However, ordinary rural houses could also have friezes and plaster decoration. In Devon, the plasterwork found in smaller houses included animals and angels executed in vernacular style, and could be as simple as finger-drawn St Andrews crosses (Beacham 1990). In Somerset, at Parsonage Farmhouse, Over Stowey, a depiction of Adam and Eve taking fruit from the serpent in the Garden of Eden was an everyday reminder of the Fall of Man, while at Binham Farm, Old Cleve, the 'Triumph of Time' in the form of a funeral cortege was a reminder of Man's inevitable end (Penoyre 2005, 88).

The 'service' areas of the house were a natural extension of the farm courtyard; in inventories, it is often difficult to discern where the listing of goods to be found in the house ends, and the listing of goods kept in the farm buildings begins. This lack of clarity is revealing – it tells us that the distinction between the interior, domestic space of the hall and parlour and the exterior space of the farmstead and farmyard was a matter not of sharp separation between the world of work and the world of the home, but rather of order and gradation. It is here, at the meeting-point of the farm buildings and the lower, service end of the house, that service rooms such as the dairy house, bakehouse, malthouse and brewhouse were placed. The kitchen could either be placed externally or 'below' the hall, or be combined with the hall itself.

Much decoration could be found around the hearth in the hall. Not only was the hall the main area where people congregated, but the hall fire was also the spiritual heart and centre of the home. At Lower Spoad Farmhouse, a medieval cruck-framed farm and possibly hunting lodge in Shropshire, the hearth beam shows hunting dogs either side of deer; the beam has been tree-ring dated to the 1540s (Riall and Hunt 2001, 172). At Thatcher's Hall, Hundon, in Suffolk, there is the painted design of an *Agnus Dei*, the lamb of Christ, on the face of the inserted chimney, itself masked by the subsequent inserted floor (Mercer 1975, 385).

The hall fireplace was much more than simply a hearth. When it also doubled as the kitchen fire, a range of hearth furniture and kitchen equipment was kept there. This might include an iron pot, spits, firehooks and irons, and other kitchen equipment are often copiously listed in inventories (cf. Steer 1950). Many houses still have holes drilled in the fireplace lintels or other signs of fireplace and kitchen equipment that have been removed, and indications of other activities such as curing through the provision of bacon hooks and curing chambers, bread ovens, separate 'bacon lofts', or the presence of milk troughs (see Penoyre 2005, 76–9 for a variety of examples from Somerset). Larger fireplaces also had areas below the lintel, to one side of the fire, termed inglenooks; in some northern houses these inglenooks have small windows of their own.

Floors might be of floorboards, paved with stone slabs, or often of beaten earth, sometimes strewn with rushes. This did not mean that they were necessarily dirty, or that they were not scrupulously swept out: on the Solway Plain, mud floors were bound with bullocks' blood to reduce the dust (Jennings 2002, 24), while in Devon floors could be of lime or ash and bound with cider. At Wharram, the earth floors of the medieval longhouses were regularly and carefully swept out, to the extent that over time they became slightly dished in profile. A 'recipe' for a lime floor made of two-thirds lime and one-third coal ash plus a little clay is given in a 1734 builder's dictionary (Beacham 1990, 28).

Figure 7.5 Fireplaces at Greenhead Farmhouse, Reedley Hallows, Lancashire. The main fireplace served a large hall; there was a partition between it and the smaller fireplace, which served a smaller and more intimate parlour. The house probably dates to the 1670s, with a compact plan two rooms deep. (English Heritage Photo Library. © Crown Copyright NMR).

The hall was still the central room in most houses; it was still termed 'the house' or 'house-body' in many inventories (Figure 7.5). It was the setting for mealtimes, the points in the day at which the whole household came together before departing to work in the fields or around the farmstead. Lighting in the evenings was provided by pewter and brass candlesticks. Inventories record a cupboard or chest in virtually every room. Goods were stored in chests, coffers and trunks, often one per room, that were again massive in appearance. They were either jointed or boarded (Slep 2004). Chests could be locked; in the seventeenth century, the locksmith gained precedence over the blacksmith in the hierarchy of trades (Berry 2001). The hall contained mugs, bowls, dishes, wooden trenchers and increasing numbers of pewter plates, dishes, vessels and silver spoons.

The parlour, still generally reached from the upper end of the hall, also had a warmer and enclosed inner space, like the hall and its fireplace inglenook. This enclosed space contained a bed, for the master and mistress of the house. Just as the master's chair took precedence in the hall, this was the best bed in the house, often of a framed four-poster form with curtains. It was the most valuable piece of furniture in the house, so it was logical to place it in the parlour where guests could admire it. Its removal to an upper floor chamber, creating the precursor to the most private and intimate space of the modern bedroom, was a shift that occurred gradually over the seventeenth century, though in any one household this must have been a sudden and profound change. In areas such as the Lancashire Pennines beds were common in parlours right up to the end of the seventeenth century (Pearson 1985, 88). Later parlours were more frequently heated, though the fireplace was considerably smaller than that of the hall and without an inglenook. Being the most enclosed and intimate area in the house, the chest found in the master's bedroom contained deeds and other documents, money, and the best silverware.

The social hierarchy that the house represented was present even in its sleeping arrangements. The master and wife characteristically had a large four-poster bed; higher status beds were decorated with heraldry signifying the lineages of the families united by marriage, and perhaps acting as an unsubtle prompt to the couple to get on with the business of ensuring its continuity (Roberts 1995). Children and others had truckle beds which could be wheeled out, or cradles on rocker stands. In some regions, for example, north Yorkshire, beds were built into the fixed architecture of the room, or fitted into the eaves space at first-floor level (Giles 1992, 129–36). Other beds were distributed around the house; the number of beds seems to have been one indicator of the wealth of the household – between four and ten beds are generally found in inventories of socially middling households. William Streaffe bequeathed seven feather beds, nine flock beds and one down bed in his will (Campbell 1942, 235). With the beds went a host of sheets, pillows and bolsters.

Cooking and Eating

The farmstead was a natural extension of the house over the wider landscape, and the house an integral part of the farmstead's embodiment of husbandry. The house was also a centre of storage and consumption. As the yeoman farmer slept in his four-poster bed, he was secure in the knowledge that his sacks of grain were safe in the upper chambers above his head, particularly before the more extensive use of upper chambers for bedrooms.

Food preparation and consumption was an active process. The housewife took natural products and transformed them, through her labour, into cultural items to be consumed. Activities such as baking, brewing, dairying, curing, salting and pickling were one small intermediate step in the progression of husbandry. This progression led inwards, from the cultivation of the landscape around the house, through harvesting, food preservation and preparation in the farmstead and service areas of the house, to the consumption of cooked food on the household table in the hall.

Bread was the most important staple of all; the wheat and rye of which it was composed, in different proportions according to region, was harvested in the fields and then stored in sacks in the barn or in the upper storeys of the house. The wheat and rye were ground into flour in the local mill and made into dough; dough bins for making bread are common (Olive 2000). Dough was then baked into loaves either in a separate bakery or, in the case of many larger farms, in a bread oven. A corn bin was kept at the rear door of the house, to be scooped out to feed the chickens.

Animals were brought in to the farmstead from surrounding fields and woodlands, and slaughtered to provide beef, mutton and pork. Mutton was salted and pickled in the kitchen and service areas of the house; bacon was salted in a trough or 'zylt', then hung up to dry and subsequently smoked and cured – separate curing chambers adjacent to the chimney-stack, or holes for fixtures and fittings for the hanging of flitches of bacon, often survive, though not in all areas (in the West Country, bacon was generally unsmoked). Fish were kept in fishponds; while most fishponds are attached to high status dwellings, in some areas such as East Anglia even yeomen had fishponds.

Beer, ale, mead, cider and perry were brewed and consumed by the household. What today would be called 'alcoholism' was rife in the English countryside, if the many anecdotal accounts are true, for example, in Richard Gough's description of Myddle at the end of the seventeenth century (Hey 1974). However, the two most important qualities of these alcoholic beverages were that they were full of calories, and in an age before refrigeration they could be easily kept. Beer was produced from the sixteenth century onwards, by the addition of hops to ale. It was served at all meals, including breakfast. Historians have calculated that beer and ale were critically important in providing the energy for daily labour, contrary to the assertions of later temperance movements (Dingle 1972). Beer could be brewed in small quantities, while cider was made in larger batches; both could be kept for weeks or months in the cool environment of the brewhouse. Dairy products were prepared in the buttery, though dairy equipment was found in some central unheated rooms at Yetminster (Machin 1978, 10).

The hall and service areas of the house, then, must be seen as centres of bustle and activity, particularly for the women of the house and their servants. These different paths of activity and preparation came together at the main meal of the day, termed 'dinner' but held at midday; supper was a light meal, often no more than raisins warmed in milk (Campbell 1942, 249). Dinner was the central point of the day, and a key event at which the lives of all elements of the household – men, women, children, servants – intersected. At dinner, all gathered round the table, which itself expressed the ordering of the household. Dinner, then, was a highly structured event. The master of the house sat in his own chair, often specified as such in inventories, which was a massive piece of furniture. Around him sat wife, family and servants, seated on lesser chairs, stools or benches. In the West Country, according to folk custom, the hall table was placed lengthways, with a form on one side and a fixed table below the hall window on the other; one end of the table would be near the end-wall fireplace, while the other end would be by the dresser. By the seventeenth century, pewter dishes had replaced wooden or 'treen' tableware in much of England; Alexander Paramore of Reculver, Kent, had both in his hall in the 1570s (Barley 1961, 42). After the meal, when the men had departed for the farm and the fields, it was the custom for the housewife to place a cloth and bowl next to the hearth end of the table to do the washing-up (Olive 1999).

Food was also a powerful metaphor for social status and identity in the early modern period. The stereotype, often presented in contemporary plays such as *Arden of Faversham* to urban audiences, was of a solid sufficiency: the yeoman's table was one of simple and unpretentious but honest, wholesome and solid fare. The contrast often drawn was with the perceived insufficiency of foreign food, particularly the recipes of the French, claimed by propagandists and other xenophobic commentators to be over-prepared and covered with sauces to disguise its insubstantial nature. This ideological portrait reached its zenith in Hogarth's famous painting *The Roast Beef of Old England* (1748) which merges satirical images of Catholics, Scots, foreigners, and royal absolutism and contrasts them all with a solid piece of English beef. Eating a meal, then, in a socially middling farmhouse, was about much more than simply satiating hunger: it gave the household a sense of who they were, in class, status and national terms. Status was reinforced through seating provision and position, but all ate the same food and drank the same beer.

Almost everything in the house was reused: food flowed in to feed the house and flowed out again as waste. Organic waste and the manure from the farmstead was scooped up into a steaming pile in the middle of the farmstead courtyard, and then carted out to fertilise the fields; wherever possible, other objects were also reused. In an age before industrial production and affluence made objects cheap, and outside elite contexts where material was often wastefully dumped, raw materials such as iron and less frequently glass were often melted down (Woodward 1985; which is why archaeologists often disproportionately emphasise pottery in their analyses; metal and other objects have been reused).

Lives of Women, Lives of Men

So far in this chapter I have emphasised how the house acted as a single unit, a component of political and cultural order and a basic building-block of society, and how the values of that unit were played out through everyday activity. This has resulted in a rather normative picture, in which the house has been presented as expressing a single set of values. However, it is equally important to emphasise the way in which different individuals and groups took different positions within the household, and took different positions towards the values it expressed. The worlds of men were different to those of women, and however much servants were part of the household, they too had their own values.

It is important to remember that seventeenth-century understandings of the differences between women and men were very different from our own. Medical texts stressed that humans were made up of the four humours, earth, air, water and fire, and that illness arose in part from an imbalance between these humours. Male and female sexual organs were seen as similar; the woman's, being less perfectly formed than the man's, being thought to have remained inside the body. Differences between women and men were seen by contemporaries to be less biological and more social and cultural in nature (Laqueur 1990). As a result, gender roles were important to peform through actions and to be materially marked through dress, for there remained an underlying fear that unless he took care to always act 'like a man', a man might turn physically effeminate, his humours might turn cold and wet. So the patterns of everyday life around the household were more than just an expression of gendered values: they created and defined them. Laura Gowing has explored how the different bodily practices of women around the home defined their gender in different ways (Gowing 1996; see also Flather 2007).

The pattern of life in and around the early modern house ensured that the worlds of women and the worlds of men were segregated for much of the day. This division, and the structure of patriarchy and male ascendancy, was central to formal political thinking in the early modern period. Some historians have even suggested that, with the sixteenth-century rise in population and the end of labour scarcity, women's positions became even more marginal and their rights rolled back (Goldberg 2004, 215). Male political commentators drew explicit links between the woman's place inside the house, her inferior political position, and the need for women to avoid gossip (the possession of a loose tongue being equated to loose control of the household and loose sexual behaviour, a misogynist stereotype that went back to the Middle Ages). This message was enforced and disseminated through popular pamphlets, which drew parallels between the understanding and control of women's bodies, household order and discipline, and political order as a whole (Fissell 2004, 10).

Women, then, were literally as well as metaphorically put in their place. However, a woman's place was also a woman's domain. The term 'housewife' itself expressed control over this domain. Even in advice books written by men, such as Gervase Markham's *The English Housewife*, women were assigned an active role around the different spaces of the house; the house could become an informal centre of power and authority. A man who was foolish enough to meddle with domestic concerns was labelled 'cotquean', and popular ballads like *The Woman to the Plow and the Man to the Hen-Roost* published in 1629 related the catastrophes that ensued when men presumed to interfere in housewifes' affairs (Mendelson and Crawford 1998, 205).

Activities such as brewing and dairying were women's domains until the eighteenth century. These were areas of what Diane Purkiss (1995, 414) calls 'cultural work', where natural products were transformed through the labour of women into cultural and marketable products – milk into curds, whey, cheese, wool into thread: 'in cooking, churning, skimming, washing and spinning, women perform an act of enculturation, turning natural materials into clean, orderly, useful objects'.

Very often, houses will have inscribed above the door a date, accompanied not as one might expect by the name or initials of the male head of household, but by the paired initials of the married couple. It has been suggested that the inscription of this pairing is often done when women bring significant property to a marriage, and/or retain rights (Laing 2005); the pairing of the initials is a material rendering of this coming-together.

If the lives of men were dominated by the values of husbandry, those of married women were dominated by the risks of childbirth and child mortality. Childbirth was a central moment in a woman's life, and it was surrounded by processes and rituals that inverted the normal order of the house and connected the house, the woman's body, and the Church (Fissell 2004, 14–16). Childbirth was also perceived to be an exceptionally dangerous moment. One in twenty women died in childbirth, and the fear among women of death, illness or other mishap was very great (Mendelson and Crawford 1998, 352–3). Traditionally, only women attended childbirth, which was supervised by a woman midwife; men were explicitly excluded from the room in which this took place for a period of weeks. Transgressions of this exclusion were treated so seriously as to end up as criminal proceedings in court (Cressy 2000, 92–115). A warm, dark room was recommended, as womb-like as possible; part of the move towards ceiled rooms with fireplaces was the immediate result of better provision for birthing mothers.

Women expressed their control and domain over the house in various ways. One particularly intriguing folk custom recorded from the north of England was the daily habit of using sand to clean the flagged stone floor of the threshold. The housewife spread the sand in a variety of complex and distinctive patterns. Often, the sand would be scattered in the morning, and not swept out till the end of the afternoon; the preservation of the patterns, then, and its link to the integrity of the household and of the wife, was made visible to the world (Brears 1988, Figure 7.6).

If the lives of women and men diverged, so too did the lives of their children. Social and cultural historians have engaged in a complex debate about the nature of childcare and parent/child relations in pre-industrial England. Philippe Aries famously argued that there was little concept of childhood as distinct from adulthood, while Lawrence Stone suggested there was a lack of affection between parents and children, in part induced by the high rate of child mortality characteristic of pre-industrial societies (Aries 1962; Stone 1977): This groundbreaking work, as so often with documentary history, tended to extrapolate from the relatively well-documented contexts of the elite and the towns. Subsequently, a generation of historians have argued for a much more diverse picture. Particularly at social levels below that of the elite, there may well have been a great deal of affection (Pollock 1983, 268). Children had their own distinct culture, seen, for example, in archaeological evidence for children's toys (Coss 1995). The revision of Aries' views is certainly well warranted, but it should be noted that however much affection there was for children, this did not stop them being sent out to service at adolescence. I suggest that this experience

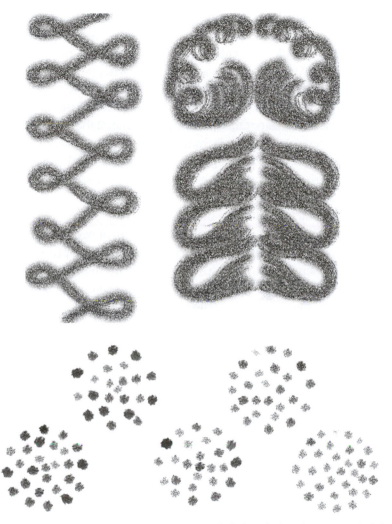

Figure 7.6 Sand patterns from the Yorkshire Dales. Folklife scholars have recorded the traditional practice of strewing sand in freehand patterns along passageways and on doorsteps, as an aid to cleaning. It was a housewife's matter of pride not to disturb the patterns before six in the evening. (Based on Brears, P.C.D., *North Country Folk Art* (John Donald Publishers, 1989).)

of moving to another household at such an age was a central part of the material experience of growing up and of learning how the culture of the house worked.

Threats to the House

The house was idealised, in contemporary writing, as a centre of hospitality: it was a matter of household honour that visitors should be welcomed and given food and drink before being asked their business. They would often be assigned a special chair to indicate their welcome status (for example, Hancock 2005 records this provision in Cumbria). However, there was always a tension between the house as part of a social network – providing hospitality and good neighbourliness – on the one hand, and its independence and self-sufficiency – as a building-block of the Commonwealth – on the other.

This tension was expressed in a number of ways, one of these being fears and anxieties about external threats. One such threat was that of the witch. Written records of early modern accusations of witchcraft, of course, reflect the anxieties and fears of the accusers, and those shadowy figures in the background directing the accusers: witchcraft accusations, then, are a revealing source not necessarily of 'what really happened' but rather of attitudes of the time. The records of these attitudes constantly refer to the way the witch attacked the boundaries and the internal order of the house.

Those accused of witchcraft were usually, though not always, women. Frequently, witches were identified in the popular consciousness as living outside the household order, as single women or widows. Accusations of witchcraft often followed incidents in which such women had come up to the door and made demands on a house of hospitality or charity, had been refused, and had muttered an oath or a curse in response. Both Keith Thomas (1971) and Alan Macfarlane (1970) linked the alleged behaviour of these women to the tensions surrounding growing differentiation between socially middling households and their poorer neighbours. The behaviour of these women was often interpreted as being demanding and aggressive rather than compliant, and was perceived as transgressing the rules of orderly households, particularly of the forms of behaviour that men held to be appropriate to a woman.

Since Thomas and Macfarlane's work, feminist scholars have established that there was much more to witchcraft than the fears of socially middling households. Beliefs in witchcraft reflected deeper anxieties about the roles of women and men within the household. Witches were depicted in records of accusations and popular pamphlets as exemplars of bad mothers, suckling their familiars rather than children, and shedding blood rather than milk (Fissell 2004, 83–4). They attacked through causing harm to women's activities and property, and could be counter-attacked in turn through those activities. In other contexts, witches could be helpful and enabling rather than being threats; they represented one form of women's traditional knowledge (Larner 1981; Purkiss 1996 and Purkiss 2006, 373–88).

Witches, it was believed, attacked the house directly; their behaviour was presented in the court depositions of their accusers as a ritualised inversion of the norm. Witches and their familiars often penetrated by flying down the chimney-stack rather than coming through the door. In this way, they attacked the hearth, the very soul of the house (Figure 3.4). Witches were also believed to perform their work by leaving items hidden in or around the house, for example, in the bedstraw.

Evidence for precautions against witchcraft are often found in vernacular houses. Precautions often centre on the hearth and stack, and may well represent for socially middling households, in particular for the housewives who were responsible for the maintaining the house, an attempt to 'seal up' the boundaries of the house. In north Yorkshire and Cleveland, and more widely, 'witch-posts' and hex signs are found (Harrison and Hutton 1984, 189; Nattrass 1956). In many houses, particularly in East Anglia, 'witch bottles' have been found buried under, or alongside, the hearth area (Merrifield 1987, 163–75). These are sixteenth- and seventeenth-century stoneware bottles, originally manufactured in the Rhine area and imported as drinking vessels and containers. Inside the bottle, nails, pins and pieces of cloth have been found.

Folklorists have recorded accounts of the use of these witch bottles, which depend on the belief that in order to attack members of the house the witch formed a magical link between the body of the witch and the body of the victim, a link which could be used in the other direction. Urine or hair from the supposed bewitched was placed in the bottle, together with nails or pins, and the bottle placed on the hearth: as the heat agitated the pins, the witch was attacked and tried to struggle free – the bottle had to be held in place. It is not clear at what point these bottles were buried under the hearth.

More generally, in recent years scholars have come to recognise a whole series of ritual and apotropaic practices in traditional buildings. Apotropaic marks can be found inscribed in the fabric of the house, and deposits of different kinds inserted into the walls and roof, either during the building process or subsequently. The 'daisy-wheel' or 'petal' patterns often found on the lintel of the hearth have been held to be explications of Vitruvian geometry to apprentices, but are equally likely to be 'ritual', a visible sign to observers that the house was protected against outside forces (Easton 1999). Mummified cats may have been trapped by accident, or in some cases may have been attempts to scare away vermin. In many cases, however, they were clearly intended as ritual precautions, for example, where they are also found with the mummified body of a rat. Other objects, particularly used garments and shoes, were buried in recesses in and around the stack, or in the body of the walls close to doors and windows; again, the concern seems to be to protect the margins of the house from magical attack, particularly in so sensitive and vulnerable a place as the hearth, or other entry and exit points. The concealed garments were usually heavily worn, and so highly personal to the wearer. In some cases, shoes have been cut or slashed in such a way as to suggest the ritual 'killing' of an object before deposition. Shoes are objects that would have had particularly personal associations. Magical curses and charms were also concealed in walls and cupboards (Figure 7.7; Eastop 2001; Merrifield 1987, 129–49).

Why were the margins of the house treated in this way? One possible explanation is beginning to emerge in the course of this book as the argument unfolds. From the later Middle Ages onwards, there was a tension between the house as a self-sufficient unit, and the cultural, social and increasingly economic and political ties that bound the house to its neighbours and to the wider world. Houses were little commonwealths, but they were also subject to the push and pull of wider market

Figure 7.7 A child's shoe, found within a house in Hursely, Hampshire, and catalogued as part of the Deliberately Concealed Garments Project (www.concealedgarments.org). (By kind permission of the Textile Conservation Centre, University of Southampton).

forces. Houses were always part of a wider mesh of relations that went beyond the threshold and the locality, but they were increasingly so over the centuries as markets and networks of consumption continued to develop. Precautionary and apotropaic treatment of the margins of the house worked through this tension between the house and the wider world. The attempt was made to seal up the boundaries of the house. Ultimately, however, the tension between house and wider world could only be resolved by the emergence of ideas and practices of domesticity in the eighteenth century, as we shall see in the following chapter.

Conclusion: Houses and Humans

In previous chapters, I sketched out the building of the house, its context, and how it changed through time; in this chapter, I wanted to populate the house, to show how its occupants experienced its spaces and textures, and to explore some of the cultural framework they used when they did so. I have tried to paint a general portrait of the early modern house and household in the English countryside. I wanted to complement dry descriptions of tie-beams and rates of rebuilding in previous chapters with accounts of the human lives within the building.

Scholars of vernacular architecture have been very good at describing the processes involved in *building* structures, but less successful at describing the processes of *dwelling* in them. This may be in part due to the nature of the evidence: building is an economic transaction, which often leaves convenient documents in its wake such as building contracts and accounts, and we have the physical fabric of the house as testament to how it was constructed and then modified or rebuilt on successive occasions. The process of dwelling in the house, on the other hand, leaves more fragmented and passing traces, though they do exist – patterns of wear on a stone floor, precautions against witchcraft around the hearth, the texture of walls, ceilings and roofs. There may also be an unconscious gender bias in the writings of scholars: building is largely perceived to be the action of men, and therefore receives disproportionate attention, while dwelling in the early modern house, as we have seen, was conceived of as a 'woman's role', and the activities involved in it (cooking, cleaning, childcare) are implicitly treated as trivial, unimportant, a matter of common sense, or somehow peripheral or marginal to the great events of history.

Dwelling in a house, however, is a profoundly important activity: it teaches us, in childhood and beyond, how to be human, how to 'get on' in the social world. Men and women learnt how to behave, how to understand themselves, how the social world worked, from observing and participating in the everyday activities around the home. Far from being trivial or unimportant, these everyday patterns and rhythms were the very bedrock and foundation of social life. They defined who people were. Cooking and eating a meal is arguably a much more profound and meaningful way of understanding the world than the better-documented 'surface froth' of history, of kings and princes and men arguing in Parliament and Star Chamber.

In the process of drawing this picture, I have probably overemphasised national uniformity at the expense of variation, both between regions and between individual households. In the eighteenth century, variation between regions was lessened. By 1800, many houses were built to a national and even international pattern and variations both between individual houses and between regions were profoundly transformed. The processes by which this happened have been termed 'Georgianisation', a process we will examine in the following chapter.

8

The Georgian Order

One of the most common, and iconic, sights in the English countryside today is that of the Georgian house. Ordered, symmetrical and refined, with sash windows arranged in a regular pattern or rhythm, often standing a little apart from the rest of the village, the Georgian house is habitually seen as the epitome of the triumph of a certain kind of civility, the archetypal expression of social order and a symbol of the English landscape (Figure 8.1).

It may seem surprising to include a discussion of Georgian building in a book on vernacular architecture. For many, the arrival of Georgian houses represents the end of the vernacular tradition. At first sight, Georgian is anything but vernacular:

Figure 8.1 The Court, Beer Hackett, Dorset, of mid-eighteenth century date. The house was extended to the right in the early nineteenth century. (Photo author's own).

it is an overtly national as well as international style, named after the reigns of the four King Georges, 1714–1830. As such, the appearance of Georgian houses might be taken as marking the moment at which regional styles rooted in the countryside ended and a national style springing from the metropolis and spreading outwards through provincial centres took over.

Such a view is at best an oversimplification. I will explore below how the arrival of Georgian did not necessarily mark the end of 'vernacular', however 'vernacular' is defined. Nevertheless, even were it to be true, it would still be necessary to consider and understand 'Georgian' architecture. If the student of vernacular architecture wants to understand the traditions that determined the building of ordinary houses before the eighteenth century, it is necessary to understand how and why those traditions came to an end, or at least were transformed or adapted. That ending, or at least transformation, is bound up with the 'rise of Georgian'. My argument is that explanations of the 'end of vernacular' and the rise of Georgian fit like lock and key, one implying the other.

The transition to Georgian architecture is also bound up with a profound set of social and cultural changes, as an initial example will illustrate.

Temple Balsall

One of thousands of early Georgian houses is Temple House, Temple Balsall, in Warwickshire (Figure 8.2; Gooder 1984, 153). Temple House deploys many of the elements of Georgian style and arrangement. Built of red brick and with a tiled roof, it has a symmetrical front and a plan two rooms deep; chimney stacks are placed at the rear. The façade has narrow sash windows with glazing bars and keystones, while the porch has Classical details of Ionic pilaster columns, an inset pediment and ball finials.

Temple House, built in the 1730s, was the residence of the Evetts family, who moved into the building from the Old Hall, where they had local standing as yeoman farmers and bailiffs since 1660. The elder Evetts, Thomas, may well have stayed in the Old Hall when his son Barlow moved into Temple House. The Old Hall represented everything the new house was trying to get away from. It was a traditional house of vernacular design, one room deep, dominated by a central hall and with an irregular plan of hall range and cross-wing, now encased in nineteenth-century brick (Figure 8.3).

But the Evetts' move was much more than a switch from an unfashionable to fashionable residence: it was a shift in the pattern and style of life of the whole household. This shift was marked not just in the different forms of the two houses, but in how the Evetts chose to prepare and consume food, drink and tobacco, as represented by the pottery and glassware they used. Either at the point of the move from one house to another or possibly upon Thomas' death a few years later, great stacks of dishes, plates and bowls, as well as beer mugs, glasses and wine bottles,

Figure 8.2 Temple Balsall, Temple House, newly built when Barlow Evetts took the lease of it in 1741. (Photo author's own).

Figure 8.3 Temple Balsall, Old Hall. Now encased in nineteenth-century brick, this was a medieval house, centre of a manor owned first by the Knights Templar and then by the Knights Hospitaller until the Dissolution. The Evetts lived here from 1660. (Photo author's own).

cups and pipkins, were carried out of the old house and thrown into a disused cellar. This great mass of rejected material, much of which was still unbroken, was excavated by archaeologists two centuries later (Gooder 1984). It bears testament to a way of life sketched out in the last chapter, and which was now being rejected. Cups and pipkins had been warmed by pushing them up against the old hall or kitchen fire, blackening the vessels with soot; brightly coloured slipware plates had been pierced for hanging on the wall as ornaments. Fragments of clay tobacco pipes were everywhere.

What is striking about this collection is what was *not* found by the archaeologists. By the middle of the eighteenth century one would expect to find new wares in such an assemblage: English and Chinese porcelain, white stoneware. These new pottery forms, often a portion of standardised, matched and mould-made sets, were part of a new structure of eating and living. Either these wares did not grace the cupboards and tables of the traditional, dark interiors of the Old House, or, more likely, these new wares had not been thrown away but rather taken across to the new Temple House, where the older material would have looked out of place in the lighter, more refined drawing and dining rooms.

The members of the older Thomas Evetts' household prepared their food over the old hearth, and ate off irregular and often brightly coloured plates and bowls. He and his family and servants enjoyed a varied diet as the bones from the excavations indicate. His son Barlow lived in a more ordered, segregated and symmetrical house, and ate off white plates that were matched and mould-made. The noise, clatter and bustle of food preparation and other household activities was, for the son Barlow's family, relegated to the back of the house, away from the main reception rooms.

This movement from old to new houses at Temple Balsall was a critical point of change in several senses. The older Thomas was known as a socially middling farmer, a yeoman of good credit and standing in the local community. His sons, however, were called gentlemen in local records. So the move to the new property was not simply a sideways shift; it could also be seen as a social move upwards, a moment of arrival into the gentry class (Gooder 1984, 163).

What the archaeology and architecture of these two houses at Temple Balsall shows us is that, when people chose to rebuild their houses to a Georgian pattern, they did so with a complex set of intentions and motivations – it was much more than a mindless urge to be fashionable. It was, in many cases, an implicit decision to live life differently, from ways of cooking and eating through the arrangement of domestic space to the location of the house in the landscape.

What happened at Temple Balsall was representative of a quite fundamental shift in the architecture and culture of ordinary people across England and beyond. In 1670, a socially middling farmer may well have built a house in regional style, one room deep, the main rooms organised from one side to another, with a carefully composed but asymmetrical exterior, and with an internal plan in which the hall, though no longer open to the roof, remained of central importance. By 1800 a socially middling farmer would have built a neat compact box, two rooms deep, of symmetrical and ordered appearance. How his family and household lived in the building is another matter.

What Temple Balsall shows us is that this pivotal change in the nature and appearance of the house accompanied a pivotal change in the nature of the everyday life and social relations that took place within and around it. There is every indication that the move to the new house was a wholesale change in the pattern and style of life of the family, not simply a new fashion. The arrival of Georgian buildings was much more than just another architectural style. If we want to understand Georgian architecture, we have to understand the Georgian order as a whole.

Georgian Architecture

At first sight, Georgian houses are easily recognised. They are characterised by order, symmetry and standardisation. In its typical form, a rural Georgian house, of large or middling size, is symmetrical, the windows and other external features organised around a central front door. Further, in the ideal model, windows and doors are arranged in a deliberate rhythm – so, with the door placed centrally, windows and doors are arranged left to right in a 2,3,2, a 3,4,3 or similar arrangement. There is, then, a mathematical or even musical pattern and rhythm to a Georgian façade, and there is an apparent visual reference in the front elevation to a system of mathematical proportions and order. Georgian facades are at least two storeys high, often more; and the roof is often less visible than that of comparable earlier houses, being either less steeply pitched, partially hidden behind a parapet, or both (Summerson 1945; Arnold 1998).

Internally, the Georgian house is often, though not always, two rooms deep. The 'hall' is now an entrance lobby and central corridor giving access to front and back, and contains a stairway leading to the upper storeys. Leading off the hall is a series of rooms, symmetrically disposed. Georgian houses have rooms that are carefully differentiated from one another by status and function, and that express a sharp division between front and back space, as well as 'upstairs, downstairs', with the kitchen and servants' spaces being moved to the basement as well as to the rear. These principles can seen across England in houses from the early- and mid-eighteenth century onwards, providing an apparent national uniformity in place of previous regional traditions. Indeed, these principles are international in nature – houses of this kind are found in different contexts around the rim of the northern Atlantic hemisphere. One of the striking things to be noted about Georgian building is its standardisation of both the overall scheme and particular elements despite a geographical distance often spanning thousands of miles. Sash windows, for example, were adopted as part of the scheme, were factory-produced, and came in a number of standard sizes. Walking down the street, an eighteenth-century observer, or a modern scholar, could recognise a 'Georgian house' from Middlesex to Maryland, from Kingston-upon-Thames to Kingston, Jamaica.

Origins of the Georgian Order

Architectural historians often tell a very detailed, but at its heart simple and progressive, story of the origins of Georgian. They see its origins centuries back in the
Renaissance 'rediscovery' of Classical architecture, and in the subsequent introduction
of Classical design into the buildings of the upper classes in England from 1500
onwards that were discussed in Chapter 6. Classical details were used in a range of
English buildings before 1600; great houses often sported columns and decorative
motifs of Classical inspiration, even if the structure and form of the house remained
of traditional or medieval form. Considerable Classical 'influence', extending from
decoration into principles of layout and design, can be seen in buildings such
as Longleat House and the great Elizabethan prodigy houses (Girouard 1983).
However, the first fully Classical buildings using the same principles as Italian
Renaissance buildings were not constructed until the time of Inigo Jones in the
earlier seventeenth century.

Jones, like many before him, had travelled in Italy, but unlike others was able
to acquire a deep understanding of the principles of Classical design. In other
words, he understood that what he was looking at was not just a series of novel
structural and decorative features but that they had deeper principles as a coherent
and ordered aesthetic system. This system integrated plan and circulation pattern
in a symmetrical and ordered layout. In particular, Jones encountered and made
detailed notes on the villas built by the sixteenth-century Italian architect Andrea
Palladio in the drained marshlands of the Veneto around Venice (Cosgrove 1983).
These great country houses referred directly to Classical models – most obviously,
they termed themselves 'villas' after the Roman pattern – and organised their facades
and elevations according to mathematical and geometrical principles. Jones used
these principles to design a series of 'polite' and metropolitan buildings now considered to be masterpieces – Whitehall Banqueting House, the Queen's House at
Greenwich and St Paul's Church in the middle of a planned Renaissance piazza
at Covent Garden (Summerson 1945, 10–19).

Jones' work, however, got a mixed reception. It was not widely imitated; in part,
this was because the style was perceived to be foreign and carrying connotations
of Catholicism and of absolute monarchy. Outside London in the provincial centres
and countryside, builders did not adopt Jones' Classical designs wholesale. The
rural houses of the gentry in the seventeenth century used elements of Classical
design, but not in the systematic and complete manner of Palladio or Jones (Cooper
1999).

Palladianism, as it was later called, reappeared in the first decades of the eighteenth
century at Wilton House, Burlington House and in a number of other urban and
elite contexts (Bold 1988). But it was a century later that Palladian 'caught on'
outside the elite and metropolitan circle. In 1732, just a few years before Temple

House was built, the satirical poet Pope complained to Lord Burlington that the publication of his designs would:

> . . . fill half the land with Imitating Fools,
> Who random Drawings from your Sheets shall take,
> And of one Beauty many Blunders make;
> Load some vain Church with old Theatric State;
> Turn Arcs of Triumph to a Garden-gate;
> Reverse your Ornaments, and hang them all
> On some patch'd Doghole ek'd with Ends of Wall,
> Then clap four slices of Pilaster on't,
> And lac'd with bits of Rustic, 'tis a Front . . .
> Conscious they act a true Palladian part,
> And if they starve, they starve by Rules of Art.
>   (Alexander Pope, 'Epistle to Lord Burlington')

Georgian architecture was, then, a distillation of the principles of Palladian design into a set of simple rules for the building of houses for a variety of social classes, socially middling as well as elite. In the provincial towns of England, most obviously and famously at the spa resort of Bath but also in smaller county towns like Warwick, the civic authorities laid down rules for the design and building of the facades of houses, to ensure a uniform and regular front (the rears of the properties at the famous Royal Crescent and Circles at Bath were more irregular, as can still be seen today: Borsay 1989 and Borsay 2000).

After its development in London and provincial cities, according to traditional scholars, Georgian building 'filtered down' the social scale, and was diffused from urban to rural contexts. Socially middling tradesmen and farmers, many of them aspiring to become members of the gentry classes, saw Georgian as a marker of urbane and elite society. They built houses that reflected Palladian principles, though not always 'correctly' (Figure 8.4). Eighteenth-century texts such as Pope's are full of comments on what the elite saw as ham-fisted attempts at social emulation by their social inferiors. Nicholas Cooper (2002) has argued powerfully that part of the reason for the success of Georgian is that elements of Classical architecture became disengaged from the question of status. In the earlier seventeenth century, Classical elements would be added to houses as a mark of gentility, or, conversely, yeoman identity would be marked by their absence, for example, amongst the Lancashire gentry and yeoman classes (Pearson 1985, 56) or in the Cotswolds (Hall 1982). However in the later seventeenth century decorative display declined. Less ostentatious heraldry and fewer inscriptions were placed on the front of buildings. Cooper suggests that by the eighteenth century this disassociation of status and display meant that socially middling farmers were free to adopt elements of the new Palladian style: 'a taste for plain facades in which status display was less favoured fostered a common architecture across the social scale' (Cooper 2002, 31).

Figure 8.4 Reddish Manor, Broad Chalke, Wiltshire, built for Jeremiah Clay, a clothier, in the early eighteenth century. In typical fashion, Pevsner describes this house as 'not at all correct or polite', though he concedes that it is 'very lively' (Pevsner and Cherry 1975, 145). The wing was added in the later eighteenth century. (Photo author's own).

The story told by architectural historians is compelling and well-documented, but it is only part of the story. Many of the elements of what came to be known as the Georgian plan – houses two rooms deep (for example, Figure 8.5), the external symmetry of the facade, increased use of the upper floor – were already present or were developing at more humble social levels in the countryside as well as the towns before the advent of Lord Burlington and his circle of civilised friends. Ordinary houses displaying symmetry or Classical features often appear to the scholar trained in polite architecture, encouraged by the evidence of texts such as Pope's and taking at face value Pope's socially exclusive and elitist views, as a vulgar attempt to 'imitate'. However, they may actually have been the result of a very different process. These may have been houses that were the expression of an active choice of people making their own history, a choice to build in a much older vernacular tradition and to adapt that tradition creatively in new ways.

The active appropriation of material forms from other social groups and contexts is well known from other situations, for example, where colonised peoples have selectively adopted elements of the colonisers' architecture. Dierdre Brown (2000),

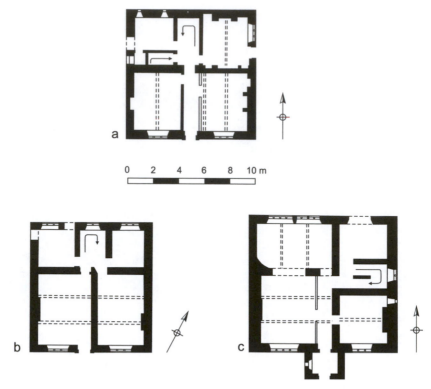

Figure 8.5 Three ground-floor plans of double-pile houses from the Lancashire Pennines. (a) Edgend House, Nelson, built c.1753 with a slightly lower and less deep rear range; (b) Nabs House, Roughlee Booth, 1756, with an entry directly on to a central room; (c) Parson Lee Farm, Wycoller, mid-eighteenth century, with a storeyed porch. (Based on Pearson, S., *Rural Houses of the Lancashire Pennines* (London: HMSO, 1985).)

for example, discusses how after the colonisation of New Zealand by the British the Maori 'appropriated Gothic timber technology, large-scale assembly spaces, cruciform plans, and trefoil designs to enhance their meeting houses and churches . . . Instead of repeating techniques and designs without question, Maori building designers developed new concepts from Gothic architecture to meet the changing needs of their tribal and pan-tribal societies' (Brown 2000, 267). When different social groups engage with wider networks of architectural and material ideas, there is a complex process of cultural traffic at work, and to label this social emulation is always at best an oversimplification. As we have seen at Temple Balsall, Georgian architecture came as part of a package. It was not simply or only a fashionable architectural style, but a much more profound shift in social attitudes and patterns of life than just a 'mere' aesthetic preference, a changing architectural 'fashion'.

Traditional accounts help us to understand the specific origins of a range of Georgian features such as Classical ornament and sash windows. To give one small example, Roberts notes how, when the Bishop of Winchester built a new hipped roof in the Classical style at Wolvesey Palace, local farmers were quick to adopt the new form in preference to the older regional tradition of half-hipped roofs (Roberts 2003). However, they are less successful in accounting for the changing relationship between polite and vernacular forms – in other words, why so many of the middling sort of people chose to abandon the solid sufficiency of their comfortable, traditional ways of living and opt in to the trappings of politeness, civility and refinement after 1700.

The Double-Pile Plan

In the later seventeenth and early eighteenth centuries, vernacular building was changing in a number of related directions. First, more houses were adopting a plan that was two rooms deep, often termed 'double-pile' (Figure 8.5). Traditionally, as we have seen, vernacular houses were only one room deep. There were a number of reasons for this. In the first place, we saw in Chapter 2 how the craft tradition rested at a very deep level on the notion of the house being composed as a series of bays in a row (Figure 2.3). These bays were structural; though they were most apparent in timber-framed buildings, bays in buildings in other materials can still be discerned at the upper level of the timber roof structure. Though bays were primarily structural in nature, they habitually corresponded to room divisions within the house, between service, cross-passage or chimney bay, hall and parlour end.

As we have seen, the correspondence between structure and room division had strong social and cultural resonance. Tie-beams or cruck pairs could only stretch across a certain width of building. The one-room-deep plan meant that windows could be opened and let in light on the side of the house away from the wind, at a time when many windows were unglazed. But most fundamentally, the one-room-deep plan laid the house open to the outside world (see Figure 4.1 p. 67). An approaching visitor could in most cases readily locate the parlour and service ends of the building, and the central position of the hall between them. The layout of the house, and the layout of the household order that the house expressed, was displayed to the world.

By the early eighteenth century, the strong structural and conceptual binding-together of the house had been weakened. In many areas and regions, rooms were built or added to the rear of the house. These often took the form of 'outshuts' or one-storey-high annexes with a lean-to roof over them. Their purpose was generally that of service and/or kitchen areas of the house. In many cases the pitch of the roof was carried down, unaltered, from the main roof of the house; such features are evocatively termed 'catslide' roofs (Figure 8.6). Some outshuts can be dated as early as the sixteenth century, for example, at Great Funtley Farm, Wickham in Hampshire (Roberts 2003, 161), but they became far more common over time. By the end of the seventeenth century, in many cases, these rear outshuts formed a continuous wing or range. The inclusion of continuous outshuts made the whole house two rooms

Figure 8.6 Duck Street, Ebbesborne Wake, Wiltshire: a seventeenth-century house with later outshuts added to the rear and to each side. The thatched roof has been extended downwards over the outshuts. (Photo author's own).

deep, with the rear range often almost as deep as the front range. The change from one-room to two-room depth was not universal: quite grand houses with Georgian facades could nevertheless be only one room deep, as at West Billingham Farmhouse on the Isle of Wight, built in 1720 (Brinton 1987, 75–6), or The Bay Tree, Fylingdales, on the North York Moors (RCHME 1987, 57 and Figure 77).

The deepening of the house from one to two rooms presented structural problems. Tie-beams, which traditionally ran from front to back of a house one room deep, now needed to be of greater length. Increasing the length made the tie-beam more prone to sag, and made it more difficult to source timber of the required length. As a result, structural solutions were often adopted, with a central strut or post extending down from the apex of the roof to hold it up (Campbell 2000, 45). At the same time, a roof of any pitch presented other problems. A steeply-pitched roof spanning a two-room-deep house of any size would be impossibly tall. Thatch requires a relatively steep pitch if water is not to penetrate, so the replacement of thatched roofs with ceramic or stone slates was partly a concomitant of this process. Often two roofs were constructed over front and back ranges, with a potentially leaky channel between them.

The deepening of the house also meant that, as in previous centuries, the hall became less and less important as a central room. The hall disappeared from probate inventories: one in 1671 and five after 1703 in the Yetminster inventories (Machin 1978, 9). It also meant that the kitchen and service areas of the house, that is, those areas which formed the traditional focus of women's and domestic servants' activities, were often relegated to the rear. In the Lancashire Pennines, for example, 'the through-passage was abandoned and service rooms were brought into direct communication with the housebody, usually through being placed at the rear of the house' (Pearson 1985, 100). The single social axis was supplemented and made more complex, then, by the addition of a front/back axis. The distinction between 'front space' and 'back space' is one that has been made much of by modern sociologists, who have seen the front parlours of contemporary houses as sites of performance, while much of the 'real action' of the household goes on behind and below. This change in axis resonated with changing roles of women and men. Women's activities were now tucked away behind the house, leaving a civilised and refined 'front space' of parlour and hall, now less and less full of activity and bustle and more and more the comfortable setting of polite conversation.

It is no coincidence that the late seventeenth century saw a profound shift in how social commentators thought and wrote about women's roles in the house. We saw in the previous chapter how advice books and commentaries saw the worlds of women and men as separate, and took patriarchy for granted, but conceived the role of the 'housewife' to be an active one. By the end of the seventeenth century, a different set of ideas of womanhood, advocating that women should behave and be treated as passive objects, part of a more polite and refined notion of domesticity, was on the rise (Fletcher 1995; Mendelson and Crawford 1998, 428–30).

Within these newly created spaces, fireplaces became more numerous, but each fireplace was smaller, and the inglenook was lost. The steady replacement of wood with coal as a fuel meant that fireplaces could be smaller, and it also meant that the kitchen range became more specialised in its functions, replacing the common hearth of many earlier houses (Roberts 1981). The separation of kitchen activities from the rest of the house was also seen in the proliferation of separate chimney-stacks. The growing multiplicity of rooms, and the more complex relations between them, meant that the compilers of probate inventories went to extra lengths to specify the location and nature of rooms (for example, Machin 1978, 8).

If the axis of the house was extended backwards, it was also extended upwards. Traditionally, the master and wife's bedstead was in the parlour on the ground floor, as we saw in the previous chapter. By the early eighteenth century, however, the majority of inventories record this principal bedstead to have moved upstairs, to the chamber over the parlour. In other words, the modern conception of the bedroom as an upper storey room evolved over this period. Again, this change varied regionally: parlours at Yetminster still generally contained beds into the 1670s

(Machin 1978, 11). In East Sussex, most beds had been moved upstairs by the middle of the seventeenth century (Martin 2000, 26). There was a general move to a full suite of rooms at upper levels, and to different roof forms that facilitated the use of the roof space for human dwelling. Gambrel roofs, often misleadingly termed 'mansard' roofs after the French architect François Mansard (Johnson 1991), were of two pitches, creating a wagon-like effect that made the most of space at attic level. Floors and ceilings between rooms at different levels were constructed in new ways to lessen the passage of sound between them, both in terms of new methods of floor construction and with the addition of ceilings (Pilling 1987).

A more complex house, with rooms divided and differentiated in new ways, needed more elaborate communication between its different elements. As a result, staircases became more important in terms of function, and more elaborate and ostentatious in form (Platt 1994, 128–32). In many seventeenth-century houses, stairs were contained in rear annexes, but by the eighteenth century elaborate stairs with rails and turned balusters were constructed at the centre of many farmhouses. These were carpentered in a new and more delicate style, and formed objects of display in their own right.

The house also contained larger numbers of movable goods, as has been shown by the very detailed studies of probate inventories undertaken by Lorna Weatherill (1988) and Carole Shammas (1990). Changes are difficult to quantify given the biases and problems in probate inventories, and much of the literature on the eighteenth century 'consumer revolution' has tended to concentrate on urban rather than rural contexts. However, just as the houses of the Great Rebuilding were less sparsely furnished that their medieval counterparts, rural houses of the eighteenth century contained many more movable goods than they had a century-and-a-half earlier. These goods materialised the ideas and practices of new ways of living: domestic clocks, for example, proliferated during this period, bringing a new precision and discipline to the working day (Lucas 1995). Furniture and other movable goods were also less heavy, and more delicate and refined in appearance. The 'Windsor chair' is a classic eighteenth-century artefact, replacing the more massive chairs of previous generations.

I have described all these changes in rather impersonal terms: it bears repeating that for any individual vernacular house, such as the older house of the Evetts, such changes were individual actions, often linked to particular moments in the life cycle (the retirement of the father as at Temple Balsall; a decision to split a house in two to provide accommodation for a widowed mother). At West Wycombe in Buckinghamshire archaeologists excavated a house that showed successive rebuildings that were associated with finds that suggested a transition to a more 'polite' and genteel lifestyle. Waste from dismembered carcasses, joints of mutton, pork and beef were found, as well as bones of a cat and a chicken; there were also red earthenware pots, stoneware, clay pipes, and wine bottles. In late periods at the site, these finds were joined by Chinese porcelain (Lucas and Regan 2003).

A 'top-down' narrative of the Georgian Order, then, is only part of the story. We can, equally plausibly, tell a 'bottom-up' story, in which the main elements of the Georgian plan, and the underlying principles of order, symmetry and segregation, evolved internally from quite humble social levels. It may well be the case that many houses that were products of the desire of ordinary people to live in different ways have been misinterpreted as attempts at 'emulation'. Byers Green Hall, in County Durham, was steadily improved over the centuries and rebuilt to a two-room-deep plan, but Adrian Green has commented that 'the house remained the most substantial tenant farmer's residence in the township and differentiated the family from the rest of the community. There was no clear attempt to ape a higher social group, and this house has more parallels with Midland farm houses than with local gentry halls' (Green 1998, 40).

However, both top-down and bottom-up elements are only part of the picture. There were other factors at work which must be considered before the full story of the Georgian order can be told. Three particularly important factors can be isolated: first, developments in building materials and techniques, second, the dissemination of pattern-books, and third, economic, political and cultural centralisation.

Building Materials

In earlier chapters we explored how one of the key reasons for regional variations was the distribution of different kinds of building materials. This situation changed fundamentally with the eighteenth-century revolution in transport.

The construction of canals in the later eighteenth century, and subsequently railways in the nineteenth century, meant that building materials could now be transported for long distances without prohibitively high transport costs (Overton 1996, 142). This transport revolution changed the distribution pattern of building materials away from one where the ease of movement was governed by sea and (natural) water routes. Materials perceived as inferior rapidly disappeared: one example among many is the disappearance of chalk buildings in the Yorkshire Wolds during the nineteenth century (Hayfield and Wagner 1998). Harder chalk can often be used as a satisfactory building material (Figure 2.6 see p. 36), but rapidly declined in popularity in many areas as other materials became available.

At the same time, new building materials made different kinds of building style possible. In particular, the more widespread use of brick was particularly appropriate for elements of the Georgian style. Georgian architecture, with its pattern of flat sash windows, horizontals and verticals, is particularly suited to being built in brick. Many of Jones' associates in London built brick gentry houses with Classical features in the 'artisan mannerist' style in the seventeenth century (Cooper 1999, 174–80); Classically derived features such as pilasters could be readily translated into bricks patterns and arrangements, and bricks could also be used to construct the segmented arched heads of Georgian design.

In places like Norfolk, where timber-framing was partly replaced by brick in the eighteenth century, the popularity of Georgian may be in part due to this ease of adaptation to the new building material. According to documentary evidence, over a third of all new Norfolk buildings were built of brick by 1790, with the proportion increasing thereafter and timber-framing being virtually extinguished a century later (Lucas 1997, Figure 1). A 'brick threshold' was crossed in 1760s Norfolk; it is often wrongly believed that this transition took place at an earlier date.

If brick was replacing timber, tiles and slates were replacing thatch as a roof cover. Pantiles were imported from Holland into Norfolk from the late sixteenth century onwards. They were at first used on estates, for example, Holkham and Felbrigg, where they were used to replace earlier thatched roofs. By the end of the eighteenth century, over half the roofs of parsonage houses in Norfolk were tiled rather than thatched. Tiles required a larger initial outlay of cash than thatched roofs, but were resistant to fire (Lucas 1998). A thatched roof required regular maintenance by the local thatcher, but a tiled roof needed relatively infrequent repair. Tiles or stone slates could also be used for a lower pitch of roof; they were thus more suitable for some forms of Georgian building, where part of the Georgian aesthetic is to hide the roof behind a parapet.

Window glass also underwent a transformation in the eighteenth century (Tarlow 2007, 172). Traditional production of window glass was in the form of small lead lites, often called 'Newcastle glas' after one of the centres of production. Newcastle glass often had 'seeds' or tiny air bubbles and other blemishes. From the mid-sixteenth century onwards crown glass was produced: crown glass was generally preferred to Newcastle glass by the eighteenth century. Crown glass could produce larger panes, of up to 50 by 30 cm, and had relatively little distortion. Developments in window glass production not only increased the ability to look out from larger sash windows but also facilitated the development of consumerism. Potential customers could now 'window-shop', look at a range of wares and products through the development of glazed shop fronts.

It should not be forgotten that the eighteenth century also saw the introduction of other building materials, for example, clay lump. This is often thought of as an ancient building material: other forms of clay walling certainly were. However, clay lump, and the earlier 'clay bats' used to build dovecots, may well have first been used structurally in the 1790s in East Anglia, and became popular thereafter through their presence in early nineteenth-century builders' manuals (McCann 1997). These building materials could also be manipulated in new ways. The development of mechanised and industrial processes like the machine saw meant that timber and stone could be cut by machine rather than finished by hand, so that many elements that had previously been traditional and variable in design became standardised. Most obviously, factories mass-produced sash windows that were often then fitted into spaces that did not quite work.

Such processes changed the texture of the surfaces of the house. A classic beginner's dating tool in considering buildings is to look at the finished surface of stone and timber. Timber is often finished with an adze; even where it has been sawn, the marks of the hand-held saw, whether of the pit saw of some other form, are quite distinctive. The more regular marks of mechanised tools, particularly those used for cutting stone, give a different finish to a window or doorway. Mechanised tools also encouraged the dissolution of certain vernacular forms. For example, the stone mullions of windows in farmhouses were traditionally chamfered and hood-moulded (see Plate 11); these hand-finished details were abandoned by the nineteenth century, and windows of the traditional form often replaced by larger, standardised windows.

Other materials were no longer prohibitively expensive to use in building. For example, iron had only rarely been extensively used in the structure of rural vernacular houses, timber frames instead being held together by complex joints and wooden pegs. The Industrial Revolution enabled the widespread use of iron as a structural building material for the first time, most famously in the great canopies of St Pancras and other Victorian railway stations. But iron could be used in a more mundane manner for iron ties in brick buildings in East Anglia or for securing joints. As a result, the complexity and wooden pegging of timber jointing was needed less and less, and timbers were more and more nailed rather than pegged in place.

In houses lower down the social scale, a whole new system of timber framing evolved. Such smaller houses were often built entirely or predominantly of reused and 'waney' timber. Tie-beams were no longer framed in to the rest of the structure, but were supported on small lintels carried in turn by pairs of (reused) posts (Johnson 1993a, 152 and Plate 4b). Braces were long and straight, rather than curved, and they were no longer halved-in to vertical studs; instead, shorter studs were jammed in around them.

Smaller houses constructed using these techniques were not simply inferior or debased versions of a formerly proud craft tradition. They are often less aesthetically pleasing to our eye, and appear less solid; but the original frame may well have been completely plastered over (the exposure of a frame is sometimes the result of modern houseowners' urge for display rather than the original intention). In their own way, they represent a highly creative and imaginative use of building materials. And these buildings have endured to the present day, giving a life of at least two centuries. But eighteenth-century changes in timber-framing technique do represent a dissolution of the pre-industrial craft tradition and mark a critical change in the way houses were built. This was also a critical moment of change in woodworking and carpentry techniques, with the emergence of modern tools and a distinctive 'British style' (Gaynor 2005).

Pattern-Books

If the Georgian Order was in part the result of new building materials, it was also in part about the rise of pattern-books. Pattern-books, and more broadly books of advice to craftsmen, developed out of Classical models, and the subsequent reprinting of Classical and Renaissance texts. The most famous of these are the works of Vitruvius and Palladio. Later pattern-books consisted not simply of advice to builders and other trades: books such as William Halfpenny's *Rural Architecture in the Gothic Taste* (1752) also contained patterns of architecture for builders to work from in the form of visual illustrations. Much of the early Renaissance details and decoration of great houses came from pattern-books: thus, for example, the central arch of the loggia at Kirby Hall is flanked by pilasters 'adorned with compositions of arabesque, candelabra and *putti* which are taken from . . . John Shute's *The First and Chief Groundes of Architecture*, of 1563; this is a particularly good example of the untutored methods of the Kirby mason, for the design comes not from any of the architectural plates in the book but from the title page' (Chettle and Leach 1984). One of the earliest and most important was Joseph Moxon's *Mechanick Exercises or the Doctrine of Handy-Works Applied To the Arts of Smithing Joinery Carpentry Turning Bricklaying* of 1681.

Pattern-books have a place in the story that was told in Chapter 6, where we saw that as a result of the rise in the conception of the 'architect' associated with the Renaissance, the work of the traditional craftsman was subordinated and ultimately became an object of elite contemplation. The literate culture of the pattern-book put in place a hierarchy of values in which the (elite) architect was above the builder, and architecture itself above 'mere building'.

However, pattern-books also worked at a more basic level than this. They changed the relationship between builder and client, and the balance of power between them. A client who wanted a house of a particular form might find it difficult to specify such from a builder, particularly if that form was out of the ordinary or outside what the traditional builder considered to be his usual repertoire. If, however, the client was in possession of, or had access to, a pattern-book, the balance of power was shifted – one could turn to a given page and say: 'I want one like that . . .'.

It is for these reasons that pattern-books and other forms of architectural advice cannot be taken at face value as objective evidence for changes in patterns of building in the seventeenth and eighteenth centuries. They represent important information on building practices in the pre-industrial period, but they are also artefacts of the shift towards national architectural models and the erosion of the vernacular tradition. A writer giving advice on how the house should be laid out was also giving advice on the cultural prioritisation of certain forms of knowledge over others, for example, between the printed word and the unspoken craft tradition. Such a writer was also therefore commenting implicitly or explicitly on the relationship between the gentry classes and the rest of the community. Therefore, the advice and classifications found in pattern-books should not be read uncritically. To take an extreme and obvious example, Sir Roger North, writing in the late seventeenth century, saw brickmakers as 'a bad, and thievish sort of men' (Colvin and Newman 1981, 36); such a statement tells us more about Roger North, and about the way he tried to draw a social distinction between architecture and crafts, than it provides neutral information about the moral qualities of brickmakers. Batty Langley's *Ancient Architecture Restored* (1742) was in turn more of an advertisement for Langley's views on Gothic architecture.

Pattern-books were not simple to-do manuals. The intellectual genealogy of the pattern-book can be traced back to the essayist Francis Bacon's call at the start of the seventeenth century to document the crafts as part of his wider project of empirical knowledge. The pattern-book became part of an ideological project to bring system and order to traditional knowledge, to create a new discourse. This discursive project ultimately imposed the same rules of order and segregation on bodies of craft knowledge that the Georgian façade and plan sought to impose on the experience of dwelling in a house. For example, Randle Holme's manuscripts (published in Alcock and Cox 2000) contain huge amounts of valuable information on living and working in seventeenth-century England. But their background intention was part of a project to document things, and the manuscripts were drawn up in an elite and urban context.

The market for, and dissemination of, pattern-books at socially middling levels depended on levels of literacy, and the ability to purchase numbers of books. By the early eighteenth century, the vast majority of the middling sort could read and write. Further, an increasing number of pattern-books turn up in inventories, indicating both a popular interest in the genre and also the ability to buy them. Where earlier households had a single Bible at most, a range and variety of books were in circulation below the levels of the elite by this period.

Centralisation

Not only could the client point to a model from a pattern-book; he or she could also draw on a much wider range of cultural and geographical experience. Eighteenth-century England was far more centralised than it had been two centuries earlier, in economic, political and cultural terms. This centralisation had a profound impact on the way architectural ideas could travel, and on the clients' view of the world.

In the first place, the traditional builder was no longer in a position of relative monopoly. If having been handed a pattern-book and asked to build in a certain way, the builder refused or was recalcitrant, the client could go to a competitor with much greater ease. Builders advertised with increasing regularity in metropolitan and provincial newspapers. Virtually every century between the fifteenth and the nineteenth has been classified by historians as 'the rise of the market', but what the rise of the market meant in this period was that alternatives beyond the local, traditional builder opened up for the client.

The client, in turn, was more likely to have an experience of the world beyond that of the local community. The isolated, self-contained rural village has always been a myth: historians have shown how rural communities have always been tied in to a range of wider networks (Dyer 2006b). However, before the seventeenth century, most of the middling sort, particularly women, travelled far from their locality only on rare occasions. Servants in husbandry would be taken on by households in a fifty-kilometre or so radius.

By 1750, the localism of previous centuries had been transformed. London had grown exponentially. Charles II famously declared that soon London would engulf all England. As a result, the masses of London had to be fed, and this need tied the farmers of the Home Counties around London more and more closely in to market demands. The economic 'pull' of London had an indirect effect on other, regional centres. For example, London's growing consumption of coal for fuel was met by shipping the coal from north-east England via the port of Newcastle down the eastern coast. As a partial result of this trade, Newcastle grew and in its turn needed to be fed by the farmers of Durham and Northumberland, who in turn were building themselves more substantial houses on the proceeds (Hodgson 1979).

The growing integration of markets meant that farmers in different regions of England could become more specialised, rather than produce a mix of arable and dairy products. In terms of lifestyle, then, a Cumbrian or Northumbrian farmer had more in common culturally, politically and socially with his Kentish counterpart in 1800 than had been the case in 1400, even though in terms of his farming practices, regional diversification meant the opposite. This meant that across much of the social scale there was a new national uniformity of culture, for example, in building, as a logical complement to growing regional diversity in farming practices.

It was also easier and less time-consuming to travel from the ends of the country to its centre. In 1663 the first Turnpike Act was applied to a section of the Great North Road; by 1750, thirteen main routes to and from London were almost complete, including the Great North Road, London-Derby-Manchester, London-Cirencester-Gloucester-Hereford, London-Bath and Bristol, and London-Dover. A frequent source of information of local topography are travellers' accounts, for example, Celia Fiennes and Daniel Defoe, but what is really interesting about these accounts is not so much what they tell us about particular localities as about the fact that, by the early eighteenth century, a growing number of individuals could make such long trips around the country with relative ease. In the process, these travellers carefully noted down local customs, habits and manners of building, and their careful descriptive notes of the different ways of life of different provinces are, somewhat ironically, harbingers of the latter's imminent dissolution.

With economic centralisation came a more general political and cultural awareness of what was going on in the capital. We saw how, with the Reformation, the London-centred state impinged itself on people's lives as never before. The political upheavals of the English Revolution had created a culture of political pamphlets that led, in the later seventeenth century, to the creation of newspapers. Newspapers and magazines gave out information and advice, not just on current affairs, but on matters of taste, and contained advertisements. By the eighteenth century, political and cultural awareness had accelerated and made possible a new consciousness of national identity (Colley 1992).

By 1750 the socially middling owner of a house in the regions was therefore embedded in a set of networks that tied the house to the wider world, and to a national culture, in a way that would have been scarcely imaginable two or three centuries earlier. It was in these circumstances that the material and cultural pattern of the Georgian Order that eliminated or downplayed regional differences, and asserted a national identity over a local specificity, became possible. There was also uniformity across classes of building: schoolhouses took on the appearance of Georgian houses, for example, Love's Charity, Froxfield, Hampshire; a small charity school built in 1733 with both the external appearance and internal arrangements of a house (Roberts 2006).

Order, Symmetry and Segregation

So far, we have explored why it was possible for a single, national style to take over, and for a national set of architectural ideas to take precedence over local and regional traditions. However, the question remains: why did that single, national style take the specific form that it did? Why were houses moving towards this specific pattern of order, symmetry and segregation, whether as a result of top-down or bottom-up influences?

We have seen at Temple Balsall that Georgian principles extended beyond the house to other classes of material culture. This point has been made most effectively by James Deetz (1977). Working with material from the English colonies of the east coast of North America, Deetz showed how Georgian principles could not just be seen in the changing pattern of building, but extended widely into all realms of everyday life. The preparation and eating of food became more ordered and segregated. The seventeenth-century yeoman family ate stews, soups and pottages, often served from large cauldrons or casseroles. When meat was served, it was cooked in large joints and roasted on spits over the fire. Individual members of the family then helped themselves from an array of communal dishes that were placed on the tables, using knives to help themselves to meat, often using messes and bread trenchers, and otherwise using their fingers.

Mealtime in a later eighteenth-century house, such as that at Temple Balsall, was very different. The family now dined off white plates rather than brightly coloured slipware dishes. The plates themselves were standardised and mould-made. Place settings were much more individualised, and included forks and other implements as well as knives and spoons. As a result, eating with the fingers came to be seen as uncivilised and unrefined. The family now sat on individual chairs, which were themselves of standardised size and shape, rather than benches or stools. This rise in order, symmetry and segregation is about the rise of a particular kind of self-conscious individual identity.

Individual identity was most obviously expressed in the activity of solitary reading. In 1500, less than half the adult male population could read and write; by 1800, the overwhelming majority could (Cressy 1980; Fox 2000). Literacy brought with it a set of cultural changes that are of direct relevance to architecture. First, the action of reading itself – a solitary activity, characteristically pursued indoors, often in private (though in many households, as in the local alehouse, pamphlets and texts could be read out loud to an informal audience). Second, literacy enabled access to new ideas, social and political (Sharpe 2000a) but also ideas about taste, the way the house should be composed, decorated and furnished, ideas about style. Given that such reading-matter was largely published in London, these ideas were by definition metropolitan and national in nature. The ability to read, then, gave access to wider, urbane and metropolitan ideas about taste, as opposed to local and regional ideas about tradition. Third, as literacy became less the preserve of the elite and more that of all social classes, such ideas were no longer the preserve of the very few, but could also be grasped and deployed by households of different social levels.

Solitary reading and the idea of 'privacy' reinforced each other. We have already seen how ordinary houses came to reflect a 'rise in privacy' – the decline of the hall, the double-pile plan, the proliferation of individual bedrooms. Women and men, and masters and servants, experienced this 'rise in privacy' differently. Men often had a study: first found in elite contexts, studies were found with increasing frequency in larger vernacular houses by the end of the eighteenth century (for example, at Wrey Manor, Lustleigh, Devon: Alcock and Carson 2007, ii). However, by the middle of the eighteenth century, many women had their own space in the form of a closet, within which they pursued solitary activities, in particular the reading of novels. In eighteenth-century novels, for example, Richardson's *Pamela* and *Clarissa*, an understanding of the (female) person is established through the literary device of looking into their private closet; the domestic spaces depicted in Defoe's novels are similarly structured. In the King James Bible of the early seventeenth century, the 'word "closet" is used to denote an inner sanctuary for a soul', for example, Matthew 6.6 (Lipsedge 2006, 109). By the time of Fielding's *Tom Jones*, published in 1749, the gamekeeper's daughter, Molly Seagram, has a 'mock' closet in her 'garret'. The closet became both a secret world and external symbol. Novels like *Pamela* and *Clarissa* provide much more, then, than simply evidence of the growing incidence of such spaces. As Robert Blair St George has shown (2006), women read this new literary form in their own closets – their own private spaces – and used the patterns of behaviour they read about very directly as models for their own behaviour. The rise of passive notions of femininity was strongly related to the rise of domestic practices and the idea of the home and the rise of the middle class – seen in novels like *Pamela* (St George 2006, 88–92). Their 'domesticity', a word that only took on its modern meaning in the eighteenth century (Kowalewski and Goldberg 2008, 2), was part of a wider separation between work and leisure.

What these developments in literature and culture tell us is not only that the domestic interior was changing, but that perhaps, more importantly, the way people were thinking about the domestic interior was changing. People were much more consciously reflective on the way in which the spatial ordering, the textures and the objects of these interiors reflected the social identities of the owners. They reflected on this ordering through the language of 'taste', and later Romanticism (Brewer 1997). Colin Campbell has argued that consumerism, in other words the urge to acquire new goods, was strongly related to a changing sense of self. Romanticism fuelled the creative imagination, and new goods offered the promise of realising that self (Campbell 1987).

Order and Discipline

The Georgian Order was about the individual; it was also about work-discipline and control of the natural world. This other side to the politeness and refinement of Georgian houses can be found in the farmsteads that went with them. The advice and pattern-books discussed above included a host of publications on the design and layout of the farmstead, and were part of a wider pattern of agricultural 'improvement': new crops, greater productivity (Robinson 1983). Greater numbers of farmsteads were laid out according to idealised plans, and termed 'model farms'. Model farms started with great landowners, who built *fermes ornées* after the French model (Wade-Martins 2002a). Model farm plans were intended to be rational and efficient: Demesne Farm Doddington, Cheshire, designed in the 1780s by Samuel Wyatt, even had radially planned shippons and stables. What these plans did was to order and systematise the organisation of labour: the symmetrical, ordered farmstead expressed a new pattern of time- and work-discipline.

Between 1550 and 1750, there was a profound shift in the employment and patterns of work of servants and labourers. In the idealised conception of the sixteenth-century household the metaphor of the family was extended to include a master's rights and duties over his servants. Servants ate at the same table, were clothed by the master and paid largely in kind. Men who did not have a master were viewed with fear, as being outside this idealised community and posing a threat to it. By the eighteenth century, however, payment of servants was proportionately more in cash than in kind (Kussmaul 1981), and the numbers of 'masterless men' and others outside or marginal to the social order had grown. The metaphor of family was weaker, and in many ways had been replaced by a gulf between the worlds of different social classes and the upper-class fear of the labouring classes. The world of master and servant had grown apart physically. Though a working farmhouse might still come together at mealtimes, servants often lived in separate dwellings, or under a different roof.

E.P. Thompson has famously shown how ideas of time- and work-discipline were necessary to the introduction and growth of the factory system (Thompson 1967).

Such discipline was equally bound up with the emergence of 'agrarian capitalism' in the eighteenth century, in the sense of the growth of large landed estates and 'the replacement of small-scale peasant cultivators by large capitalist farms, specialist producers for the market'. Discipline was bound up with new forms of knowledge: 'The middle decades of the eighteenth century saw the elaboration of, and growing familiarity with, new legal forms which could remove even the most complex of common field systems' (Williamson 1998, 109 and 111).

In place of the metaphor of family, then, came modern patterns of work-discipline, and a much sharper distinction between work time and leisure time (Burke 1995). A sharp distinction between work and leisure also meant a sharper distinction between family members and the labouring poor employed as day-workers on the farm. In the eighteenth century 'the poor came to take on the status of an undifferentiated class, whose need for charity was their most distinguishing characteristic' (Barrell 1980, 3). In this sense, then, the regular Georgian house and the artistic depictions of pastoral cottages went hand in hand: a romantic, undifferentiated image of the labouring poor and the heightened segregation of middle-class life were opposite sides of the same coin.

Labourers were not necessarily poorer than their counterparts in earlier centuries, but they had lost much of their economic independence through enclosure. The model farm sought to enforce patterns of discipline on a socially distant workforce. Threshing floors in newly built brick barns were often hollow, so that the sound of threshing resonated and the farmer could be sure work was progressing when he was on another part of the farmstead. There was large-scale rebuilding of farm buildings in many regions in the later eighteenth century, for example, Devon (Beacham 1990). Although large numbers of earlier barns and some earlier buildings survive, the farm buildings surrounding most farmhouses today commonly date from the late eighteenth century onwards, reflecting this rebuilding (Wade-Martins 2002b).

The Georgian farmhouse, then, has to be seen as one element of a web of wider changes across the landscape, changes that were tied up with the feeding of a population that doubled from six million in 1760 to twelve million sixty years later (Barnwell and Giles 1997, 4). The eighteenth and early nineteenth centuries were the time of parliamentary enclosure. The open fields of communities across the champion belt of England were swept away. The process as a whole took over a century, and in any one community was usually the end result of a longer process of piecemeal change. Parliamentary enclosure in any one place nevertheless swept away an entire landscape in one sudden reorganisation. The familiar and traditional landscape was replaced by one of straight hedges and ditches; earlier common rights were swept away. Even the old and familiar naming of the landscape – fields, routeways, boundaries – vanished in a reformation of the landscape that left the naming of the landscape civil, polite and sanitised (Thomas 1983). At the same time, new crops were introduced: English agriculture has doubled its productivity since 1500, with the introduction not just of new farming methods but of new crops such as potatoes, rape, turnips and swedes (Overton 1996). Georgian farmhouses were part of this shift. They often stood in isolated locations, in the middle of the new enclosed fields, their newly-built brick farm buildings organised in a rational pattern (Barnwell and Giles 1997). Their order, symmetry and segregation was part and parcel of the wider forces of 'improvement' and Enlightenment rationality sweeping across the English countryside (Tarlow 2007).

The transformation of the eighteenth-century countryside also produced large numbers of labourers' cottages, often built to a standardised plan that itself reflected Georgian principles, which were also seen in workers' housing of the Industrial Revolution (Caffyn 1986). By the end of the eighteenth century, many servants were accommodated not under the master's roof, but either in separate cottages or in other accommodation, for example, over the stables. Rows of cottages were newly built, the result of piecemeal additions to earlier houses, or the result of subdivision of earlier houses (Alcock 1993, 128–9; Johnson 1993a, 152–5).

Conversations Between Classes

One of the remarkable things about Georgian building is its uniformity, when compared to either the seventeenth or nineteenth centuries. The visitor taking a walk up and down the street of a village or small town in England may well see a lot of very different Victorian houses, but remarkably uniform Georgian facades. Where houses from earlier centuries have survived, the visitor will often find that they have been adapted to Georgian uniformity (Plate 14). In the sense of expressing a common order or pattern that could be deployed at different social levels, Georgian architecture materialised a conversation between classes, and a subtle commentary on the gradations of class and how to negotiate these gradations, at a time when what social status and class meant was changing profoundly, during the Industrial and agrarian Revolutions.

Georgian uniformity reflected a new national discourse of 'taste' in the eighteenth century. Good taste was seen as universal; it was not different for people of different social positions – though different social classes might, elite writers implied, be more or less able to appreciate or understand it. Good taste, then, was reflected in architectural principles that were uniform, and good taste facilitated conversations between classes. Georgian architecture was one way in which this discourse of taste was materialised. 'Taste', writes Bernard Herman, 'can be read as a system of social and cultural values focused in the eighteenth century on regularity, hierarchy, order, and standardisation, all materially grounded in and made visible through architecture and an astonishing range of artefacts and social behaviours . . . taste serves as an instrument that simultaneously privileges processes of social cohesion and social distinction. Taste in this context informs material and visual representations of power' (Herman 2006, 43).

One of the best ways to understand how social ideas are mapped on to the appearance of the house and the space within the household is to read the literature of the period. Jane Austen's novels are above all about social class, and the way class is constructed and negotiated through manners. When the heroine of *Mansfield Park*, Fanny Price, returns to her parents' house in Portsmouth, Austen indicates Fanny's consciousness of their slightly lower social status than herself through little details: for example, she notes how doors are left open through the house, so that the noise and clatter of household activities, and particularly the smell of the kitchen, permeate the parlour, impinging on any attempt at 'civilised' conversation (Lascelles ed. 1978, 288–92).

What the order, symmetry and segregation of the Georgian house did was to orient and position these different individuals very carefully towards one another, in ways that enabled them to communicate across boundaries of gender, status and class. Individuals from different social classes, both men and women, could meet together in spaces that no longer had overt markers of distinction within them, such as the upper and lower end of the open hall had had. It became a mark of incivility to comment overtly on the relative social grading of different members of a dining party or excursion, as Elizabeth's initial impressions of a prideful and snobbish Mr Darcy, standing aloof from the rest of the party at the ball in Meryton, exemplify in *Pride and Prejudice*.

Continuities

It would be all too easy to conclude, from a rapid survey of a village or small town, that the triumph of the Georgian Order was complete by the end of the eighteenth century. However, the truth is a little more complex. Even in the great metropolis of London itself, there was more variety in the forms of smaller houses than the Georgian façade might indicate. Peter Guillery has shown how even in the nineteenth century, a variety of plans derived from pre-Georgian models continued to be built in London (Guillery 2004). In the countryside, particularly in the north, a variety of rural plans continued earlier forms. The laithe-house form of west Yorkshire, mostly built after c.1750, 'encompasses under one roof a combined barn and byre' after the older, traditional pattern (Mercer 1975, 45). Regional differences in building materials remained. For example, when Daniel Garrett published his *Designs and Estimates of Farmhouses &c. for the County of York, Northumberland, Westmoreland and Bishoprick of Durham* in 1747 it was 20 per cent more costly to build in brick than in stone in mid-eighteenth century north England (Airs and Broad 1998, 53), and so building in stone remained popular in these latter areas.

Many earlier timber-framed houses were encased in brick 'skins' in this period, or were adapted as rear ranges to symmetrical Georgian front halls and parlours. In the process, of course, earlier phases of house were entirely obscured to the casual eye. It is due to later stone and brick encasing, for example, that timber-framed houses in the southern Pennines were relatively unknown before internal examination. But more fundamentally, the Georgian façade often concealed the survival of a more traditional plan. It is easily forgotten that all those thousands of medieval conversions, and conversions of the sixteenth and seventeenth century houses discussed in previous chapters, survived throughout the eighteenth century and indeed to the present day, albeit often heavily modified to something very like a Georgian appearance (Plate 14). The actual experience of changes in and around houses may have been different for men and for women: behind the fine Georgian façades, and behind even the mannered conversation and dining taking place in the front space of the Georgian house, different patterns of life carried on in women's and servants' realms: in the kitchen and in what was now 'back space'.

It is revealing of the persistence of other ways of life and their architectural expression that the addition of a Georgian façade only produced a perfectly symmetrical exterior in a few cases. More frequently, there was some slight asymmetry in the façade. A front door might be placed slightly off-centre, or not placed centrally at all; the bays to either side of the front door could be of slightly different widths; an annexe or farm building would be placed off to one side (Plate 15; see also RCHME 1987, 58–9, for examples). In many cases, these slight asymmetries or irregularities are produced by the needs of 'fitting' a Georgian façade to an earlier core; but in others, particularly in the Pennines and in Northumbria, the slight irregularities suggest a more subtle interpretation. The façades of these houses suggest a familiarity with Georgian principles of design and a subscription to the values of taste that go with it. Certainly, completely symmetrical façades can be found from the later seventeenth century onwards, integrated with a traditional plan, for example, at Thirley Beck Farm on the North York Moors (RCHME 1987, 35 and Figure 39); so these later houses are not simply ignorant of Georgian principles. However, they also and at the same time give the reassuring visual clues to a visitor or outsider to understand the house from the outside, and act as a subtle rejection of the rules of symmetry. Anne Palkovich observed this phenomenon in excavating the Morris Pound House in eighteenth-century Chesapeake where 'examination of the interior walls . . . shows that careful attention was paid to their construction. Irregularities inherent in the building materials project to the outside of the structures. The interior walls are straight, smooth, carefully built – and irregular in their dimensions. . . . Simply concluding that an incomplete transition in construction style is being observed does not explain why these structures could violate well-known rules of construction' (Palkovich 1988, 301).

Conclusion

The Georgian house, then, did not mark the 'death of vernacular' and the end of regional variation and traditions. It did, however, mark a critical horizon in building. Most local communities, from Northumberland to Cornwall and from Kent to

Cumbria, have prominent examples of Georgian houses; in most of these cases, again, a large number of older houses have been 'Georgianised', from the addition of sash windows to the wholesale addition of a brick or stone casing or a second range of rooms, either at front or rear.

This critical horizon was linked in turn to a fundamental social transformation, a shift in patterns of material life and culture. Previous chapters have shown how the roots of this transformation can be traced right back into the sixteenth century. The following, concluding, chapter will consider how that transformation has to be understood, not just within the narrow confines of England but across the Atlantic world as a whole.

9
Conclusions

The last chapter looked at the rise of Georgian houses and the alleged 'end of vernacular' over the course of the eighteenth century. I have suggested that a wide range of factors were involved in the creation of symmetrical, segregated houses at middling social levels. Changing architectural style and 'Classical influence' was only part of the picture; one also had to consider changing building patterns, changing farming practices, changing patterns of work-discipline, changing class relations, and a host of other factors. Most fundamentally, 'Georgian' was about changing patterns of ordering everyday life, and ordering everyday relations between human beings. Order, symmetry and segregation were not just architectural and material principles; they materialised a new pattern of living and a new way of thinking.

This pattern of living was woven together, and made sense to people, over a much wider geographical spread and scale than simply 'England'. Georgian architecture, and the Georgian world-view that it materialised, was a production not of 'England', but of the British Isles, and of the Atlantic world. It expressed a system of ideas about how to live that bound people together across what had been very different local contexts, and across much older national boundaries.

To put it very crudely, Georgian houses were more than simply nationally uniform. They were material expressions of a sense of common identity that worked across the British Isles and the Atlantic. It is no coincidence that such a pattern of architecture can be found uniting upper and middling classes across all areas of 'Britain', *just at the moment when Britain was being created*. When the American scholar Bernard Herman talks about 'taste' in the towns, his words can be taken as a statement about Georgian houses and ways of life as a whole:

> When we look at the dynamic practice of taste . . . we find visual differences that synthesise local practice and polite ideas around fragmented but shared desires for economic and social expression. The ethos for advancement, however, lay not necessarily in a desire to emulate elite affectations, but in the very nature of the competitive and acquisitive culture of trade that defined the eighteenth century Atlantic world. Given significant physical distances, strong local cultures, and movement of individuals of all classes in and out of cities, there was a deep need for a visual and material lingua franca that communicated effectively in local and international contexts. Taste worked as a strategy that lent itself to situational deployment in the slippery world of eighteenth-century urban demotic culture.
>
> (Herman 2006, 52)

It does not make sense, then, to tell the story of vernacular architecture in exclusively 'English' terms. 'Georgian' was, among other things, about a wider network. It was an architectural language that spanned the Atlantic world.

'Georgian' was a distinctive set of material principles that marked out different classes of objects, architecture, and landscape. It was in a sense the cultural counterpart to the political Act of Union of 1707. This was a pivotal moment in British political history, when England and Scotland became one nation; though Scotland and England had had the same monarch since 1603, they had remained separate nations until this date. In a sense, it can be seen as a 'cultural horizon'. Archaeologists talk about a horizon when they see a distinctive, relatively sudden moment of transformation that spreads very rapidly and can be seen as a key marker of change in different places – a new pottery style, or a new set of farming techniques. Georgian marks such a horizon.

We have seen how consciousness of 'England' as a nation was materialised in the architectural changes of the sixteenth and seventeenth centuries, in particular in the creation of 'vernacular' as a distinctive category and its opposition to 'polite' architecture and culture. Political and cultural historians have long emphasised how 'England' never existed in splendid isolation, and how, contrary to popular myth, 'England' was never a stable unit with a fixed identity and boundaries. 'England' was the result of conquest and continuous interaction with its neighbours in the rest of the British Isles: Wales, Ireland and Scotland. The kingdom of Wales had been assimilated politically into the kingdom after the conquest of Gwynedd at the end of the thirteenth century. Two centuries later, much of Wales was carved up into counties along the same lines as the rest of the kingdom of 'England'. The presence of hundreds of standing vernacular farmhouses, particularly in the Marches, and in North Wales, is in part a materialisation of the identities and aspirations of a Welsh-speaking middling sort of people (Smith 1975; Suggett 2005).

In Scotland, Wales, and Ireland, the creation of Georgian houses and landscapes was in some ways a more sudden horizon than in England. In many areas, particularly in the uplands of the north and west of the British Isles, the eighteenth century was the first point at which large numbers of ordinary houses were built that still survive today. Much of Wales now, particularly upland areas, can be seen as a landscape of what elite contemporaries called 'improvement' (Tarlow 2007). Symmetrical, Georgian farmhouses sit in isolated locations, surrounded by drystone walls of eighteenth- or nineteenth-century date. The traditional Radnorshire farmhouses discussed by Richard Suggett (2005), for example, were replaced by symmetrical houses after 1750.

In Scotland, symmetrical, ordered farmhouses again went with eighteenth-century landscapes of enlightenment and 'improvement' – in the southern Scottish highlands, for example, neat, ordered farmhouses and courtyard and linear built farmsteads went with ordered, geometrically laid out enclosures (Dalglish 2003). At the same time, landscape change went hand-in-hand with the break-up of old kin groups and, ultimately, migration to the New World. Infield-outfield systems were replaced by enclosed landscapes, culminating in the Highland Clearances. Earlier one-storey, drystone houses were replaced by mortared, storeyed farmhouses by the later eighteenth century, for example in Argyll (MacKie 1997; Fraser 2000).

The Irish rural landscape and its houses are similarly the result, in part, of the eighteenth-century Georgian horizon. The famous Georgian town houses of Dublin were matched in the countryside by symmetrical, ordered boxes, surrounded by enclosed fields (Aalen et al. 1997, 159). More subtly, the transition from undifferentiated longhouse to divided longhouse occurred between the late eighteenth and early twentieth centuries (Aalen et al. 1997, 148). Again, landscape, cultural and political change went together: in 1801, the Irish Parliament was abolished and Ireland became part of the United Kingdom of Great Britain and Ireland, a status not to be changed until 1922.

Georgian, then, was not just about the subsuming of regional variability within a national tradition. It was also about the creation of a tradition beyond England – in particular, the creation of an idea of Britain. Linda Colley's famous and controversial book, *Britons*, explored how the idea of 'Britain' was actively created by the Protestant elite and middle classes in the four nations in the eighteenth century. Georgian architecture can be seen as an architectural expression of this creation (Colley 1992). In many contexts, Georgian architecture represented a 'British' identity, just as other classes of material objects, such as the images found on transfer-printed ceramics, also came to represent Britishness (Brooks 1999).

Georgian Horizons

Georgian architecture across the Atlantic materialised elements of this British identity, though not in a straightforward or simple way. The seventeenth-century houses of the colonies of New England and Virginia were products of different English vernacular traditions, alongside other European and African traditions, adapted to a variety of new environments and conditions (Cummings 1979; Horn 1993). In the context of the American colonies, Georgian houses appeared as a cultural horizon even more sharply than in Scotland, Wales and Ireland. T.H. Breen has argued that they were part of a wider 'package' of architectural and material forms that pulled the American colonies back from relative isolation into the British Atlantic world as part of an 'empire of goods' (Breen 1986 and Breen 2004).

The idea of the Georgian Order as a way of life, and as a common set of principles, extended beyond architecture to other material forms as discussed in the previous chapter, was actually first explored by scholars working on the American colonies. The folklorist Henry Glassie drew a compelling portrait of a transformation in the 'folk housing' of rural Virginia. He showed how symmetrical, ordered houses arrived in the middle of the eighteenth century, a transformation whose immediate causes he attributed to the arrival of pattern-books from England. Glassie drew a wider picture, however, linking the order of Virginian folk housing to the fearful control of the social and natural world of the Virginian farmer (Glassie 1975).

The archaeologist James Deetz saw the power of Glassie's vision of folk housing, and related it outwards to other classes of material culture – pottery, gravestones, refuse disposal (Deetz 1977 and Deetz 1996). Deetz saw clearly that Georgian principles applied to patterns of eighteenth-century life as a whole, not simply to questions of architectural style. In his other work as an archaeologist, Deetz talked about 'pattern' and 'horizon' in the archaeological record, and in many ways he saw Georgian as a distinctive horizon in the material culture and life of the American colonies.

Mark Leone and his students (Leone 2005) grasped the power of Deetz's insight and applied it to an understanding of the social structure of the American colonies. For Leone, Georgian principles of order, symmetry and segregation were linked to the rise of capitalism. He emphasised how eighteenth-century life in the colonies was increasingly unequal. The American colonies were divided along class, gender and racial lines. The symmetrical Georgian façades and elegant gardens of the colonial elite masked these divisions and inequality. It made the social order appear harmonious, and made social divisions appear natural. Behind the apparent harmony and civility of Georgian architecture and landscape, then, lay social division and segregation, just as it did in England (Borsay 2006).

In the last chapter, I stressed how Georgian had to be seen as much more than an architectural style, and I have continued in this chapter to look at how it materialised British identity. In the context of the American colonies, Georgian materialised a sense of British and Protestant identity, but it took on new and other meanings as well. Leone's most famous example is that of William Paca of Annapolis in Maryland. The symmetry and segregation of his house, and the principles of harmony and natural order that could be seen in his formal garden, reinforced Paca's position as a member of the local elite. Paca was a man who signed the Declaration of Independence proclaiming the ideal of liberty and equality for all men; yet he owned over a hundred slaves.

Georgian, then, is about the first British Empire, the empire that was lost with the American colonies after 1776. It is also about the most intimate ordering of common life (Glassie 2000), the placing of a kitchen at the back of a small farmhouse rather than at the side. Principles of symmetry, order and segregation were successful in part because they offered a way of spanning these two extremes, of creating a common architectural and material language that took in these two scales and points in between, from individual, household and regional identities to affiliations of class, nation and empire.

At the same time, Georgian subsumed and transformed vernacular tradition; it did not replace it. Even at the apex of the social scale, the relationship between polite and vernacular was more complex than this. Dell Upton has discussed how Thomas Jefferson's great house at Monticello in Virginia presents a Classical façade, but behind that façade its plan is more traditional. Monticello's relationships of different spaces which govern its internal plan (basement to upper floors, front/back, left/right) resonates with vernacular traditions (Upton 1998, 20–38).

A century later in the back lanes of England, the architect Edwin Lutyens and others were building Vernacular Revival houses for the affluent middling sort of the Surrey commuter belt: 'Lutyens' childhood in Thursley and the country lanes of West Surrey had given him ample time to absorb the intricacies of the local vernacular and the mysteries of carpentry and brickwork. His subsequent mastery of whatever style was required and his later triumph in the raising of New Delhi was all built on the foundation of the rural building craft of West Surrey' (Budgen 2002, 7). The idea of local 'character' continues to hold a central place in modern planning and design, and in 'management' of the countryside.

Houses and Context

I originally intended to conclude this book with a much more detailed and comparative account of the creation of this 'Georgian horizon' that spanned national borders and boundaries, and the prehistory of the process which culminated in the Georgian Order which, this book has argued, went back to the later middle ages. I wanted to show how the very smallest and most intimate detail of an English vernacular house could be related outwards to historical processes and currents that embraced the Atlantic world as a whole. Perhaps inevitably in what I have written above this story remains imperfectly sketched out rather than told in detail.

To do justice to such a story, one would need to engage with a detailed account of local and indigenous contexts in Scotland, Wales and Ireland, as well as in the regions of England. One would need a frame of reference that encompassed urban as well as rural contexts (cf. Quiney 2004), and great castles and houses as well as ordinary dwellings. Such a study would also be incomplete without examining changing landscapes as a whole, and it would need to engage with a variety of other colonial contexts – the Caribbean, Virginia, the Chesapeake, New England. The story of the estate and landscapes of the Atlantic world would have to be told (Finch and Giles 2007). Finally, the story would have to be taken back to the framing of the landscape in the earlier Middle Ages – Georgian houses were, after all, built in the interstices of fields, routes and trackways that were centuries and sometimes millennia old.

In some ways, this book is a preface to this larger project, an interim statement. Here, instead, are some passing reflections on some of the key themes thrown up by this study.

National Unity?

Is the topic of English vernacular houses a coherent one? Chapter 2 discussed what Richard Harris called a national language of timber-framing, with different dialects. Box-framing, however, is also found in Wales, while surviving crucks have a distribution across the British Isles rather than just England, being common across Wales. Open halls have elements that can be considered to be distinctive to England, but the phenomenon of the hall as central to medieval architecture is found across Europe. At the same time, the cultural distance between different regions of England was very great, particularly at the opening of our history. A Kentish yeoman may well have had more in common, in terms of farming practices, level of prosperity, and experience of the world, with his northern French counterpart than he did with the Northumbrian owner of a bastle.

Eric Mercer constructed a coherent story for English vernacular houses by stressing a common pattern between regions:

> Regional peculiarities had not been wholly eliminated by the end of the eighteenth century, nor by the mid nineteenth century for that matter, but they had become of minor importance against the background of national conformity brought about by a sequence of changes common to all parts. If the development in the south-east is regarded as the classic norm, then those in the rest of the country fall into place. The stages occurred in different regions at different times, occupied longer or shorter periods, or were even omitted altogether, but the same road was followed to the same end, and that early uniformity which began to break up in the later Middle Ages had re-established itself on a wholly different level by the early nineteenth century. Looked at in this way the subject ceases to be a bundle of independent themes, connected only when one area happens to influence another, but becomes a national theme with local variations. Instead of giving a geographical account of vernacular houses in England it becomes possible to attempt a history of English vernacular houses which may perhaps be related to the history of English society.
>
> (Mercer 1975, 33)

Until the publication of *English Vernacular Houses*, much of the discussion of vernacular traditions had stressed regional tradition and peculiarity, moreover in a rather unsystematic way. Differences between one area and another were understood in terms of local tradition or simply not thought through or explained at all. Mercer's thesis in *English Vernacular Houses* was very simple: all areas of England went through the same fundamental transition between the fourteenth and the eighteenth centuries, and had the same start points and end points. However, they went through this transition at different paces and in different ways. As a result, what appeared as regional differences were actually symptoms of a fundamental, single social change affecting the whole of England.

It is very striking that after the great syntheses of Mercer, Barley, Hoskins, Clifton-Taylor and others, a later generation of writers on vernacular architecture have been increasingly hesitant to tell a single national story of this kind, though regional studies continue apace. Part of the reason for this reluctance is the sheer quantity of information that now has to be marshalled. If there is so much more information, it is also true that its interpretation – what the information might be held to mean – is not so straightforward as it appeared thirty years ago. The work of Currie (1988) and others suggesting that there is no automatic link between surviving houses and waves of rebuilding in the past has also given the project of national synthesis a severe jolt. The reader will have noticed, and probably been frustrated and irritated by, the many careful qualifications I have had to make every time I discussed a particular trend, type or group of houses. These qualifications are irritating to read but necessary, and many experts on the subject will feel that I should probably have inserted many more of them along the way in this text.

One area in particular has been neglected: that of the urban experience. Ordinary houses in London and the provincial towns of England tell stories that are very different from that of the countryside, but which are also closely interrelated. Felicity Riddy, for example, has argued that the distinctively socially middling outlook which I have identified in the sixteenth-century rebuilding in the countryside is actually two centuries older; she locates its origins in the lifestyles of burgess households in towns such as York (Riddy 2008). At the other end of the story told here, both the development of the Georgian style, and the way smaller houses came to adopt elements of both Georgian and vernacular, has an important metropolitan and urban component to it (Guillery 2004). However, most would agree with Sarah Pearson when she remarks that 'urban buildings are very often a separate species from rural ones' (Pearson 1994, 4); a book that encompassed town as well as country would be a fat and heavy volume indeed.

The answer to the question of synthesis is also about that of national identity, and the place of England, and later Britain, in the Atlantic world. Mercer, and the generation of Marxist historians of which he was a part, wrote about England and the Civil War, which they termed the 'English Revolution', as if English history were largely driven by internal forces of class conflict. Scotland, Wales and Ireland, and the world beyond, often seemed to play little role in the story that they told. It was straightforward, then, for such a generation of scholars to speak of 'English houses' as a stable category and single process of development. This view, however, was challenged on two fronts. Historians of the English Civil War came to stress its origins in the relationships between the four nations of Ireland, Scotland, Wales and England (Morrill 1993; Stoyle 2005); at the same time postcolonial historians rightly insisted that the development of class relations in England fitted like lock and key with the development of colonies, and in particular the institution of slavery, across the British colonies (Williams 1944). As much as scholars of vernacular architecture would like their subject to be neatly packaged, we cannot write in such an innocent fashion any more.

Discussions of architectural styles and values that make claims about what was or is 'distinctively English' are popular currency, but they tend to fall very rapidly into platitudes. In his Reith lectures, later published as *The Englishness of English Art*, Nikolaus Pevsner (1955) pointed to two elements: a middle-class rationality, and a Romantic sensibility, epitomised by what he referred to as the 'flaming line' of the art of William Blake. But it is very difficult to conceive of a piece of European architecture that could not fit into one of these two categories, or somewhere between them, any more or less than English examples or specimens. Roy Strong, in *The Spirit of Britain*, identifies two 'great centralities' in what he calls the 'spirit of Britain', which he later qualifies as, for him, 'essentially the story of England and the English' (Strong 1999, 1–2 and 679). Again, what is specifically nationally distinctive in these two characteristics, as opposed to European, is very hard to identify here. Meditative ruminations by the chattering classes on the essential quality of Englishness fill the Sunday papers, but are of very little use when trying to understand traditions of building in any depth.

My contribution to this question is to suggest that anyone writing about 'English houses' has to acknowledge three things. First, that ideas of the English and British nation have been actively constructed. There is no predefining essence to them. In particular, ideas of the nation were constructed in the Renaissance and in the eighteenth century as part of a wider set of cultural transformations. 'England', then, is a problematic concept. To talk about 'the buildings of England', we now realise, is to talk about a series of images, concepts and ideas that are both complex and ideologically loaded.

Second, that ideas of the nation-state were built – literally as well as metaphorically – with reference to houses. Traditional ideas of the 'commonwealth' were given material form in the structuring of the house and household. The patterns of building and dwelling in an early seventeenth-century house, or particularly of a Georgian house, were part of an emerging national unity, part of a subscription to a set of common values and meanings on the part of the builder and owner.

Third, that houses were active places in this construction of national identity. They did not just 'reflect' or 'express' a wider national consciousness; they materialised and framed it. The active creation of opposed categories of 'polite' and 'vernacular' architecture, with the latter being held to be rooted in the soil and in a particular place, was a central part of this active process.

To return to the Preface: our visitors to an English village reflect on the houses around them as active creations; they are not simply 'distinctively' or 'quintessentially' 'English'. They must be understood in terms of the way they created, and were created by, different scales of human action, from the individual and household, through the identities of village and regional communities, to the nation and to the Atlantic world beyond. Gazing upon the warm colours of a Cotswold village is not a nostalgic meditation on the essential, unchanging quality of Englishness; it is part of a critical exercise in understanding how England came to be created. As such, it lends itself to critical thought on how England might be recreated in the future.

Bottom-Up Versus Top-Down

One of the aims of this book has been to write a view of architectural and social change that gives back to the builders and dwellers of vernacular houses in the past a sense of agency, of making their own history. I have tried to write a 'bottom-up' as much as a 'top-down' account of how houses changed, and how people's lives changed with them.

One of the habitual statements found in popular history books that should arouse the mental alarm-bells of any reader is: 'English people felt that . . .' How does the writer know? He or she cannot 'know' from the documents alone, because as we have seen, these were mostly written by a very small minority of the population, who claimed to speak for the rest or claimed to be simply transcribing the testimony of the rest. Where the voices of others appear in these documents, they appear in the context of court records or other classes of material which, to state the obvious, are drawn up with very specific objects and purposes in mind, and only 'reflect' beliefs and values of other groups in a very complex and indirect way (as Diane Purkiss demonstrates, for example, in relation to women's testimony on witchcraft: Purkiss 1995). For example, many of the ritual and apotropaic practices mentioned in Chapter 7 have very little direct documentary evidence, although indirect hints can be gleaned from more recent oral history and folklore (for example, Ewart Evans 1966).

But this does not mean that documents should be ignored. Rather, the view I have tried to argue for in this book is that documents are best understood, and help us understand the past most effectively, if their role as technologies of power is placed at centre stage. In other words, the first question to be asked of an historical document is not, 'What evidence does this data give, and what are its biases?' but rather, 'Why was this document drawn up? What power required this information?' As such, the silences in documents, far from being 'frustrating' or 'elusive' in their silences and omissions, are as revealing as what they say, for example, about processes of state formation. As Michel Foucault pointed out, this is an archaeological view of documents, which looks in an archaeological way at their form, their physical presence, the way they pile up in archives (Foucault 1972). So, for example, the question to be asked of probate inventories is not simply, 'What have they omitted – what are their biases?' but rather, 'Why was it that just at the moment that the middling sort were acquiring and consuming material goods, did the church courts acquire a new interest in classifying, listing and valuing those goods?' As the early modern historian Kevin Sharpe has insisted, documents are different kinds of representations; they relate in a complex way to different kinds of performance (Sharpe 2000a).

At one point I wanted to frame the whole book around a response to Kevin Sharpe's powerful characterisation of the social and cultural history of early modern England. Sharpe suggests that sixteenth- and early seventeenth-century political culture and its representations emerged as an attempt to paper over the cracks that had emerged in late medieval society, in particular the divisions created by the Reformation. After the death of Elizabeth, the Stuart monarchs failed in this task, leading to civil war: 'men fought for and about monarchy because they could not accommodate reasoned differences concerning it'. A new political and cultural settlement around 'a new political culture – of politeness' only emerged at the end of the seventeenth century (Sharpe 2000b, 22 and 23). Sharpe's view is compelling, but he is careful to qualify it as only one of various possible ways of seeing early modern history.

What vernacular houses show us is that the narrative of political culture and debate that Sharpe presents was not simply or only a matter of royal and elite culture. Elite representations were not just passively consumed by everybody else. Monarchy, after all, was but one manifestation of much broader ideas about patriarchy and commonwealth that stretched down the social scale, but which were responded to in different ways by different people. Houses expressed ideas about social order as powerfully as royal portraits – in some ways more powerfully, because their textures and spaces were implicit and unexamined. The performances that went on every day within vernacular buildings were restatements, in a very small way, of the values of household and patriarchy, just as royal ceremony was a grand statement of the values of monarchy. The emergence of new patterns of symmetrical and segregated architecture at vernacular levels, then, materialised the cultural counterpart of Sharpe's political settlement framed around 'politeness'.

Long Term Versus Short Term

In this book, I have tried to expand the question of temporal scale in two ways. First, I have sketched out change in the very long term, from the later Middle Ages to the end of the eighteenth century. This has been a daunting, but, I think, a necessary task. Many books take a tighter focus, looking, for example, only at the later Middle Ages, or at the seventeenth century or Georgian era. By doing so, they are able to provide great depth and detail, but at the expense of leaving the wider sweep of historical processes implicit and unexamined.

I have tried to tell this larger narrative by constructing the book around archaeological ideas of pattern and horizon. Archaeologists are good at seeing patterns on the ground and ordering those patterns into stages or phases. They are also good at seeing critical horizons – moments of very rapid transformation, at which everything seems to change very suddenly. The middle of the sixteenth century and the middle of the eighteenth century were two critical horizons in the patterning of English houses.

Before about 1540, and after about 1750, houses of a wide range of social classes were articulated according to a set of common principles. Between these dates, there were a range of different pathways that the development of houses took in different areas of England. Some have explained this variation in terms of regional differences. Mercer explained it in terms of the varying pace of a broader evolutionary process. In this book, I have tried to stress agency – in other words, how houses are material evidence for ordinary people making their own lives in their own ways, rather than being dictated to by 'region', 'historical process', or being governed by a mad rush to emulate or 'follow fashion'.

The student of vernacular buildings is faced with a paradox. On the one hand, houses materialise very small-scale actions that need to be understood in their own terms – the replacement of a window, the addition of a porch, even the daily sweeping-out of a floor, the setting and clearing of a table at mealtime. On the other hand, it is necessary to be sensitive to the fact that the context of these actions is one of a very long time-span, spanning several centuries at least – the rise of plans two rooms deep, the move away from medieval patterns of living towards Georgian ways of life. To make things more complicated, a long-term process may manifest itself very suddenly in an individual case – thus, although it may have taken more than a century for open halls to disappear, in the case of any individual house and its inhabitants, the conversion associated with the insertion of a ceiling and chimney-stack might be very sudden, to create a profound change in lived experience.

Vernacular and Polite

To make things more complicated still, I have tried to show that the opposed terms 'vernacular' and 'polite' are problematic. To draw together and summarise some of the points made in earlier chapters: though there were larger and smaller houses in the later Middle Ages, from a two-bay cruck-framed cottage to Westminster Hall, at this point in time we cannot talk of separate architectural traditions of vernacular and polite. The definition and opposition of vernacular and polite traditions was an historical process with its origins in the sixteenth century. Georgian building was in part about materialising a politeness and civility that framed and defined the vernacular in its turn.

The study of vernacular architecture is therefore problematic. Though it is pursued by the most 'practical' of scholars, it is a modern theoretical imposition that does not fit past historical realities. The buildings of England have to be studied in their wider social and cultural context, and as part of this project, smaller houses must be studied in terms of their changing relationship to contemporary larger buildings. Instead of a world divided in two where polite buildings express culture and meaning, and vernacular buildings are 'just' about function, I have tried to delineate different building traditions changing in a complex way, as part of an historically evolving 'building culture' (Davis 2006).

Conclusion

In late medieval and early modern England, we see a vernacular construction of authority, a material expression by the middling sort of people of their view of their world. Such a view is not easily approximated to either an unquestioning acceptance of the elite construction of authority, but neither is it a complete rejection. The top-down changes of the Reformation led to changes in the constitution of that authority; the bottom-up response was active, and led to unintended consequences and patterns of change.

This book has come a long way from its original tableau, a casual visit to an English village. I have argued that the houses found in the English landscape do not just form part of a pretty picture: they tell a story. It is a story of transformation; of change and transition; of material 'improvement'; of the clash between different systems of economic, social and cultural values; of the development of different kinds of cultures of building; and a story of the growing articulation of households and local communities within wider structures and processes, processes that spread out across, and integrated, different elements not just of the English and British nation but of the Atlantic world beyond.

Part of my aim in writing this book was to address the myth that traditional or vernacular houses are artefacts of some kind of unchanging, conservative authenticity. Many contemporary critics, most notably Prince Charles (1989), condemn modern architecture by appealing to a past tradition which is constructed as somehow more authentic, more secure and, it is suggested, more 'humane'. This view was always highly selective: the 'Georgian Vernacular' so beloved of Charles and his followers at Poundbury in Dorset was, in the past, never an architecture for the whole community – it was always an architecture and a landscape from which the poor and those outside the exclusive circle of 'politeness' were marginalised and excluded (Borsay 2006).

Vernacular houses in England may be held to carry meanings of 'tradition' and 'authenticity' now, for complex social and cultural reasons to do with the Romanticism so prevalent and so characteristic of an alienated modern society. But to state the obvious, when they were built, many of these buildings were very new. In its own way, a newly built house in the sixteenth century that did not have an open hall, or even a medieval house that was converted with chimney-stack and ceiling, was a radical restatement of cultural values and ideals. In its own way, it was as radical and arresting as a piece of modern architecture such as Richard Rogers' Lloyd's Building or Norman Foster's 'Gherkin'.

The main aim of this book has been very simple: it is to ensure that no visitor to the English countryside can look at a timber-framed or a Georgian house in the same way ever again. In place of the rather cosy series of myths outlined in the Introduction, in which houses are viewed in a Romantic way, I have tried to show houses and human actions involved in complex and dynamic relationships, relationships that played their part in the creation of the modern world.

Houses were settings that structured and defined the way people staged performances. These performances were mundane, everyday and habitual, but they defined who people were, and how they understood the world around them. People staged those performances actively, in part by building and adapting new forms of house, in part by their chosen manner of dwelling within spaces inherited from the past. Through these everyday rhythms of life, punctuated by episodes of transformation, the house came to materialise ideas about individual identity, household and social life, and wider cultural and political understandings of the world. If this wider story is borne in mind, a walk around a village or a rural landscape becomes not just a pastime of delighting in pretty buildings but an exercise in understanding the pattern and structure of history, and in understanding the human past.

Glossary

The study of vernacular architecture is bedevilled by technical jargon. This glossary covers not merely specialist terms from the field of architecture, but also specialist terms from economic, social and legal history. I have tried to minimise the use of such terms in this book, and so scarcely a fraction of the terms found in *Vernacular Architecture* and other specialist journals will be found here; the reader is referred to Alcock et al. 1996 for more guidance on specialist terminology.

Many of the architectural definitions have been adapted from Mercer (1975, 229–32), Alcock et al. (1996) and www.lookingatbuildings.org.uk. Historical terms have been adapted from Wrightson (2003).

Agnus Dei: a Christian symbol (the lamb of Christ).

Aisle: a space, usually lower, alongside the body of a building, separated by posts or columns.

Anchor-beam: a beam functioning like a tie, but at cross-rail rather than wall-plate level.

Andirons: metal supports used for holding up logs in a fireplace.

Apotropaic: having the power to prevent evil or bad luck (for example, precautions against witchcraft).

Ashlar: stone that has been squared, coursed and jointed.

Axial: at right-angles to the main axis of the structure.

Bacon loft: a space, usually within the chimney, where flitches of bacon are hung to be smoked.

Baluster: the support to a hand-rail on a stair.

Bastle: farmhouse with thick stone walls and living quarters over accommodation for animals, found in the northern borders.

Bay: the space between two trusses or cross-frames.

Bolster: a piece of bed furniture.

Box-frame: where the frame apart from the roof and braces consists of upright and horizontal members.

Brace: a diagonal timber supporting the frame. An **arch-brace** is between post and plate above. A **tension-brace** is between post and plate below. A **wind-brace** is in the roof, between principals and side purlins.

Bressumer: a plate resting on, or in front of, the joists to form a jetty and supporting the posts over.

Cambered: pertaining to a beam, often a tie-beam, whose centre is higher than its ends.

Canopy: the curving hood over the upper end of an open hall.

Cell: the unit of a house, often corresponding to bay and room divisions.

Chamber: a room, though sometimes used to designate its upper-floor counterpart: thus the 'hall chamber' can be the room over the hall.

Chamfer: the planing away of the corner of the profile of a timber. A 'chamfer-stop' is the carved end to a chamfer.

Clay-lump: a technique of construction using unfired clay bricks.

Collar: a beam coupling a pair of rafters above the wall-plate.

Competence: a set of mental rules, implicitly understood and applied by the builders, that generated house forms.

Coppice: a tree is coppiced when its trunk is cut off near the base, so that young shoots grow quickly from the stump that remains.

Cottage: though often used today to refer indiscriminately to smaller vernacular houses, the more precise term refers to the dwellings of those holding little or no land, usually labourers, often built and owned by the landlord from the eighteenth century onwards.

Couple: a pair of rafters, often halved together at the apex.

Cross-frame: see **truss**.

Cross-rail: a main plate between sill-beam and wall-plate, often receiving ceiling joists.

Crown-post: a post resting on a tie supporting a collar purlin and collar, and often braced to these.

Cruck: a pair of curved timbers or 'blades' bearing a structural load (see Figure 2.6). Base crucks rise from ground level to a tie-beam or collar-beam. Full crucks rise from ground level to the apex of the roof. Jointed crucks have blades formed from more than one piece of timber. Middle crucks rise from halfway up the walls to a tie or collar-beam. Raised crucks rise from halfway up the walls to the apex of the roof. Upper crucks are supported on a tie-beam and rise to the apex.

Cupboard: either a table upon which items were placed, or similar to a sideboard.

Dais: a raised platform at the upper end of a hall.

Diocese: the district under the jurisdiction of a bishop.

Donjon: the great tower or 'keep' of a castle.

Dormer: a window above the eaves line, either with its own gable or surmounted by a curve in the thatch (eyebrow dormer).

Double-pile: pertaining to a house plan that is two rooms deep.

Dragon beam: a diagonal beam supporting jetties on two adjacent sides of an upper floor.

Dressing: the working of stone or brick to a finished face, for example, around a corner or opening.

Facing-in: the placing of timbers so that the 'fair face' or external face of the timber, with the heads of the pegs, is facing the upper end of the hall.

Ferme Ornée: an 'ornamented farm'; a farming estate laid out to aesthetic principles.

Finial: the highest ornamental feature, for example, above a gable.

Firehood: a timber and plaster hood over a hearth, to control and channel the smoke upwards.

Flushwork: the combination of dressed stone and worked flint to form patterns.

Gable: the external wall, rising to a point, at the end of a roof.

Galleting: small stones set in a mortar course.

Gentry: a class of substantial landowners and agents of government, below the aristocracy but above yeomen.

Half-hipped: pertaining to a roof, gabled in the lower part and hipped in the upper.

Hall-house: a term applied to houses in many regions of England in the pre-industrial period; sometimes used to refer to open-hall houses in modern literature (in this book, I have preferred the longer 'open-hall houses').

Halved: pertaining to two timbers, cut back to half their depth to join one another.

Hammerbeam: a roof carried on horizontal brackets projecting at wall-plate level. The brackets support hammerposts, which in turn support collars and purlins (see Figure 4.2).

Heck: in Northern usage, a short screen between the doorway and the fireplace, characteristically ended by a 'heck-post'.

Hipped: pertaining to a roof, built with a slope at the ends as well as the sides.

Husbandmen: a class of small farmers, below that of yeomen.

Inglenook: a recess adjoining a fireplace.

Inventory: see **probate inventory**.

Jetty: the projection of an upper storey over that below.

Joint: a **lap-joint** is the junction of two timbers at different angles, often halved. A **scarf-joint** is the junction of two end-on timbers. A **straight-joint** or **butt-joint** is the unbonded junction of two parts of a structure, often indicating two phases.

Jowl: the enlarged head of a vertical post.

Keystone: the central stone in an arch.

Laithe-house: a building combining a low-house, storage space for crops, and an attached house.

Linhay: an open-fronted cattle shed.

Lintel: a horizontal timber or stone over a door, fireplace or other opening.

Loggia: a gallery with regular openings along one side.

Longhouse: a house where the human living space and byre are in the same range, with internal access between them.

Lynchets: earthen terraces in a hillside, often the remains of past cultivation.

Manor: the district over which a lord had domain (the manor house being his residence, from which domain was exercised).

Marches: loosely borderlands; more specifically, areas controlled by English 'lords of the March', tasked with maintaining border control between England and neighbouring areas of Scotland and Wales.

Messuage: a legal term referring to a dwelling-house and associated outbuildings and land.

Mortice: socket in a piece of timber, to receive a tenon.

Moulding: the carved profile of a timber or masonry features.

Mullion: an upright dividing a window into lights.

Nogging: brick infill in a timber frame.

Oast: a drying kiln, for example, for hops, malt or tobacco.

Outshut: extension to a building under a lean-to roof.

Over: on the floor above.

Pantile: a roof tile with an S-shaped profile.

Pargetting: moulded patterning in plaster, either patterned or figurative.

Pediment: a tall block carrying a classical column or feature.

Pilaster: flat representation of a column in shallow relief.

Plate: any horizontal timber.

Polite: pertaining to architecture that is of basically high status, showing national and international influence; to be understood as a paired term with 'vernacular'.

Pollard: as with coppicing, the cutting-off of a tree trunk to encourage the growth of shoots from the stump, but pollarding is done at a sufficient height to stop animals grazing on the shoots.

Post: any vertical timber forming part of the main frame.

Principals: rafters over the main posts, often larger than common rafters, though rarely so in Suffolk.

Probate inventory: a list of movable goods and their values drawn up on a person's death, often compiled room-by-room.

Purlin: a horizontal timber between the wall-plates and the apex of the roof to provide longitudinal support.

Quoin: dressed stone at the angle of a building.

Rail: a horizontal timber.

Recusant: pertaining to those who remained Roman Catholics after the English Reformation who refused to attend the services of the Church of England.

Rendering: covering, for example, of plaster and/or of lime.

Roof: Catslide: the main slope descending without change in pitch, for example, over an outshut. **Hipped**: with a sloping rather than gabled end. **Gambrel**: with a pitch of two angles, the steeper one below.

Scantling: dimensions of a timber.

Screens passage: a screened-off passage, usually linking opposed doors, between hall and service rooms.

Shippon: a cowhouse.

Sill: the lower member of a window frame, or the rail at the foot of the frame.

Skep: a domed beehive made of twisted straw.

Slabbing: an outside piece cut from a log when squaring it for timber.

Smoke bay: see Chapter 5. A bay that has been left open to the roof to allow the smoke from a hearth to rise and disperse.

Soffit: the underside of a lintel or arch.

Solar: withdrawing room.

Spere: a truss at the lower end of an open hall with a partition screen at the two sides but not in the middle (seen in plan on Figure 4.1); the open space may have been occupied by a movable screen.

Stack: abbreviation of 'chimney-stack'.

Staddle stones: mushroom-shaped stone blocks upon which the superstructure of a granary is placed; the shape prevents vermin from getting into the granary.

Stud: common vertical timbers set between posts, closely or widely spaced (hence 'close studding').

Tenon: the diminished end of a timber to fit in a mortice.

Tenure: a form of landholding, of various forms and degrees of security (for example, freehold and copyhold tenure).

Tie-beam or **tie**: the horizontal timber of a truss at wall-plate level connecting the tops of the posts.

Toft: the farmyard around the medieval peasant house, often defined by a bank and ditch.

Truss: a pair of posts and principals and the frame connecting them, such that the timber frame is made of up a series of trusses (see Figure 2.4).

Vernacular: pertaining to architecture that uses local materials in traditional ways, to be understood as a paired (and changing) term with 'polite'.

Wainscotting: the wooden lining to interior walls.

Wall-plate: a rail running along the top of the wall.

Waney: pertaining to timber with its curved edge left on, usually due to insufficient scantling.

Weald: an area of Sussex and Kent characterised by heavy clay soil, areas of woodland, and dispersed settlement.

Wealden: pertaining to a particular type of open-hall house with both upper and lower ends jettied to the front. The wall-plate over the jetties continues over the front of the unjettied hall, creating an overhang. Wealdens are found in, but not confined to, the Weald of Kent and Sussex.

Yeomen: a socially middling class of tenant farmers of reasonable security and wealth.

Further Reading

In what follows, I will first list suggestions for further reading and research before appending a full bibliography. Suggestions for further reading have been made on a highly selective basis – they are meant as a few places to start, and are not authoritative reading lists.

Places to Visit

The best way to start learning about old houses is to go and look at them. However, no house can be fully understood without looking at it inside as well as outside, and as most traditional houses are still occupied and functioning buildings, surviving houses in the countryside have been modified over and over again. You will get a better idea of how the much-changed and fragmentary buildings you are looking at relate to different types in the past by visits to the Weald and Downland Museum (http://www.wealddown.co.uk/); Avoncroft Museum of Historic Buildings (http://www.avoncroft.org.uk/); Ryedale Folk Museum (http://www.ryedalefolkmuseum.co.uk); and the National Museum of Wales at St Fagans (http://www.museumwales.ac.uk/en/stfagans/). The Museum of English Rural Life at Reading (http://www.reading.ac.uk/merl/) also has relevant material. For other museums see http://www.ruralmuseumsnetwork.org.uk/members/. The properties of English Heritage and the National Trust are generally larger buildings, but a selection of houses that could be termed vernacular can be found in their care.

In North America, visits to Plimoth Plantation (http://www.plimoth.org/) and to Colonial Williamsburg (http://www.colonialwilliamsburg.com/) are fascinating experiences, though, as the curators themselves will affirm, they should be treated with critical caution.

In planning visits to villages and other settlements, the county Pevsner is helpful, particularly if it has recently been revised (the revised editions include more vernacular buildings than Pevsner originally listed); in any case, only the narrowest of minds would refuse to visit the local church alongside the houses, and Pevsner is essential for the former. I have also found the Images of England website useful in deciding where to go (www.imagesofengland.org.uk). Do bear in mind that most vernacular houses are still private homes, and show consideration in respecting the owners' privacy. Barns are the best place to study timber-framing as the structure of the frame is less obscured by partitions – and also easier to gain access to than people's homes.

Relevant Societies

The Vernacular Architecture Group (VAG) is the most important relevant organisation. They are friendly and extremely welcoming to newcomers (I am grateful to the group for much of my early training as a young student). Their 'spring meetings' take several days to visit a series of houses in a given area, usually, though not always, in England or Wales; they are consistently oversubscribed, and for good reason. The spring meetings are a fantastic opportunity to look at houses in the company of more experienced researchers. The VAG also holds a themed winter meeting of lectures, often the focus of lively debate (http://www.vag.org.uk/). There is also an Historic Farm Buildings Group (www.hfbg.org.uk). The Society for the Protection of Ancient Buildings, founded by William Morris, also plays an important role (www.spab.org.uk). A full list of local, regional and other societies with a web presence can be found on the VAG website, including links to societies around the world such as the North American Vernacular Architecture Forum (www.vernaculararchitectureforum.org).

General Reading

If you have time to read five books they should be the following:

1. Glassie 2000, *Vernacular Architecture*, is my favourite book on traditional buildings; there is more thoughtful insight packed into a few of Glassie's pages than there is to be found on most books on the subject.
2. Wilkinson 2000, *The Shock of the Old*, is an exciting account of the general history of architecture in Britain, which stresses that old buildings, 'rather than being part of a quaint homogenous British landscape, were dramatic statements of modern form, technology and occasional eccentricity' (front flyleaf). For more depth, move on to Davis 1999.
3. Much of the literature on timber framing techniques is a forest of technical jargon in which, very often, the human beings seem to have been lost. Easily the best introduction that avoids this is Richard Harris' brilliant *Discovering Timber-Framed Buildings* (1993), which as well as its clarity and brevity contains a great deal of deep thinking and subtle insights. The newcomer to the field is advised to read this book three or four times carefully before moving on to Harris' articles, especially Harris 1989, which informs much of the explication of timber-framing in Chapter 2.
4. W.G. Hoskins, *The Making of the English Landscape* (1955), is now out of date, but is still essential to read: see also Johnson, *Ideas of Landscape* (2007) for my assessment of Hoskins' contribution.
5. Keith Wrightson, *Earthly Necessities* (2000), is an introduction to the changing social and economic basis of life across England, Scotland and Wales; a reading of Wrightson will also correct some of the Anglocentric and rural bias of this book.

Books to avoid: there is a genre of 'chocolate-box' writing with titles like *The Charm of the English Country Cottage*, often authored by a celebrity, that needs to be avoided. Often beautifully photographed and produced, they are seductive in their appeal to a vision of an 'Olde Englande' but tend to replicate traditional ideas of an unchanging countryside rather than questioning them.

The best books for those interested in researching the history of their own homes are Alcock 2003, Barratt 2000 and Cunnington 1999. (See the Bibliography for further details.)

Houses Around the World

There is a huge comparative literature on the anthropology and history of houses around the world: places to start are Oliver 1997 and Oliver 2006; Beck 2007; Knapp 1989; Locock 1994; Maran et al. 2006; Ardener 1993 for a feminist perspective.

Introduction

An authoritative history of the study of vernacular architecture has yet to be written. On different approaches to the subject, see different articles in *Vernacular Architecture* 28, including Johnson 1998, and Pearson and Meeson (eds) 2001; Pearson's article in that latter volume includes much more historical detail than space allows here. Arnold 2002 discusses different approaches to architectural history.

There is a huge theoretical literature on performance, materiality and agency: here are a few places to start. Performance and performativity are discussed extensively by, among many others, Goffman 1959 and Butler 1993; Arnold 2001, 129–33, discusses performativity in relation to architecture. John McGavin 2007, 5–11, discusses how difficult it is to capture the nuances of performance from the written record alone. On materiality see Miller 2005; on agency see Giddens 1984, though Cressy 2000 is good as a practical illustration; see also Dobres and Robb 2000.

Building Traditional Houses

The Pattern of English Building, by Clifton-Taylor 1972, is an engaging and beautifully written account of the building materials used in England and their influence on architectural patterns. Harvey 1984 and Salzman 1952 are best on building accounts; see also Binding 2004, Hislop 2000 and Barnwell et al. 2004. Airs 1995 is a masterly synthesis of information on sixteenth- and seventeenth-century building practices, albeit at the polite rather than vernacular level.

For timber-framing, read Harris 1993; also read the various books by Brunskill (for example, Brunskill 2000 and 2004) on building materials generally.

Houses in the Landscape

Readers wanting to explore the medieval structuring of the English landscape might start with three recent books on the subject which take differing approaches to the issue: Williamson 2002, Roberts and Wrathmell 2002, and Jones and Page 2006. These are the three latest, and most impressive, statements on a set of issues that have generated a vast literature.

Overton (1996) is the best introduction to changing farming practices in the early modern period. Johnson (1996) is my attempt to put housing changes in the context of landscape and society as a whole.

The Medieval House

For deeper analysis and discussion of Bayleaf and the other houses at the Weald and Downland, see Tankard 2009. I am very grateful to Danae Tankard for letting me have prior sight of her chapter on Bayleaf (see also Tankard 2007).

Coldstream (2002) is a lucid and beautifully illustrated introduction to medieval architecture in general. Grenville (1997) is the clearest introduction, placing vernacular medieval houses in the context of other classes of building. Two recent articles are particularly important in changing our view of medieval houses: Pearson 2005 and Gardner 2000.

There is a huge literature on late medieval rural economy and society. Some places to start are Dyer 2002 and Dyer 2005, Goldberg 1997 and 2004, Horrox and Ormrod 2006. Bennett 1987 and Mate 1998 are good on women's status and experiences.

Rebuilding and Reformation

Maurice Howard (2007) is the best recent discussion of changes in sixteenth-century architecture as a whole. I have discussed the origins and development of Hoskins' idea of the
rebuilding in Johnson 1993b, and look at Harrison's comments in Johnson 1996, 154–78.

For the Little Ice Age, read Fagan 2000 for an accessibly written introduction, and Grive
1990 for more detail. On the Reformation read Gaimster and Gilchrist 2003. Overton 1996
is the best introduction to enclosure and related changes.

Polite and Rustic

The best writers on sixteenth- and seventeenth-century polite architecture are Mark Girouard,
Maurice Howard, and Nicholas Cooper. Nicholas Cooper's *The Houses of the Gentry in England*
(1999) is a definitive text. I disagree with Cooper's conclusions but his scholarship is beyond
question. For a much-needed feminist perspective, see the essay by Alice Friedman in Arnold
(ed.) 2002. On state formation, see Braddick 2000 and Hindle 2002. Green 2007 is a short
but crucial study of the origins of 'vernacular' as a category.

Everyday Life in the Early Modern House

The discussion of Yetminster is largely based on Machin (1978).

This chapter tries to bring together a very complex literature from feminist history, folklife,
and other studies. Fletcher (1995) and Mendelson and Crawford (1998) are good introduc-
tions to men's and women's roles; see also Fletcher 2008 on children. Cressy 2000 is an accessible exploration of the culture of early modern England, and brings across the way ideas of
household and political order intersected with people's lives. Hutton 1994 is a classic on the
ritual year. Thirsk 2007 emphasises the importance of both the production and preparation
of food in early modern England. Wade Martins 2002b is a valuable summary of current
research into farm buildings.

On culture of the middling sort, Campbell 1942 remains a classic; Brooks and Barry 1994
is more up-to-date. St George 1998 is good on Puritan culture as expressed in architecture.
For folklife, the best book remains that of the great George Ewart Evans (1966).

For furnishings and fittings, see the publications of the Regional Furniture Society; also
Mercer 1969, Hall 2006 and Gilbert 1991. Thornton 1978 and Thornton 1984 are beautifully
illustrated but, despite their titles, are confined to elite and urban/metropolitan interiors.
Recent publications by the AHRC Centre for the Study of the Domestic Interior are, for
example, Styles and Vickery 2006; their database of images is an invaluable resource though
it concentrates on metropolitan and eighteenth-century material (http://csdi.rca.ac.uk/).

For witchcraft, see Macfarlane 1970, Thomas 1971, Larner 1981 and Purkiss 1996. These
are four classic books, all which take rather different approaches to witchcraft. Merrifield
1987 brings together the copious archaeological evidence for ritual and apotropaic practices.

Georgianisation

Summerson 1945 and Gloag 1944 are classic statements of the traditional view: see the
first chapter of Hughes 1987 for an alternative view to Gloag's. Arnold 1998 provides new
perspectives at the 'polite' level.

In the last twenty years, much exciting and theoretically aware research has been published on material objects from this period, but, with exceptions, it is largely elite, metropolitan and urban in its focus, and it does not tackle the rural and the vernacular. Nevertheless Bermingham and Brewer (eds) 1995, Brewer and Porter 1993 and Brewer and Staves 1995, are essential places to start; see also Brewer 1997 and Wilson 2008. Styles and Vickery (eds) 2006 is a wonderful collection of essays reflecting the state of the art in the field of Georgian material culture, particularly the articles by Herman and Blair St George.

The ideas of Peter Guillery are extremely important in understanding housing in this period, though he has worked in urban rather than rural contexts (Guillery 2004; see also his work with Bernard Herman, 2006).

Tarlow 2007 discusses the 'archaeology of improvement' for the period 1750–1850.

Conclusions

For the Georgian Order in the American colonies, see Leone 2005. Green and Leech 2006 is a valuable collection of studies from around the Atlantic world. Deetz 1977 draws many of its ideas from Glassie (1975), a more complex book; Glassie 2000 is an easier place to start. No discussion of the Atlantic world is meaningful without discussion of the slave trade and Britain's role in it: see Schama 2005.

Key figures in American vernacular architecture are Bernard Herman, Cary Carson and Robert Blair St George (1998); all have essays in *Common Places* (Upton and Vlach 1986), a reader on American vernacular architecture, which includes a classic essay by Fred Kniffen. Upton 1998 is a subtle and insightful account of architecture in the United States, placing houses and vernacular traditions in a wider, thematic frame.

Bibliography

Aalen, F., Whelan, K. and Stout, M. (eds) 1997. *Atlas of the Irish Rural Landscape*. Cork, Cork University Press

Aberg, F.A. (ed.) 1978. *Medieval Moated Sites*. CBA Research Report 17. London, Council for British Archaeology

Adams, M. 2005. 'The Bernoulli Principle and Smoke Control'. *Vernacular Architecture* 36, 61–5

Addy, S.O. 1898. *The Evolution of the English House*. London, Swan Sonneschein

Airs, M. 1975. *The Making of the English Country House, 1500–1640*. London, Allen and Unwin

Airs, M. 1995. *The Tudor and Jacobean Country House: A Building History*. Stroud, Sutton

Airs, M. and Broad, J. 1998. 'The Management of Rural Building in Seventeenth-Century Buckinghamshire'. *Vernacular Architecture* 29, 43–56

Albert, W. 1972. *The Turnpike Road System in England 1663–1840*. Cambridge, Cambridge University Press

Alcock, N.W. 1981. *Cruck Construction: An Introduction and Catalogue*. London, Council for British Archaeology

Alcock, N.W. 1993. *People At Home: Living in a Warwickshire Village, 1500–1800*. Chichester, Phillimore

Alcock, N.W. 1994. 'Physical Space and Social Space: The Interpretation of Vernacular Architecture'. In Locock (ed.) (1994), 207–30

Alcock, N.W. 1997. 'A Response To Cruck Distribution: A Social Explanation by Eric Mercer'. *Vernacular Architecture* 28, 92–3

Alcock, N.W. 1998. 'Smoke Bay or Open Hall? Cuttle Pool Farm, Knowle, Warwickshire'. *Vernacular Architecture* 29, 82–4

Alcock, N.W. 2002. 'The Distribution and Dating of Crucks and Base Crucks'. *Vernacular Architecture* 33, 67–70

Alcock, N.W. 2003. 'Documenting the History of Houses'. *Archives and the User*, 10. London, British Records Association

Alcock, N.W. 2006. 'The Origins of Crucks: Innocence or Naivete? A Response'. *Vernacular Architecture* 37, 50–3

Alcock, N.W., Barley, M.W., Dixon, P.W. and Meeson, R.A. 1996. *Recording Timber-Framed Buildings: An Illustrated Glossary*. York, Council for British Archaeology

Alcock, N.W. and Carson, C. 2007. *West Country Farms: House-and-Estate Surveys, 1598–1764*. Oxford, Oxbow

Alcock, N.W., Child, P. and Laithwaite, M. 1972. 'Sanders, Lettaford: A Devon Long-house'. *Transactions of the Devon Archaeological Society* 30, 227–33

Alcock, N.W. and Cox, N. 2000. 'Living and Working in Seventeenth-Century England: An Encyclopaedia of Drawings and Descriptions from Randle Holmes'. Orginal Mansuscripts for The Academy of Armory. CD-ROM, British Library

Alcock, N.W. and Laithwaite, M. 1973. 'Medieval Houses in Devon and their Modernization.' *Medieval Archaeology* 17, 100–25

Alcock, N.W. and Woodfield, C.T.P. 1996. 'Social Pretensions in Architecture and Ancestry: Hall House, Sawbridge, Warwickshire and the Andrewe Family'. *Antiquaries Journal* 76, 51–72

Alfrey, J. 2006. 'The Language of its Builders: Stone in the Vernacular of Rural Wales During the Nineteenth Century'. *Vernacular Architecture* 37, 54–60

Amussen, S. 1995. 'Punishment, Discipline and Power: The Social Meanings of Violence in Early Modern England'. *Journal of British Studies* 34, 1–34

Anderson, S. 2003. 'Architectural Terracotta from Westhorpe Hall, Suffolk. *Archaeological Journal* 160, 125–59

Archer, R. 1997. ' "How Ladies . . . Who Live on Their Manors Ought to Manage their Households and Estates": Women as Landholders and Administrators in the Later Middle Ages'. In Goldberg (ed.), 1997, 149–81

Ardener, S. (ed.) 1993. [Second edition.] *Women and Space: Ground Rules and Social Maps*. Oxford, Berg

Aries, P. 1962. *Centuries of Childhood*. London, Cape

Arnold, D. 1998. *The Georgian Country House: Architecture, Landscape and Society*. Stroud, Sutton

Arnold, D. 2001. *Reading Architectural History*. London, Routledge

Aston, M., Austin, D. and Dyer, C.C. (eds) 1989. *The Rural Settlement of Medieval England*. Oxford, Blackwell, 247–67

Baird, K. 2003. Secular Wall Paintings in the Sixteenth and Seventeenth Centuries. Unpublished PhD thesis, University of Oxford

Barley, M.W. 1961. *The English Farmhouse and Cottage*. London, Routledge

Barnwell, P. and Adams, J. 1994. *The House Within: Interpreting Medieval Houses in Kent*. London, Her Majesty's Stationery Office

Barnwell, P. and Airs, M. (eds) 2006. *Houses and the Hearth Tax: The Later Stuart House and Society*. CBA Research Report 150. London, Council for British Archaeology

Barnwell, P. and Giles, C. 1997. *English Farmsteads 1750–1914*. London, Her Majesty's Stationery Office

Barnwell, P., Palmer, M. and Airs, M. (eds) 2004. *The Vernacular Workshop from Craft to Industry, 1400–1900*. CBA Research Report 140. London, English Heritage

Barratt, N. 2000. *Tracing the History of Your House*. London, Public Records Office

Barrell, J. 1980. *The Dark Side of the Landscape: The Rural Poor in English Painting 1730–1840*. Cambridge, Cambridge University Press

Beacham, P. (ed.) 1990. *Devon Building: An Introduction to Local Traditions*. Exeter, Devon Books

Bebb, R. 2007. *Welsh Furniture 1250–1950: A Cultural History of Craftsmanship and Design*. Aberystwyth, Saer Books

Beck, R. (ed.) 2007. *The Durable House: House Society Models in Archaeology*. Carbondale, Southern Illinois University Press

Beier, A.L. 1985. *Masterless Men: The Vagrancy Problem in England 1560–1640*. London, Methuen

Benjamin, W. 1968 [1936]. *Illuminations*. New York, Schosken

Bennett, J.M. 1987. *Women in the Medieval English Countryside*. Oxford, Oxford University Press

Beresford, M.W. and Hurst, J.G. (eds) 1971. *Deserted Medieval Villages*. Woking, Lutterworth Press

Bermingham, A. and Brewer, J. (eds) 1995. *The Consumption of Culture 1600–1800: Image, Object, Text*. London, Routledge

Bernard, G. 2006. *The King's Reformation: Henry VIII and the Remaking of the English Church*. New Haven, Yale University Press

Berry, J.A. 2001. 'English Furniture Locks'. *Regional Furniture* 15, 64–71

Betjeman, J. 1970 [1933]. *Ghastly Good Taste: Or, A Depressing Story of the Rise and Fall of English Architecture*. London, Anthony Blond

Binding, G. 2004. *Medieval Building Techniques*. Stroud, Tempus

Blaylock, S. 2004. *Bowhill: The Archaeological Study of a Building Under Repair in Exeter, Devon, 1977–95*. London, English Heritage

Blomley, N. 2007. 'Making Private Property: Enclosure, Common Right and the Work of Hedges'. *Rural History: Economy Society, Culture*. 18:1, 1–21

Bold, J. 1988. *Wilton House and English Palladianism: Some Wiltshire Houses*. London, Her Majesty's Stationery Office

Borsay, P. 1989. *The English Urban Renaissance: Culture and Society in the Provincial Town 1660–1770*. Oxford, Clarendon Press

Borsay, P. 2000. *The Image of Georgian Bath: Towns, Heritage and History*. London, Oxford University Press

Borsay, P. 2006. 'From Bath to Poundbury: The Rise, Fall and Rise of Polite Urban Space 1700–2000'. In Green and Leech (eds), 2006, 97–116

Bourdieu, P. 1990. *The Logic of Practice*. Cambridge, Polity

Braddick, M. 2000. *State Formation in Early Modern England*. Cambridge, Cambridge University Press

Brears, P.C.D. 1988. *North Country Folk Art*. Edinburgh, John Donald

Breen, T.H. 1986. 'An Empire of Goods: The Anglicisation of Colonial America, 1690–1776. *Journal of British Studies* 25:4, 467–99

Breen, T.H. 2004. *The Marketplace of Revolution: How Consumer Politics Shaped American Independence*. Oxford, Oxford University Press

Brewer, J. 1997. *The Pleasures of the Imagination: English Culture in the Eighteenth Century*. London, HarperCollins

Brewer, J. and Porter, R. (eds) 1993. *Consumption and the World of Goods*. London, Routledge

Brewer, J. and Staves, S. (eds) 1995. *Early Modern Conceptions of Property*. London, Routledge

Brinton, M. 1987. *Farmhouses and Cottages of the Isle of Wight*. Newport, Isle of Wight County Council

Britnell, R. 2004. *Britain and Ireland 1050–1530: Economy and Society*. Oxford, Oxford University Press

Britnell, W.J. and Suggett, R. 2002. 'A Sixteenth-Century Peasant Hallhouse in Powys: Survey and Excavation of Tyddyn Llwydian, Pennant Melangell, Montgomeryshire'. *Archaeological Journal* 159, 142–69

Britton, J. (ed.) 1847. *The Natural History of Wiltshire, by John Aubrey*. London, no publisher stated

Brooks, A. 1999. 'Building Jerusalem: Transfer-Printed Finewares and the Creation of British Identity'. In Tarlow and West (eds), 1999, 35–50

Brooks, C. and Barry, J. (eds) 1994. *The Middling Sort of People: Culture, Society and Politics in England, 1550–1800*. Basingstoke, Macmillan

Brown, D. 2000. 'The Maori Response to Gothic Architecture'. *Architectural History* 43, 253–70

Brunskill, R.W. 2000. *Vernacular Architecture: An Illustrated Handbook*. London, Faber

Brunskill, R.W. 2004. *Traditional Buildings of Britain: An Introduction to Vernacular Architecture and its Revival*. London, Cassell

Budgen, C. 2002. *West Surrey Architecture 1840–2000*. Woking, Heritage of Waverley

Burke, P. 1995. 'The Invention of Leisure in Early Modern Europe'. *Past and Present* 146, 136–51

Burt, R. and Archer, J.M. (eds) 1994. *Enclosure Acts: Sexuality, Property and Enclosure in Early Modern England*. Ithaca, Cornell, 17–33

Bushaway, R. 1982. *By Rite: Custom, Ceremony and Community in England 1700–1880*. London, Junction Books

Butler, J. 1993. *Bodies that Matter: On the Discursive Limits of 'Sex'*. London, Routledge

Caffyn, L. 1986. *Workers' Housing in West Yorkshire, 1750–1920*. London, Her Majesty's Stationery Office.

Camille, M. 1998. *Mirror in Parchment: The Luttrell Psalter and the Making of Medieval England*. London, Reaktion

Campbell, C. 1987. *The Romantic Ethic and the Spirit of Modern Consumerism*. Oxford, Blackwell

Campbell, J.W.P. 2000. 'Naming the Parts of Post-Medieval Roof Structures'. *Vernacular Architecture* 31, 45–51

Campbell, J.W.P. and Saint, A. 2002. 'The Manufacture and Dating of English Brickwork 1600–1720'. *Archaeological Journal* 159, 170–93

Campbell, M. 1942. *The English Yeoman Under Elizabeth and the Early Stuarts*. New Haven, Yale University Press

Carson, C. 1978. 'Doing History with Material Culture'. In Quimby, I.M.G. (ed.) *Material Culture and the Study of American Life*. New York, Norton

Carson, C., Barka, N., Kelso, W., Stone, G.W. and Upton, D. 1988. 'Impermanent Architecture in the Southern American Colonies'. In St George (ed.), 1988, 135–96

Charles, Prince of Wales, 1989. *A Vision of Britain: A Personal View of Architecture*. London, Doubleday

Chatwin, D. 2003. 'Variations in the Survival Rate of Timber-Framed Buildings in Two Sussex Parishes'. *Vernacular Architecture* 34, 32–6

Chettle, G.H. and Leach, P. 1984. *Kirby Hall, Northamptonshire*. London, English Heritage

Clarke, J. 2005. 'An Early Vernacular Hammer-Beam Structure: Imberhorne Farm Cottages, East Grinstead, West Sussex'. *Vernacular Architecture* 36, 32–40

Clarkson, L. 1975. *Death, Disease and Famine in Pre-Industrial England*. London, Macmillan

Clifton-Taylor, A. 1972. [Third edition.] *The Pattern of English Building*. London, Faber

Coldstream, N. 2002. *Medieval Architecture*. Oxford, Oxford University Press

Colley, L. 1992. *Britons: Forging the Nation*. New Haven, Yale University Press

Colman, S. 1982. '"Weepers": A Small Late Medieval Aisled Hall in Cambridgeshire'. *Medieval Archaeology* 26, 158–62

Colvin, H. (ed.) 1963. *The History of the King's Works*. Vols 1 and 2. London, Her Majesty's Stationery Office

Colvin, H. and Newman, J. (eds) 1981. *Of Building: Roger North's Writings on Architecture*. Oxford, Clarendon

Cooper, N. 1999. *Houses of the Gentry 1480–1680*. New Haven, Yale University Press

Cooper, N. 2002. 'Display, Status and the Vernacular Tradition'. *Vernacular Architecture* 33, 28–33

Cormack, L. 1991. '"Good Fences Make Good Neighbours": Geography as Self-Definition in Early Modern England'. *Isis* 82, 639–61

Cosgrove, D. 1983. *The Palladian Landscape: Geographical Change and its Cultural Representations in Sixteenth-Century Italy*. Leicester, Leicester University Press

Coss, P.R. 1995. 'The Culture of Children in Medieval England'. *Past and Present* 148, 48–88

Cousins, N. 2000. *Lincolnshire Buildings in the Mud and Stud Tradition*. Heritage Lincolnshire

Cox, J. and Thorp, N. 2001. *Devon Thatch: An Illustrated History of Thatching and Thatched Buildings in Devon*. Cheltenham, Devon Publishing

Cressy, D. 1976. 'Educational opportunity in Tudor and Stuart England'. *History of Education Quarterly* 16, 501–6

Cressy, D. 1980. *Literacy and the Social Order in Tudor and Stuart England*. Cambridge, Cambridge University Press

Cressy, D. 2000. *Agnes Bowker's Cat: Travesties and Transgressions in Tudor and Stuart England*. Oxford, Oxford University Press

Cummings, A.L. 1979. *Framed Houses of Massachusetts Bay 1625–1725*. Cambridge, Harvard University Press

Cunnington, P. 1999. *How Old is Your House?* Yeovil, Marston

Currie, C.R.J. 1988. 'Time and Chance: Modelling the Attrition of Old Houses'. *Vernacular Architecture* 19, 1–9

Currie, C.R.J. 1992. 'Larger Medieval Houses in the Vale of White Horse'. *Oxoniensia* 57, 81–244

Currie, C.R.J. 2004. 'The Unfulfilled Potential of the Documentary Sources'. *Vernacular Architecture* 35, 1–11

Dalglish, C. 2003. *Rural Society in the Age of Reason: An Archaeology of the Emergence of Modern Life in the Southern Scottish Highlands*. New York, Kluwer

Davis, H. 2006. *The Culture of Building*. Oxford, Oxford University Press

Davies, K. 2008. *Artisan Art: Vernacular Wall Paintings in the Welsh Marches, 1550–1650*. Logaston, Herefordshire, Logaston Press

Deadman, J. 2004. *Langton House and the Carlen Brewery: A History 1751–2004*. Great Ayton, Great Ayton Community Archaeology Project

Deetz, J.F. 1996 [1977]. [Second edition.] *In Small Things Forgotten: An Archaeology of Early American Life*. New York, Anchor

Demos, J. 1999. [Second edition.] *A Little Commonwealth: Family Life in Plymouth Colony*. Oxford, Oxford University Press

De Selincourt, E. (ed.) 1906 [1835]. [Fifth edition.] *Wordsworth's Guide to the Lakes*. Oxford, Oxford University Press

Dingle, A.E. 1972. 'Drink and Working-Class Living Standards in Britain, 1870–1914'. *Economic History Review* 25:4, 608–22

Dixon, P. 1979. 'Towers, Pelehouses and Border Society'. *Archaeological Journal* 136, 240–52

Dobres, M-A. and Robb, J. (eds) 2000. *Agency in Archaeology*. London, Routledge

Dobson, R.R. 1973. *Durham Priory 1400–1450*. Cambridge, Cambridge University Press

Dorson, R.M. 1972. *Folklore and Folklife: An Introduction*. Chicago, University of Chicago Press

Duffy, E. 1992. *The Stripping of the Altars: Traditional Religion in England, c.1400–1580*. New Haven, Yale University Press

Duffy, E. 2001. *The Voices of Morebath: Reformation and Rebellion in an English Village*. New Haven, Yale University Press

Dyer, C.C. 1986. 'English Peasant Houses in the Later Middle Ages'. *Medieval Archaeology* 30, 19–45

Dyer, C.C. 2002. *Making a Living in the Middle Ages: The People of Britain 850–1520*. New Haven, Yale University Press

Dyer, C.C. 2003. 'The Archaeology of Medieval Small Towns'. *Medieval Archaeology* 30, 85–114

Dyer, C.C. 2005. *An Age of Transition? Economy and Society in England in the Later Middle Ages*. Oxford, Oxford University Press

Dyer, C.C. 2006a. 'Vernacular Architecture and Landscape History: The Legacy of "The Rebuilding of Rural England" and "The Making of the English Landscape"'. *Vernacular Archiecture* 37, 24–32

Dyer, C.C. (ed.) 2006b. *The Self-Contained Village? The Social History of Rural Communities 1250–1900*. Hatfield, University of Hertfordshire Press

Dyer, C.C. 2008. 'Building in Earth in Late Medieval England'. *Vernacular Architecture* 39, 63–70

Dymond, D. 1998. 'Five Building Contracts from Fifteenth-Century Suffolk'. *Antiquaries Journal* 78, 269–87

Dymond, D. and Paine, C. (eds) 1992. *The Spoil of Long Melford Church: The Reformation in an English Parish*. Bury St Edmunds, Suffolk Borough Council

Easton, T. 1999. 'Ritual Marks on Historic Timber'. *Weald and Downland Open Air Museum Journal*, unnumbered, spring 1999, 22–8

Eastop, D. 2001. 'Garments Deliberately Concealed in Buildings'. In Wallis and Lymer (eds), 2001, 79–84

Eaton, T. 2000. *Plundering the Past: Roman Stonework in Medieval Britain*. Stroud, Tempus

Ebbatson, L. 1994. 'Context and Discourse: Royal Archaeological Institute Membership 1845–1942'. In Vyner (ed.), 1994, 22–74

Edelen, G., ed. 1968. *The Description of England by William Harrison*. Ithaca, Cornell University Press

Elton, G.R. 1953. *The Tudor Revolution in Government: Administrative Changes in the Reign of Henry VIII*. Cambridge, Cambridge University Press

Emery, A. 1985. 'Ralph, Lord Cromwell's Manor at Wingfield (1439–c.1450): Its Construction, Design and Influence'. *Archaeological Journal* 142, 276–339

Evans, D.H. and Jarrett, M.G. 1987. 'The Deserted Village of West Whelpington, Northumberland, Part II'. *Archaeologia Aeliana* 16, 139–92

Evans, N. (ed.) 1987. *Wills of the Archdeaconry of Sudbury 1630–1635*. Bury St Edmunds, Suffolk Records Society, 29

Ewart Evans, G. 1962. *Ask the Fellows Who Cut the Hay*. London, Faber

Ewart Evans, G. 1966. *The Pattern Under the Plough: Aspects of the Folk-Life of East Anglia*. London, Faber

Fagan, B. 2000. *The Little Ice Age: How Climate Made History, 1300–1850*. New York, Basic Books

Ferguson, M. 2003. *Dido's Daughters: Literacy, Gender and Empire in Early Modern England and France*. Chicago, University of Chicago Press

Ferris, I.M. 1989. 'The Archaeological Investigation of Standing Buildings'. *Vernacular Architecture* 20, 12–17

Ferris, I.M. 1991. 'I Am Not a Camera'. *Vernacular Architecture* 22, 1

Finch, M. and Giles, K. (eds) 2007. *Estate Landscapes: Design, Improvement and Power in the Post-Medieval Landscape*. Woodbridge, Boydell

Fissell, M.E. 2004. 'The Politics of Reproduction in the English Reformation'. *Representations* 87, 43–81

Flather, A. 2007. *Gender and Space in Early Modern England*. Woodbridge, Boydell

Fleming, J. 2001. *Graffiti and the Writing Arts of Early Modern England*. London, Reaktion

Fletcher, A. 1995. *Gender, Sex and Subordination in England 1500–1800*. New Haven, Yale University Press

Fletcher, A. 2008. *Growing Up in England: The Experience of Childhood, 1600–1914*. New Haven, Yale University Press

Fletcher, A. and Stevenson, J. (eds) 1985. *Order and Disorder in Early Modern England.* Cambridge, Cambridge University Press

Foster, L. and Alcock, L. (eds) 1963. *Culture and Enviromment: Essays in Honour of Sir Cyril Fox.* London, Routledge

Foucault, M. 1972. *Archaeology of Knowledge.* London, Tavistock University Press

Fox, A. 2000. *Oral and Literature Culture in England, 1500–1700.* Oxford, Clarendon Press

Fox, Sir C. 1938. *The Personality of Britain: Its Influence on Inhabitant and Invader in Prehistoric and Historic Times.* Cardiff: National Museum of Wales

Fox, H.S.A. and Butlin, R.A. (eds) 1979. *Change in the Countryside: Essays on Rural England, 1500–1900.* Special Publication No. 10. London, Institute of British Geographers, 88–93

Fox, Sir C. and Raglan, Lord. 1951–4. *Monmouthshire Houses: A Study of Building Techniques and Smaller House-Plans in the Fifteenth to Seventeenth Centuries.* Three volumes. Cardiff, National Museum of Wales

Frantzen, A.J. and Moffat, D. (eds) 1994. *The Work of Work: Servitude, Slavery, and Labor in Medieval England.* ADD PLACE OF PUBLICATION, Cruithne Press

Fraser, S.M. 2000. 'The Materiality of Desire: Building Alternative Histories for a Hebridean Crafting Community'. *Archaeological Journal* 157, 375–98

French, H. 2000. 'The Search for the "Middle Sort" of People in England, 1600–1800'. *The Historical Journal* 43, 277–93

Friedman, A.T. 1997. 'Wife in the English Country House: Gender and the Meaning of Style in Early Modern England'. In Lawrence (ed.), 1997, 111–25

Furnivall, F.J. (ed.) 1877. *Harison's Description of England in Shakspere's Youth: Being the Second and Third Books of his Description of Britain and England.* London, New Shakspere Society

Gaimster, D. and Gilchrist, R. (eds) 2003. *The Archaeology of Reformation 1480–1580.* London, Society for Post-Medieval Archaeology

Games, N. (ed.) 2002. *Pevsner on Art and Architecture: The Radio Talks.* London, Methuen

Gardiner, M. 2000. 'Vernacular Buildings and the Development of the Later Medieval Domestic Plan in England'. *Medieval Archaeology* XLIV, 159–80

Gardiner, M. 2008. 'Buttery and Pantry and their Antecedents: Idea and Architecture in the English Medieval House'. In Kowalewski and Goldberg (eds), 2008, 37–65

Gaynor, J.M. 2005. 'Seventeenth- and Eighteenth-Century Woodworking Tools: The Evolution of a British Style'. *Tools and Trades* 14, 1–29

Gee, E. 1987. 'Heating in the Later Middle Ages'. *Transactions of the Ancient Monuments Society* 31, 88–105

Gent, L. (ed.) 1995. *Albion's Classicism: The Visual Arts in Britain 1550–1660.* New Haven, Yale University Press

Gent, L. and Llewellyn, N. (eds) 1990. *Renaissance Bodies.* London, Reaktion

Giddens, A. 1984. *The Constitution of Society: Outline of the Theory of Structuration.* Berkeley, University of California Press

Gilbert, C. 1991. *English Vernacular Furniture 1750–1900.* New Haven, Yale University Press

Gilchrist, R. 1994. *Gender and Material Culture: The Archaeology of Religious Women.* London, Routledge

Giles, C. 1992. *Rural Houses of West Yorkshire 1400–1830.* London, Her Majesty's Stationery Office

Giles, K. and Dyer, C. (eds) 2005. *Town and Country in the Later Middle Ages: Contrasts, Contacts and Interconnections, 1100–1500.* SMA Monograph 22. London, Society for Medieval Archaeology

Giles, K. and Giles, M. 2007. 'The Writing on the Wall: The Concealed Communities of the East Yorkshire Horselads'. *International Journal of Historical Archaeology* 11, 336–57

Girouard, M. 1978. *Life in the English Country House.* New Haven, Yale University Press

Girouard, M. 1983. *Robert Smythson and the Elizabethan Country House.* New Haven, Yale University Press

Girouard, M. 2000. *Life in the French Country House.* London, Cassell

Glassie, H. 1975. *Folk Housing in Middle Virginia, A Structural Analysis of Historic Artifacts.* Knoxville: University of Tennessee Press

Glassie, H. 2000. *Vernacular Architecture.* Bloomington, University of Indiana Press

Gloag, J. 1944. *The Englishman's Castle: A History of Houses, Large and Small.* London, Eyre and Spottiswoode

Goffman, E. 1959. *The Presentation of Self in Everyday Life.* New York, Doubleday

Goldberg, P.J.P. (ed.) 1997. *Women in Medieval English Society.* Stroud, Sutton

Goldberg, P.J.P. 2004. *Medieval England: A Social History 1250–1550.* London, Hodder

Gooder, E. 1984. 'The Finds from the Cellar of the Old Hall, Temple Balsall, Warwickshire'. *Post-Medieval Archaeology* 18, 149–250

Goody, J. 1987. *The Interface Between the Written and the Oral.* Cambridge, Cambridge University Press

Gowing, L. 1996. *Domestic Dangers: Women, Words and Sex in Early Modern London.* Oxford, Clarendon Press

Gowing, R. and Pender, R. (eds) 2007. *All Manner of Murals: The History, Techniques and Conservation of Secular Wall Paintings.* London, Archetype

Graves, C.P. 2000. *The Form and Fabric of Belief: An Archaeology of the Lay Experience of Religion in Medieval Norfolk and Devon.* BAR British Series 311. Oxford, British Archaeological Reports

Graves, C.P. 2008. 'From an Archaeology of Iconoclasm to an Anthropology of the Body: Images, Punishment, and Personhood in England, 1500–1660'. *Current Anthropology* 49:1, 35–60

Green, A. 1998. 'Tudhoe Hall and Byers Green Hall, County Durham: Seventeenth- and early Eighteenth-Century Social Change in Houses'. *Vernacular Architecture* 27, 33–42

Green, A. 2007. 'Confining the Vernacular: The Seventeenth-Century Origins of a Mode of Study'. *Vernacular Architecture* 38, 1–7

Green, A. and Leech, R. (eds) 2006. *Cities in the World 1500–2000.* Leeds, Maney

Grenville, J. 1997. *Medieval Housing.* Leicester, Leicester University Press

Grenville, J. 2008. 'Urban and Rural Houses and Households in the Late Middle Ages: A Case Study from Yorkshire'. In Kowalewski and Goldberg (eds), 2008, 92–123

Grive, J.M. 1990. *The Little Ice Age.* London, Routledge

Groves, C. 2000. 'Belarus to Bexley and Beyond: Dendrochronology and Dendro-Prevenancing of Conifer Timbers'. *Vernacular Architecture* 31, 59–66

Guillery, P. 2004. *The Small House in Eighteenth Century London.* New Haven, Yale University Press

Hall, L. 1982. *The Rural Houses of North Avon and South Gloucestershire 1400–1700.* Bristol, City of Bristol Museum and Art Gallery

Hall, L. 2006. *Period House Fixtures and Fittings 1300–1900.* Newbury, Countryside Books

Hamilton, A.H.A. 1878. *Quarter Sessions from Elizabeth to Anne.* London, Samson Low

Hamling, T. 2007. 'To See or Not to See? The Presence of Religious Imagery in the Protestant Household'. *Art History* 30:2, 170–97

Hancock, L. 2005. 'A Dug Out Chair from the South Lake District'. *Regional Furniture* 19, 80–2

Harding, J.M. 1976. *Four Centuries of Charlwood Houses: Medieval to 1840*. Charlwood, The Charlwood Society

Harris, R. 1989. 'The Grammar of Carpentry'. *Vernacular Architecture* 20, 1–8

Harris, R. 1993. [Third edition.] *Discovering Timber-Framed Buildings*. Princes Risborough, Shire

Harrison, B. and Hutton, B. 1984. *Vernacular Houses of North Yorkshire and Cleveland*. Edinburgh, Donald

Harvey, J. 1984. *English Mediaeval Architects: A Biographical Dictionary Down to 1550*. London, Alan Sutton

Harvey, N. 1984. *A History of Farm Buildings in England and Wales*. Newton Abbott, Devon, David and Charles

Hayfield, C. and Wagner, P. 1998. 'The Use of Chalk as a Building Material on the Yorkshire Wolds'. *Vernacular Architecture* 27, 1–12

Heal, F. 1990. *The Idea of Hospitality in Early Modern England*. Oxford, Clarendon Press

Herman, B. 1987. *Architecture and Rural Life in Central Delaware, 1700–1900*. Knoxville, University of Tennessee Press

Herman, B. 2006. 'Tabletop Conversations: Material Culture and Everyday Life in the Eighteenth-Century Atlantic World'. In Styles and Vickery (eds), 2006, 37–60

Hervey, F. (ed.) 1902. *Suffolk in the Seventeenth Century: the Breviary of Suffolk by Robert Reyce, 1618*. London, Murray

Hettinger, M. 1994. 'Defining the Servant: Legal and Extra-Legal Terms of Employment in Fifteenth-Century England'. In Frantzen and Moffat (eds), 1994, 190–210

Hewett, C.A. 1973. 'The Development of the Post-Medieval House'. *Post-Medieval Archaeology* 7, 60–78

Hewett, C.A. 1980. *English Historic Carpentry*. Sussex, Phillimore

Hey, D. 1974. *An English Rural Community: Myddle under the Tudors and Stuarts*. Leicester, Leicester University Press

Hill, J.E.C. 1962. *Puritans and the 'Dark Corners of the Land'*. Transactions of the Royal Historical Society, fifth series, 13, 77–102

Hill, J.E.C. 1966. *Society and Puritanism in Pre-Revolutionary England*. London, Heinemann

Hill, N. 2005. 'On the Origins of Crucks: An Innocent Notion'. *Vernacular Architecture* 36, 1–14

Hill, R. 2007. *God's Architect: Pugin and the Building of Romantic Britain*. London, Allen Lane

Hilton, R. 1975. *The English Peasantry in the Later Middle Ages. The Ford Lectures for 1973, and Related Studies*. Oxford, Clarendon Press

Hilton, R. 1979. *The English Peasantry in the Later Middle Ages*. Oxford, Clarendon Press

Hindle, S. 2002. *The State and Social Change in Early Modern England, 1550–1640*. London, Macmillan

Hines, J. 2004. *Voices in the Past: English Literature and Archaeology*. Cambridge, Brewer

Hinton, D. 1967. 'A Cruck House at Lower Radley, Berkshire'. *Oxoniensia* 32, 13–33

Hinton, D. 2005. *Gold and Gilt, Pots and Pins: Possessions and People in Medieval Britain*. Oxford, Oxford University Press

Hislop, M. 2000. *Medieval Masons*. Princes Risborough, Shire

Hislop, M. 2003. 'Rock House Farm, Great Haywood: A Fifteenth-Century Staffordshire Farm?' *Vernacular Architecture* 34, 75–8

Hodgson, R.I. 1979. 'The Progress of Enclosure in County Durham, 1550–1870'. In Fox and Butlin (eds), 1979,

Hooke, D. (ed.) 2000. *Landscape: The Richest Historical Record*. Society for Landscape Studies Supplementary Series 1. Amesbury, Society for Landscape Studies

Horn, J. 1993. *Adapting to a New World: English Society in Seventeenth Century Chesapeake*. Chapel Hill, NC, UNC Press

Horrox, R. and Ormrod, M. (eds) 2006. *A Social History of England 1200–1500*. Cambridge, Cambridge University Press

Hoskins, W.G. 1953. 'The Rebuilding of Rural England, 1570–1640'. *Past and Present* 4, 44–59

Hoskins, W.G. 1955. *The Making of the English Landscape*. London, Hodder & Stoughton

Hoskins, W.G. 1966. *English Local History: The Past and the Future*. Leicester, Leicester University Press

Howard, M. 1987. *The Early Tudor Country House: Architecture and Politics 1490–1550*. London, Philip

Howard, M. 2007. *The Building of Elizabethan and Jacobean England*. New Haven, Yale University Press

Hughes, R. 1987. *The Fatal Shore: A History of the Transportation of Convicts to Australia, 1787–1868*. London, Collins Harvill

Hurd, J. and Gourley, B. (eds) 2000. *Terra Brittanica: A Celebration of Earthen Structures in Great Britain and Ireland*. London, English Heritage

Hurst, J.G. 1971. 'A Review of Archaeological Research (to 1968)'. In Beresford and Hurst (eds), 1971, 76–144

Hutton, R. 1994. *The Rise and Fall of Merry England: The Ritual Year 1400–1700*. Oxford, Oxford University Press

Ingram, M. 1987. *Church Courts, Sex and Marriage in England, 1570–1640*. Cambridge, Cambridge University Press

Innocent, C.F. 1916. *Development of English Building Construction*. Cambridge, Cambridge University Press

James, D. 2003. 'An Investigation of the Orientation of Timber-Framed Houses in Herefordshire'. *Vernacular Architecture* 34, 20–31

James, S., Marshall, A. and Millett, M. 1984. 'An Early Medieval Building Tradition'. *Archaeological Journal* 141, 182–215

Jennings, N. 2002. 'The Building of the Clay Dabbins of the Solway Plain: Materials and Man-Hours'. *Vernacular Architecture* 33, 19–27

Johnson, B.H. 1991. 'Not "Mansard or Gambrel"'. *Vernacular Architecture* 22, 24–6

Johnson, M.H. 1993a. *Housing Culture: Traditional Architecture in an English Landscape*. London, University College London Press

Johnson, M.H. 1993b. 'Rethinking the Great Rebuilding'. *Oxford Journal of Archaeology* 12, 117–25

Johnson, M.H. 1996. *An Archaeology of Capitalism*. Oxford, Blackwell

Johnson, M.H. 1998. 'Vernacular Architecture: The Loss of Innocence'. *Vernacular Architecture* 28, 13–19

Johnson, M.H. 1999. 'Reconstructing Castles and Refashioning Identifies in Renaissance England'. In Tarlow and West (eds), 1999, 69–86

Johnson, M.H. 2002. *Behind the Castle Gate: From Medieval to Renaissance*. London, Routledge

Johnson, M.H. 2007. *Ideas of Landscape*. Oxford, Blackwell

Jones, R. and Page, M. 2006. *Medieval Villages in an English Landscape: Beginnings and Ends*. Macclesfield, Windgather Press

King, C. 2003. 'The Organisation of Social Space in Late Medieval Manor Houses'. *Archaeological Journal* 104–24

Kirk, J.C. 2003. 'Butts Cottage, Kirdford: The Conversion of Trees to Timber in the Rural Sussex Weald'. *Vernacular Architecture* 35, 12–20

Kirkham, A. 2007. 'Pattern and Colour in Late Sixteenth- and Seventeenth-Century Secular Wall and Panel Paintings in Suffolk: An Overview'. In Gowing and Pender (eds), 2007,

Knapp, Ronald G. 1989. *China's Vernacular Architecture: House Form and Culture*. Honolulu, University of Hawaii Press

Kniffen, F.B. and Glassie, H. 1986. 'Building in Wood in the Eastern United States: A Time-Place Perspective'. In Upton and Vlach (eds), 1986, 159–81

Kowalewski, M. and Goldberg, P.J.P. (eds) 2008. *Medieval Domesticity: Home, Housing and Household in Medieval England*. Cambridge, Cambridge University Press

Kumin, B. 2005. 'Drinking and Public Space in Early Modern German Lands'. *Contemporary Drug Problems* 35, 9–27

Kussmaul, A. 1981. *Servants in Husbandry in Early Modern England*. Cambridge, Cambridge University Press

Laing, F. 2005. Higher Status Domestic Buildings of Lancashire and Cheshire: Social Context and Actors Influencing the Choice of Building Materials. Unpublished PhD thesis, University of Liverpool

Laithwaite, M. 1977. *Sanders, Lettaford*. Transactions of the Devon Archaeological Society 35, 84

Lake, J. and Edwards, R. 2006. 'Buildings and Place: Farmsteads and the Mapping of Change'. *Vernacular Architecture* 37, 33–49

Lamb, H.H. 1982. *Climate, History and the Modern World*. London, Methuen

Laqueur, T. 1990. *Making Sex: Body and Gender from the Greeks to Freud*. Cambridge, Harvard University Press

Larner, C. 1981. *Enemies of God*. London, Chatto & Windus

Lascelles, C. (ed.) 1978. *Mansfield Park*. London, Dent

Lawrence, C. (ed.) 1997. *Women and Art in Early Modern Europe*. University Park, Pennsylvania University Press

Leone, M. 2005. *The Archaeology of Liberty in an American Capital: Excavations in Annapolis*. Berkeley, University of California Press

Leone, M. and Potter, P.B. (eds) 1988. *The Recovery of Meaning: Historical Archaeology in the Eastern United States*. Washington, Smithsonian

Leslie, M. and Raylor, T. (eds) 1992. *Culture and Cultivation in Early Modern England: Writing and the Land*. Leicester, Leicester University Press

Letts, J.B. 2000. *Smoke Blackened Thatch: A Unique Source of Late Medieval Plant Remains from Southern England*. London, English Heritage

Lewis, M. 2002. 'Impact of Industrialisation: Comparative Study of Child Health from Medieval and Postmedieval England (AD 850–1839)'. *American Journal of Physical Anthropology* 119, 211–23

Lipsedge, K. 2006. ' "Enter Into Thy Closet": Women, Closet Culture, and the Eighteenth-Century English Novel'. In Styles and Vickery (eds), 2006, 107–23

Lloyd, N. 1931. *A History of the English House: From Primitive Times to the Victorian Period*. London, Architectural Press

Locock, M. (ed.) 1994. *Meaningful Architecture: Social Interpretations of Buildings*. Aldershot, Avebury

Longcroft, A. (ed.) 2005. *The Historic Buildings of New Buckenham*. Norwich, University of East Anglia

Longcroft, A. 2006. 'Medieval Clay-Walled Houses: A Case Study from Norfolk'. *Vernacular Architecture* 37, 61–74

Lucas, G. 1995. 'The Changing Face of Time: English Domestic Clocks from the Seventeenth to the Nineteenth Centuries'. *Journal of Design History* 8, 1–10

Lucas, G. and Regan, R. 2003. 'The Changing Vernacular: Archaeological Excavations at Temple End, High Wycombe, Buckinghamshire'. *Post-Medieval Archaeology* 37, 165–206

Lucas, R. 1994. 'Ships' Timbers: Some Historical Evidence from Norfolk for Their Use'. *Vernacular Architecture* 25, 1–3

Lucas, R. 1997. 'When did Norfolk Cross "The Brick Threshold"'? *Vernacular Architecture* 28, 68–80

Lucas, R. 1998. 'Dutch Pantiles in the County of Norfolk: Architecture and International Trade in the Seventeenth and Eighteenth Centuries'. *Post-Medieval Archaeology* 32, 75–94

Luckyj, C. 1993. ' "A Moving Rhetoricke": Women's Silences and Renaissance Texts'. *Renaissance Drama* 24, 33–56

Macfarlane, A. 1970. *Witchcraft in Tudor and Stuart England: A Regional and Comparative Study*. New York, Harper and Row

Machin, R. 1977a. 'The Great Rebuilding: A Reassessment'. *Past and Present* 77, 33–56

Machin, R. 1977b. 'The Mechanism of the Pre-Industrial Building Cycle'. *Vernacular Architecture* 8, 815–19

Machin, R. 1978. *The Houses of Yetminster*. Bristol, University of Bristol, Department of Extra-Mural Studies

MacKie, E.W. 1997. 'Some Eighteenth-Century Houses in Appin, Lorn, Argyll'. *Antiquaries Journal* 77, 243–89

Maran, J., Juwig, C., Schwengel, H. and Thaler, U. (eds) 2006. *Konstruction der Macht: Architektur, Ideologie und Soziales Handeln*. Berlin, Lit Verlag

Marks, R. 2004. *Image and Devotion in Late Medieval England*. Stroud, Sutton

Marsh, C. 2005. 'Order and Place in England, 1580–1640: The View from the Pew'. *Journal of British Studies* 44, 3–26

Martin, D. 2000. 'End Reversal During the Conversion of Medieval Houses in Sussex'. *Vernacular Architecture* 31, 26–31

Martin, D. 2003. 'The Configuration of Inner Rooms and Chambers in the Transitional Houses of Eastern Sussex'. *Vernacular Architecture* 34, 37–41

Martin, D. and Martin, B. 1997. 'Detached Kitchens in Eastern Sussex: A Reassessment of the Evidence'. *Vernacular Architecture* 28, 85–91

Mate, M.E. 1998. *Daughters, Wives and Widows after the Black Death*. Woodbridge, Boydell

McCann, J. 1987. *Brick Nogging in the Fifteenth and Sixteenth Centuries, with Examples Drawn Mainly from Essex*. Transactions of the Ancient Monuments Society 31, 107–33

McCann, J. 1997. 'The Origin of Clay Lump in England'. *Vernacular Architecture* 28, 57–67

McCann, J. 2007. 'Clay-Walled Houses in Norfolk: Some Comments'. *Vernacular Architecture* 38, 58–60

McCracken, G. 1983. 'The Exchange of Children in Tudor England: An Anthropological Phenomenon in Historical Context'. *Journal of Family History* 8:4, 303–13

McGavin, J. 2007. *Theatricality and Narrative in Medieval and Early Modern Scotland*. London, Ashgate

McRae, A. 1996. *God Speed the Plough: The Representation of Agrarian England, 1500–1660*. Cambridge, Cambridge University Press

Meeson, R.A. 2000. 'Detached Kitchens or Service Blocks?' *Vernacular Architecture* 31, 73–5

Meeson, R.A. 2005. 'Ritual Marks and Graffiti: Curiosities or Meaningful Symbols?' *Vernacular Architecture* 36, 41–8

Mendelson, S. and Crawford, P. 1998. *Women in Early Modern England*. Oxford, Oxford University Press

Mercer, E. 1969. *English Furniture 700–1700*. London, Weidenfeld & Nicolson

Mercer, E. 1975. *English Vernacular Houses: A Study of Traditional Farmhouses and Cottages*. London, Her Majesty's Stationery Office

Mercer, E. 1996. 'Cruck Distribution: A Social Explanation'. *Vernacular Architecture* 27, 1–2

Mercer, E. 1998. 'Cruck Distribution: A Brief Note'. *Vernacular Architecture* 29, 57

Merrifield, R. 1987. *The Archaeology of Ritual and Magic*. London, Batsford

Miele, C. (ed.) 1996. *William Morris on Architecture*. Sheffield, Sheffield University Press

Miles, D.H.W. and Russell, H. 1995. 'Plumb and Level Marks'. *Vernacular Architecture* 26, 35–8

Miller, D. (ed.) 2005. *Materiality*. Durham, Duke University Press

Moir, J. and Letts, J. 1999. *Thatch: Thatching in England 1790–1940*. English Heritage Research Transactions 5. London, English Heritage

Moran, M. 1989. 'Re-Erecting Houses in Shropshire in the Late Seventeenth Century'. *Archaeological Journal* 146, 538–53

Moran, M. 2003. *Vernacular Buildings of Shropshire*. Little Logaston, Herefordshire, Logaston Press

Morrill, J. 1993. *The Nature of the English Revolution*. London, Longman

Muldrew, C. 1998. *The Economy of Obligation: The Culture of Credit and Social Relations in Early Modern England*. Basingstoke, Macmillan

Munby, J. 1974. 'A Dated Wealden House in Oxford From a Buckler Sketchbook'. *Vernacular Architecture* 5, 26

Nattrass, M. 1956. 'Witch Posts and Early Dwellings in Cleveland'. *Yorkshire Archaeological Journal* 39, 136–46

Olive, G. 1999. 'English West Country Tables and Forms'. *Regional Furniture* 13, 39–51

Olive, G. 2000. 'English West Country Cupboards'. *Regional Furniture* 14, 4–24

Oliver, P. (ed.) 1997. *Encyclopaedia of Vernacular Architecture*. Cambridge, Cambridge University Press

Oliver, P. 2006. *Built to Meet Needs: Cultural Aspects of Vernacular Architecture*. London, Architectural Press

Olwig, K. 2002. *Landscape, Nature and the Body Politic: From Britain's Renaissance to America's New World*. Madison, University of Wisconsin Press

Overton, M. 1996. *Agricultural Revolution in England: The Transformation of the Agrarian Economy 1500–1850*. Cambridge, Cambridge University Press

Pacey, A. 2005. 'Some Carpenter's Marks in Arabic Numerals'. *Vernacular Architecture* 36, 59–72

Palkovich, A.M. 1988. 'Asymmetry and Recursive Meanings in the Eighteenth Century: The Morris Pound House'. In Leone and Potter (eds), 1988, 293–306

Pantin, W.A. 1962–3. 'Medieval Town-House Plans'. *Medieval Archaeology* 6–7, 202–39

Parry, G. 2006. *The Arts of the Anglican Counter-Reformation: Glory, Laud and Honour*. Woodbridge, Boydell

Peachey, S. 1990. 'A Possible Duck Wall in Gwent'. *Journal of the Historic Farm Buildings Group* 4

Pearson, S. 1985. *Rural Houses of the Lancashire Pennines*. London, Her Majesty's Stationery Office

Pearson, S. 1994. *The Medieval Houses of Kent: An Historical Analysis*. London, Her Majesty's Stationery Office

Pearson, S. 2001. 'The Chronological Distribution of Tree-Ring Dates, 1980–2001: An Update'. *Vernacular Architecture* 32, 68–9

Pearson, S. 2005. 'Rural and Urban Houses 1100–1500: "Urban Adaptation" Reconsidered'. In Giles and Dyer (eds), 2005, 43–64

Pearson, S. and Meeson, R. (eds) 2001. *Vernacular Buildings in a Changing World: Understanding, Recording and Conservation*. York, Council for British Archaeology

Pennell, S. 1999a. 'The Familiar Past? Archaeologies of Later Historical Britain'. In Tarlow and West (eds), 1999, 35–50

Pennell, S. 1999b. 'Consumption and Consumerism in Early Modern England'. *Historical Journal* 42, 549–64

Penoyre, J. 2005. *Traditional Houses of Somerset*. Tiverton, Somerset Books

Penoyre, J. and Penoyre, J. 1993. *Decorative Plasterwork in the Houses of Somerset 1500–1700*. Taunton, Somerset County Council

Pevsner, N. 1942. 'The Term "Architect" in the Middle Ages'. *Speculum* 17

Pevsner, N. 1955. *The Englishness of English Art*. London, British Broadcasting Corporation

Pevsner, N. 1963. *An Outline of European Architecture*. Harmondsworth, Penguin

Pevsner, N. and Cherry, B. 1975. [Second edition.] *The Buildings of England: Wiltshire*. Harmondsworth, Penguin

Pilling, R. 1987. 'Wooden Floors in Evolution'. *Traditional Homes* 3, 10–17

Platt, C. 1994. *The Great Rebuildings of Tudor and Stuart England*. London, University College London Press

Pollock, A. 1983. *Forgotten Children: Parent–Child Relations From 1500 to 1900*. Cambridge, Cambridge University Press

Poos, L.R. 1991. *A Rural Society after the Black Death: Essex 1350–1525*. Cambridge, Cambridge University Press

Purkiss, D. 1995. 'Women's Stories of Witchcraft in Early Modern England: The House, the Body, the Child'. *Gender and History* 7:3, 408–32

Purkiss, D. 1996. *The Witch in History: Early Modern and Twentieth Century Representations*. London, Routledge

Purkiss, D. 2006. *The English Civil War: A People's History*. London, HarperCollins

Quiney, A. 1994. 'Medieval and post-medieval vernacular architecture'. In Vyner (ed.), 1994, 228–43

Quiney, A. 2004. *Town Houses of Medieval England*. New Haven, Yale University Press

Rackham, O. 1972. 'Grundle House: On the Quantities of Timber in Certain East Anglian Buildings in Relation to Local Supplies'. *Vernacular Architecture* 3, 3–8

Rackham, O. 1986. *The History of the Countryside*. London, Dent

Rackham, O. 1990. [Second edition.] *Trees and Woodland in the British Landscape*. London, Dent

Rackham, O. 1994. *The Illustrated History of the Countryside*. London: Weidenfeld & Nicolson

Ramm, H.G., McDowall, R.W. and Mercer, E. 1970. *Shielings and Bastles*. London, Her Majesty's Stationery Office

Reed, M. 1986. *The Age of Exuberance 1550–1700*. London, Routledge

Riall, N. and Hunt, R. 2001. 'A Tudor Cupboard at Cotehele, Cornwall'. *Archaeological Journal* 163, 147–79

Riddy, F. 2008. '"Bourgeois" Domesticity in Late-Medieval England'. In Kowalewski and Goldberg (eds), 2008, 14–36

Rigold, S. 1963. 'The Distribution of the Wealden House'. In Foster and Alcock (eds), 1963, 351–4

Roberts, B.K. 2008. *Landscapes, Documents and Maps: Villages in Northern England and Beyond, AD 900–1250*. Oxford, Oxbow

Roberts, B.K. and Wrathmell, S. 2002. *Region and Place: A Study of English Rural Settlement*. London, English Heritage

Roberts, E. 2003. *Hampshire Houses 1250–1700: Their Dating and Development*. Winchester, Hampshire County Council

Roberts, E. 2006. 'The Architecture of Love's Charity, Froxfield'. *Hampshire Field Club and Archaeological Society Newsletter* 45, 12–13

Roberts, H.D. 1981. 'Downhearth to Bar Grate: An Illustrated Account of the Evolution in Cooking Due to the Use of Coal Instead of Wood'. Avebury, Wiltshire Folk Life Society

Roberts, M. 1994. *Durham*. London, Batsford

Roberts, S. 1995. 'Lying among the Classics: Ritual and Motif in Elite Elizabethan and Jacobean Beds'. In Gent (ed.), 1995, 325–60

Roberts, W.E. 1986. 'The Tools Used in Building Log Houses in Indiana'. In Upton and Vlach (eds), 1986, 182–203

Robinson, J.M. 1983. *Georgian Model Farms: A Study of Decorative and Model Farm Buildings in the Age of Improvement 1700–1846*. Oxford, Oxford University Press

Roffey, S. 2001. 'Constructing a Vision of Salvation: Chantries and the Social Dimension of Religious Experience in the Medieval Parish Church'. *Archaeological Journal* 163, 122–46

Rose, E.J. 1998. 'Man Set Over the Animals'. *Vernacular Architecture* 29, 18–21

Royal Commission on Historical Monuments of England (RCHME) 1987. *Houses of the North York Moors*. London, Her Majesty's Stationery Office

Ruskin, J. 1884. *The Stones of Venice*. Three volumes. Orpington, Allen

Ryan, P.R. 1986. 'Fifteenth-Century Continental Brickmasons'. *Medieval Archaeology* 30, 112–13

Ryan, P.R. 2000. 'The Buildings of Rural Ingatestone, Essex, 1556–1601: "Great Rebuilding" or "Housing Revolution"?' *Vernacular Architecture* 31, 11–25

Ryder, P. 1979. *Timber-Framed Buildings in South Yorkshire*. Barnsley, South Yorkshire County Council

Ryder, P. 1990. 'Fortified Medieval and Sub-Medieval Buildings in the North-East of England'. In Vyner (ed.), 1990,

Sahlins, M. 1972. *Stone Age Economics*. Chicago, Aldine

Salzman, L.F. 1952. *Building in England Down to 1540: A Documentary History*. Oxford, Oxford University Press

Samson, R. (ed.) 1990. *The Social Archaeology of Houses*. Edinburgh, Edinburgh University Press

Sandall, K. 1986. 'Aisled Halls in England and Wales'. *Vernacular Architecture* 17, 21–35

Schama, S. 2005. *Rough Crossings: Britain, The Slaves and the American Revolution*. London, BBC Books

Schofield, P. 2003. *Peasant and Community in England, 1200–1500*. Basingstone, Palgrave Macmillan

Sciama, L. 1993. 'The Problem of Privacy in Mediterranean Anthropology'. In Ardener (ed.) 1993, 87–111

Shammas, C. 1990. *The Pre-Industrial Consumer in England and America.* Oxford, Clarendon Press

Sharpe, K. 2000a. *Reading Revolutions: The Politics of Reading in Early Modern England.* New Haven, Yale University Press

Sharpe, K. 2000b. *Remapping Early Modern England: The Culture of Seventeenth-Century England.* Cambridge, Cambridge University Press

Siemon, J.R. 1994. 'Landlord not King: Agrarian Change and Interarticulation'. In Burt and Archer (eds), 1994,

Slep, Janet 2004. 'Chests, Coffers and Trunks in East Anglia 1650–1730: A Step Towards Defintition'. *Regional Furniture* 18, 62–7

Smith, J.T. 1993. *English Houses 1200–1800: The Hertfordshire Evidence.* London, Her Majesty's Stationery Office

Smith, J.T. 2002. 'The Miles Standish House, Duxbury, Mass., and its British Antecedents'. *Vernacular Architecture* 33, 57–66

Smith, P. 1975. [Second edition.] *Houses of the Welsh Countryside: A Study in Historical Geography.* London, Her Majesty's Stationery Office

Spufford, M. 1984. *The Great Reclothing of Rural England: Petty Chapmen and Their Wares in the Seventeenth Century.* London, Hambledon

Spufford, M., Green, A. and Parkinson, E. (eds) 2006. *Country Durham Hearth Tax Assessment Lady Day 1666.* British Record Society

St George, R.B. (ed.) 1988. *Material Life in America, 1600–1800.* Boston, Northeastern University Press

St George, R.B. 1998. *Conversing by Signs: Poetics of Implication in Colonial New England Culture.* Chapel Hill, University of North Carolina Press

St George, R.B. 2006. 'Reading Spaces in Eighteenth Century New England'. In Styles and Vickery (eds), 2006, 81–106

Steer, F. 1950. *Farm and Cottage Inventories of Mid-Essex, 1635–1749.* Chelmsford, Essex Record Office

Stenning, D.F. 1997. 'Arch Braces or Tension Braces?' *Vernacular Architecture* 28, 81–3

Stenning, D.F. 2003. 'Smaller Aisled Halls in Essex'. *Vernacular Architecture* 34, 1–19

Stone, L. 1977. *The Family, Sex and Marriage in England, 1500–1800.* London, Weidenfeld & Nicolson

Stoyle, M. 2005. *Soldiers and Strangers: An Ethnic History of the English Civil War.* New Haven, Yale University Press

Strong, R. 1999. *The Spirit of Britain: A Narrative History of the Arts.* London, Hutchinson

Styles, J. and Vickery, A. (eds) 2006. *Gender, Taste and Material Culture in Britain and North America, 1700–1830. Yale Studies in British Art* 17. New Haven, Yale University Press

Suggett, R. 2005. 'Houses and History in the March of Wales: Radnorshire 1400–1800'. Aberystwyth, Royal Commission on the Ancient and Historical Monuments of Wales (RCAHMW)

Summerson, J. 1945. *Georgian London.* New Haven, Yale University Press

Tankard, D. 2007. 'Bayleaf – A Wealden Hall House from Chiddingstone, Kent'. Weald and Downland Open Air Museum spring 2007, no issue no. stated, 9–13

Tankard, D. 2009. *Houses of the Weald and Downland.* Lancaster, Carnegie Publishing Ltd in association with the Weald and Downland Open Air Museum

Tankard, D. and Harris, R. 2008. 'The House from Walderton, West Sussex'. Weald and Downland Open Air Museum unnumbered issue, autumn 2008, 9–13

Tarlow, S. 2007. *The Archaeology of Improvement in Britain, 1750–1850*. Cambridge, Cambridge University Press

Tarlow, S. and West, S. (eds) 1999. *The Familiar Past? Archaeologies of Later Historic Britain, 1500–1900*. London, Routledge

Tawney, R.H. 1926. *Religion and the Rise of Capitalism: A Historical Study*. London, Murray

Tawney, R.H. 1941. 'The Rise of the Gentry 1558–1640'. *Economic History Review* 11, 1–38

Taylor, A.J. 1974. *The King's Works in Wales 1277–1330*. London, Her Majesty's Stationery Office

Taylor, R. 1992. 'Population Explosions and Housing, 1550–1850'. *Vernacular Architecture* 23, 24–9

Thirsk, J. 1957. *English Peasant Farming*. London, Routledge

Thirsk, J. 1992. 'Making a Fresh Start: Sixteenth-Century Agriculture and the Classical Inspiration'. In Leslie and Raylor (eds), 1992, 15–34

Thirsk, J. 2000. *Alternative Agriculture: A History from the Black Death to the Present Day*. Oxford, Oxford University Press

Thirsk, J. 2007. *Food in Early Modern England: Phases, Fads and Fashions*. London, Hambledon

Thomas, K. 1971. *Religion and the Decline of Magic*. New York, Scribner's

Thomas, K. 1983. *Man and the Natural World: Changing Attitudes in England 1500–1800*. London, Allen Lane

Thompson, E.P. 1963. *The Making of the English Working Class*. London, Gollancz

Thompson, E.P. 1967. 'Time, Work-Discipline and Industrial Capitalism'. *Past and Present* 38, 56–97

Thompson, E.P. 1991. *Customs in Common*. London, Merlin Press

Thompson, M.W. 1995. *The Medieval Hall: The Basis of Secular Domestic Life 600–1600*. Aldershot, Scolar Press

Thornton, P. 1978. *Seventeenth-Century Interior Decoration in England, France and Holland*. New Haven, Yale University Press

Thornton, P. 1984. *Authentic Décor: The Domestic Interior 1620–1920*. London, Weidenfeld & Nicolson

Turner, S. 2007. 'Fields, Property and Agricultural Innovation in Late Medieval and Early Modern South-West England'. In Finch and Giles (eds), 2007, 57–74

Tyson, B. 1993. 'Low-Cost Housing in Cumbria 1665–1721: Documentary Evidence for Three Cottages'. *Vernacular Architecture* 24, 20–8

Tyson, B. 1998. 'Transportation and the Supply of Construction Materials: An Aspect of Traditional Building Management'. *Vernacular Architecture* 29, 63–81

Underdown, D. 1985a. 'The Taming of the Scold'. In Fletcher and Stephenson (eds), 1985, 116–36

Underdown, D. 1985b. *Revel, Riot and Rebellion: Popular Politics and Culture in England 1603–1660*. Oxford, Clarendon Press

Underdown, D. 1993. *Fire From Heaven: Life in an English Town in the Seventeenth Century*. London, Fontana

Underdown, D. 1996. *A Freeborn People: Politics and the Nation in Seventeenth-Century England*. Oxford, Oxford University Press

Upton, D. 1998. *Architecture in the United States*. Oxford, Oxford University Press

Upton, D. and Vlach, J.M. (eds) 1986. *Common Places: Readings in American Vernacular Architecture*. Athens, University of Georgia Press

Virágos, G. 2006. *The Social Archaeology of Residential Sites: Hungarian Noble Residences and Their Social Context From the Thirteenth Through to the Sixteenth Century: An Outline for Methodology*. BAR International Series 1583. Oxford, British Archaeological Reports

Vyner, B. (ed.) 1990. *Medieval Rural Settlement in North-East England*. Durham, Architectural and Archaeological Society of Durham and Northumberland, 127–40

Vyner, B. (ed.) 1994. *Building on the Past*. London, Royal Archaeological Institute

Wade Martins, S. 2002a. *The English Model Farm: Building the Agricultural Ideal, 1700–1914*. Windgather Press

Wade Martins, S. 2002b. 'Reboiling the Cabbage? The Present State of Research on Historic Farm Buildings'. *Journal of the Historic Farm Buildings Group* 16, 9–47

Walker, J.L. 1999. 'Fyfield Hall: A Late Twelfth-Century Aisled Hall Rebuilt c.1400 in the Archaic Style'. *Archaeological Journal* 156, 112–42

Walker, J.L. 2000. 'Detached Kitchens – A Comment and an Essex Example'. *Vernacular Architecture* 31, 75–77

Walker, J.L. 2003. 'A Lobby-Entrance House of 1615: Model Farm, Linstead Magna, Halesworth, Suffolk'. *Vernacular Architecture* 34, 79–83

Wallis, R. and Lymer, K. (eds) 2001. *A Permeability of Boundaries? New Approaches to the Archaeology of Art, Religion and Folklore*. BAR International Series S936. Oxford, British Archaeological Reports

Weatherill, L. 1988. *Consumer Behaviour and Material Culture in England 1660–1760*. London, Routledge

Weber, M. 1965. [First published 1904.] *The Protestant Ethic and the Spirit of Capitalism*. London, Unwin

Wilkinson, P. 2000. *The Shock of the Old: A Guide to British Buildings*. Basingstoke, Macmillan

Williams, E. 1944. *Capitalism and Slavery*. Chapel Hill, University of North Carolina Press

Williams, R. 1973. *The Country and the City*. London, Chatto & Windus

Williams, T. 1990. '"Magnetic Figures": Polemical Prints of the English Revolution'. In Gent and Llewellyn (eds), 1990, 86–110

Williamson, T.M. 2000. 'The Rural Landscape, 1500–1800: The Neglected Centuries'. In Hooke (ed.), 2000, 85–132

Williamson, T.M. 2002. *Shaping Medieval Landscapes: Settlement, Society, Environment*. Macclesfield, Windgather Press

Wilson, R.J. 2008. '"The Mystical Character of Commodities": The Consumer Society in Eighteenth-Century England'. *Post-Medieval Archaeology* 42:1, 144–56

Winchester, S. 2001. *The Map that Changed the World: The Tale of William Smith and the Birth of a Science*. London, Viking

Woodward, D. 1985. '"Swords into Ploughshares": Recycling in Pre-Industrial England'. *Economic History Review* 38, 175–90

Woodward, D. 1995. *Men at Work: Labourers and Building Craftsmen in the Towns of Northern England, 1450–1750*. Cambridge, Cambridge University Press

Woolgar, C. 2006. *The Senses in Medieval England*. New Haven, Yale University Press

Wrathmell, S. 1984. 'The Vernacular Threshold of Northern Peasant Houses'. *Vernacular Architecture* 15, 29–33

Wrathmell, S. 1989. 'Peasant Houses, Farmsteads and Villages in North-East England'. In Aston, Austin and Dyer (eds), 1989,

Wrightson, K. 2000. *Earthly Necessities: Economic Lives in Early Modern Britain*. New Haven, Yale University Press

Wrightson, K. 2003. [Second edition.] *English Society 1580–1680*. London, Routledge

Wrigley, E.A. and Schofield, R.S. 1981. *The Population History of England, 1541–1871: A Reconstruction*. Cambridge, Cambridge University Press

Zell, M. 1994. *Industry in the Countryside: Wealden Society in the Sixteenth Century*. Cambridge, Cambridge University Press

List of Websites Mentioned in the Text

http://csdi.rca.ac.uk
http://www.avoncroft.org.uk/
http://www.colonialwilliamsburg.com/
http://www.concealedgarments.org
http://www.hfbg.org.uk
http://www.imagesofengland.org.uk
http://www.museumwales.ac.uk/en/stfagans/
http://www.plimoth.org/
http://www.reading.ac.uk/merl/
http://www.ruralmuseumsnetwork.org.uk/members/
http://www.ryedalefolkmuseum.co.uk
http://www.spab.org.uk
http://www.vag.org.uk
http://www.vernaculararchitectureforum.org
http://www.wealddown.co.uk/

Index